Research and Devel Tax Reliefs

Research and Development Tax Reliefs

Maria Kitt

Bloomsbury Professional

For Eleanora

Bloomsbury Professional Ltd, Maxwelton House, 41–43 Boltro Road, Haywards Heath, West Sussex, RH16 1BJ

© Bloomsbury Professional Ltd 2014

Bloomsbury Professional is an imprint of Bloomsbury Publishing Plc

A CIP Catalogue record for this book is available from the British Library.

ISBN: 978 1 78043 353 0

Typeset by Phoenix Photosetting, Chatham, Kent
Printed and bound in Great Britain by CPI Group (UK) Ltd, Croydon, CR0 4YY

Preface

UK R&D tax reliefs are among the most effective and generous tax allowances in the world. Yet many companies, entitled to the incentive, do not claim reliefs that are due, either through a lack of awareness or because the reliefs seem complex and inappropriate to their business. But the significant increases in the value of the incentive make the R&D tax relief even more important, whilst at the same time, the growth in HMRC powers and penalty-based tax regime highlight the importance of accurately documented claims. For the first time, this comprehensive book brings together the many aspects of the R&D tax relief framework and its alternatives into a readable and manageable reference point.

UK R&D tax relief has traditionally been dominated by large Pharma and biotechnologies, but this picture is changing. The definition of 'Research and Development' for tax purposes is a universal one and can apply in almost any industry. It may apply to any type of technology or science and any area of technical uncertainty.

The rise in popularity of the R&D relief schemes began to emerge in 2008. The SME rate of relief was increased for the first time since its introduction in 2000; and in that year, the number of tax relief claims processed by HMRC reached a record 8,000. Tax relief support administered by HMRC reached a record breaking £1,000 million, again a 'first'. Extensive expert studies, conducted on a much more informed scale than mine, concluded that R&D trends, ie project activity and investment in new R&D ventures, is relatively unresponsive to uplifts in the absolute rate of tax reward. This shows the ability of innovation not only to gather and sustain its own pace, but to draw into it many more innovative companies and expertise. But the new 'Tech Cities' and 'Science Parks', are only part of the picture as the real pattern of the tax relief over recent years has been its cascade across a variety of business sectors and activity.

Knowledge-transfer and commercialisation of innovative ideas are strongly supported by the R&D tax credit scheme. For the first time since the reliefs were introduced, a cash credit is available to larger companies and to SMEs performing subcontracted activity.

It is clear then that the R&D relief scheme offers something to almost any innovative company seeking a technical 'first of class', and at last there is a publication drawing together the many strands of legislation and requirements making up a competent claim into a single reference point.

Summary of Contents

In **Chapter One,** I outline a brief history of the reliefs and the schemes on offer to SME and Large Companies and their context. There have been many, many developments for companies within the R&D arena, since 2000. These include the large increase in the cash value of these reliefs announced over the last four Finance Acts. But the wider corporate environment for innovative companies has also changed dramatically. These changes include the introduction of the new R&D Expenditure Credit for large companies, the advent of the new Creative Sector reliefs and the introduction of a UK/EEA Patent Box. As the Dyson Review, 'Ingenious Britain' foresaw, a catalogue of reliefs and non-fiscal incentives provides a springboard for the Tech Economy if the UK is to compete with emerging Tiger Economy technologies and have an EEA equivalent fiscal incentive for innovation.

In **Chapter Two,** I look at the detail of the R&D tax relief framework. Any claim to tax relief must have a legislative basis. The UK has twelve disparate strands of legislation and interpretations that make up the relief matrix. Each aspect is taken sequentially and explained on a step by step basis. Frustratingly, a claim to R&D tax relief can fail or be significantly reduced at any stage of this process, perhaps because the company's accounts do not identify costs that are eligible for relief or perhaps because of the influence of a range of commercial circumstances in which the company performs R&D activity. A number of worked examples and Case Studies draw out the importance of each stage making up the claim.

In **Chapter Three,** the BIS Guidelines, which have provides the core definition of 'Research and Development' for tax purposes since 2000, are considered in depth. The definition of work eligible for tax relief is in reality, extremely broad. It is characterised by a 'Gateway test' which requires research and/or development work to target an advance in science or technology through the resolution of an area of specific technical uncertainty. The practical application of what is, at first sight, an opaque terminology will in practice draw in a wide range of commercial development work far beyond traditional IT and Pharma based technologies. A number of Case Studies and practical examples highlight the opportunities and restrictions found within the current tax definition, and answer the important question, 'What is R&D'? The Guidelines contain a number of examples to develop what is meant by an 'advance' and these move through a number of further key terms which are discussed through worked examples.

In **Chapter Four,** the reliefs available to SME companies are detailed. The cash value of the relief is shown in a number of worked examples. For most advisors and innovative companies, familiar with the rules of the Chapter 2 SME Scheme, the detailed requirements of Chapters 3 and 4 may also be encountered at some point within a company's project work. These are explained clearly showing the impact on the relief calculation where R&D activity is subsidised or subcontracted. Commercial considerations underline the R&D tax relief framework and these are brought together to enable a full reference point for the reader. But what is an SME for the purposes of R&D tax relief? This is completely different to familiar and commonly encountered corporate tax scenarios such as the provisions for associated companies and ordinary control. Here, the impact of EC Legislation in defining the SME Enterprise is clearly explained to provide the reader with a quick reference point for linked and partner enterprises which are relevant to the SME claimant.

In **Chapter Five,** I look at the reliefs on offer to Large Company Scheme claimants and consider the enormity of the move toward the 'Above the Line' R&D Expenditure Credit from 1 April 2016. The special rules of the Large Company Scheme are outlined through a number of worked examples, including the detailed rules for large companies engaged within subcontractor relationships. The impact of the Patent Box is particularly exciting and enables the Large Company to claim both R&D tax relief incentives and reduced corporation tax charges upon UK/EEA Patented relevant income streams. The legacy Chapter Five relief for Large Companies will be withdrawn from 31 March 2016 and the transitional rules up to that period are outlined in detail.

In **Chapter Six,** the administration of the relief schemes is outlined. The work of HMRC has become both more difficult and more significant as claims grow in volume and value. This has certainly gained momentum from a surge in the number of 'No win/No fee' 'advisors'. As these R&D Units struggle with claims that are incorrect or incomplete, the chapter provides clear and concise guidance upon common errors and misconceptions and the significance of key HMRC interpretations. R&D records form a vital part of the company's record keeping requirements for CTSA and practical guidance is given on the minimum standards of documentation and support. The parallels drawn from key cases such as Gripple Ltd and BE Studio's is an important part of the HMRC interpretation of R&D tax relief administration and the key practical points are explained in detail.

In **Chapter Seven,** ways through the funding 'Innovation Gap' are outlined. Non fiscal support for R&D activity has grown very significantly over the past seven years and a number of programmes, including the key Horizon 2020 programme have been allocated large funding budgets for innovative businesses. The contrasting application processes and their benefits are summarised. Practical tips on alternatives to tax relief are brought together in this chapter providing a 'handbook' of R&D support for 2014 and beyond.

In **Chapter Eight,** I look at the very exciting worldwide trends in R&D from the UK context. R&D Expenditure has sustained itself through global recession and continued to produce innovative change in a variety of micro circumstances. This leads to the key question – what is the impact of tax relief upon innovation? A number of studies are brought together in this chapter to provide some interesting answers and commentary. The performance of the UK R&D Economy compares favourably with its European counterparts, and it is very exciting to see the growth in key engineering and technology based

R&D activities mirroring the traditional Pharma and biotechnology growth which has traditionally dominated the UK innovation base.

In **Chapter Nine**, a number of Industry Case Studies bring the R&D rules alive across a number of innovative industries. These include development work in the engineering and construction sectors, manufacturing and 'traditional' development sectors, and software and ICT based business. As the UK innovation growth cascades across a variety of SME companies, the importance of emerging technologies is summarised. Against this industry background, a number of common scenario's such as how to identify R&D project work, the impact of the R&D budget funding, the impact of employee and consultancy hire, the effect of group dynamics and subcontracting relationships are explained.

In **Chapter Ten**, I am delighted to outline the introduction of the new Creative Sector tax reliefs for companies engaged in gaming technologies and television/animation production companies. The Creative Sector is estimated to employ over 1.5 million talented people in the UK and have an economic significance of around £36 billion. Last minute EC approval has also enabled gaming companies to have a valid alternative to R&D tax relief as expenditure is eligible for the new VGTR from 1 April 2014.

The **Appendices** to the book provide an at-a-glance summary of the key reference points for the relief and up to date tables of rates and allowances.

I hope that the book will provide an interesting acknowledgement to the work of an army of skilled and talented innovators, as well as a pathway through the complexity of the tax relief framework currently making up the R&D incentive.

This book has been inspired by the new generation of 'Tech Entrepreneurs', many of whom I have been able to help with practical tax advice. The UK has some truly breath-taking technologies emerging into the innovation race and I am delighted that the R&D Tax Relief Scheme can now play such a significant part in moving towards an 'Ingenious Britain'.

This book would not have been written without the kind encouragement of my publisher Dave Wright and his team at Bloomsbury Professional. I must also acknowledge my friends Lesley, Carole, Jane, Harry and Buster, whom have helped with this manuscript in so many ways.

As ever, suggestions for how the publication can be further developed are always welcome and I can be contacted through maria@tax-insight.co.uk.

Maria Kitt
July 2014

Contents

Contents

Contents

Table of Statutes

[All references are to paragraph numbers.]

Table of Statutory Instruments

[All references are to paragraph numbers.]

Table of Cases

[All references are to paragraph numbers.]

Table of Examples

[All references are to paragraph numbers.]

Table of Examples

Chapter 1

UK research and development tax reliefs: Introduction

Contents

SIGNPOSTS

- UK R&D tax reliefs are a recent feature of the corporation tax 'roadmap'. They also form just one part of a number of incentives on offer in the UK to innovators (see **1.1**). The tax definition of R&D for UK tax purposes is complex and differs to the definitions used in EU territories and by bodies providing grant funding or indirect support. It is only partly based on the *Frascati* Model and applies universally to any type of innovation by any size of company (see **1.6, 1.11**).

- *Finance Act 2014* is the culmination of a number of enhancements to the relief framework. The UK SME can now obtain 225% relief on eligible R&D costs, and loss making companies a repayable tax credit of 14.5% (see **1.4, 1.12**)

- This builds on the enhancements made to the large company relief scheme in *FA 2013*, which introduced the expenditure credit as an 'above the line' relief (see **1.5**).

- UK R&D tax relief has a broad legislative basis and is administered by HMRC. Both aspects have led to complexity. With the potential for significant tax relief on the one hand and tax-geared penalties on the other, it is essential any claim is correctly formulated (see **1.6, 1.7, 1.9**).

- The Dyson review led to sweeping changes from the key *FA 2012* amendments, but it is widely felt there is some way to go for the relief to be absorbed freely into the innovative economy (see **1.10**).

INTRODUCTION

1.1   This book is about UK tax reliefs for research and development (R&D) activity. It is intended to help both the innovative company and the professional tax adviser to claim reliefs in an informed and effective way. Tax reliefs are also commonly called 'tax credits', for example, in National Statistics publications about HMRC R&D tax relief claims, but this is not the correct terminology. A tax credit is available in some circumstances, but this is only one of the many forms the relief can take.

This history of UK tax incentivisation for R&D is a recent one. Fourteen years on, competent use of the relief is still weak. This is not helped by the legislation being both complex and piecemeal. The aim of the book is to cut through the many obscurities and traps in the framework and to provide a practical guide to maximise the relief opportunity.

R&D tax relief can be a very valuable tax incentive, particularly for SME companies. But many large company UK R&D performers have found the relief ineffective and irrelevant to their R&D strategy. For example, loss bound large companies were not able to access a tax credit for surrenderable losses until very recently, making the R&D incentivisation more apparent than real. In any case, overseas ownership or funding for much UK R&D prevents relief being advantageous or even available to the UK entity.

The role of HMRC in administering the relief has been criticised as querulous and quarrelsome. But experience shows that technical policy upon R&D tax relief has been fairly responsive to an almost constant feedback from both R&D companies and their advisers. In particular, the Dyson Review, 'Ingenious Britain', published in March 2010, very quickly paved the way for the important Finance Act reforms of 2011 and 2012.

Funding for R&D activity in the UK does not comprise tax incentivisation alone, of course. A raft of direct incentives is available to UK companies from both UK and EU agencies. These are both technology-specific and general reliefs to the innovative business. The lead UK grant agency is the Technology *TSB* Strategy Board, which states it has provided funding for innovation of £2.5 billion in the past five years for UK R&D companies. Many SMEs find these incentives very useful and an outline of available schemes is discussed at **Chapter 7**.

Despite the diversity of R&D activity in the UK, the Guidelines underlying the legislation are generic, applying equally to all industries and all scales of project work. This universality is illustrated in the case studies at **Chapter 9** which put the R&D legislation into practice and provide a number of useful tips on maximising the R&D opportunity and overcoming significant pitfalls for the unwary.

Finally, the book needs to reflect the fact that R&D tax relief was partly triggered by its international context. The relief was introduced as a responsive measure. Much of the motivation for the introduction of the reliefs was to place the UK in an internationally competitive advantage, leading the export of technology in the EU. **Chapter 8** of the book considers the performance of the UK on international R&D scoreboards. In particular the context and challenges for UK R&D companies and their ability to capitalise on emerging technologies.

UK R&D

1.2 UK innovation has a very strong science base, relatively low R&D intensity across business sectors and relatively high intangible investments. The UK's R&D environment also has well-developed financial and venture capital markets, and high international integration.

Compared with other economies, the UK is well-placed, but not amongst, the global innovation leaders. This is borne out by a number of major R&D studies such as the Thompson Reuters Innovator Index and the 2013 EU R&D

Scoreboard. The trends are also borne out by the dominance of SME activity in claims for R&D tax relief which are filed to HMRC.

A common commentary upon UK R&D activity is that it displays a historically low level of intensity. Business expenditure in R&D is certainly lower than the *Organisation for Economic Co-operation and Development* (OECD) average at about 1.6 to 1.9% of GDP overall. But this must be interpreted carefully, because the real difference between the UK and other major countries lies not in the level of R&D but in its industrial structure. For example, the UK performs well in high-tech industries (such as pharmaceutical, aerospace and ICT). The UK's R&D intensity in these industries is below France and the US, but higher than Japan, Germany and Korea. It is in the large, medium, and low-tech industries, such as vehicles, metal products or food processing, that the UK is *comparatively* weaker – significantly below Germany, Japan and Korea. In other words, a distinctive feature of the UK innovation system appears to be strong performance in a small group of high-tech industries, but relatively weak innovation performance across the average of 'high-tech' sectors when taken together.

The malaise is also the result of the UK having to catch up with decades of de-industrialisation and the surge of new digital and precision-based technologies. Many UK SMEs are engaged upon R&D work within such emerging technologies, but activity on this scale this will take time to materialise upon EU and worldwide scoreboards.

The effectiveness of UK R&D tax reliefs therefore has to be measured against a number of extraneous factors.

Brief history of the reliefs

1.3   UK R&D tax reliefs have been introduced and updated through successive Finance Acts. *FA 2000* introduced a scheme for small and medium-sized enterprises (SMEs) to obtain 150% relief for R&D work that met the tax definition of R&D (*FA 2000, s 69* and *Sch 20*). A second scheme for large companies and SMEs performing R&D in certain circumstances was introduced in April 2002 (*FA 2002,s 53* and *Sch 12*).

The SME scheme is regarded as a State Aid under European law. This complicates the relief. For example, it affects a number of the definitions applied to the 'enterprise' performing the R&D and applies an overall cap to the amount of incentive funding a project can receive.

The SME legislation is now consolidated at *CTA 2009, Pt 13, Chs 2–4. Part 13 of CTA 2009* is the principal source for UK R&D legislation once the definition of R&D for tax purposes has been established.

The rules for SME relief are different from those for large company relief schemes. Several of the rules for large company relief are more stringent than those applying to SME activity, such as the restricted ability to claim relief for subcontractor expenditure. Other features of the scheme are more progressive, such as the ability to claim relief for contributions to independent research and subsidised expenditure. The large company scheme is not a State Aid but the overall definition of what is a large company derives from the EC Regulations applying to SMEs.

The large company scheme was extended in 2003. Smaller enterprises unable to claim R&D tax relief under the SME scheme where activity was performed in a subcontracting relationship were able to make claims under what is now *CTA 2009, Pt 13, Ch 3* at the large company rate of relief (*FA 2003, Sch 31, para 15*).

The legislation then underwent annual amendments to the rates of relief and definition of expenditure categories for each *Finance Act* from 2003 without exception. An overview of the history is at **Appendix 6**.

FA 2011 and *FA 2012* introduced the most important reforms to the reliefs, and formulate the current state of play in UK R&D relief today. The reforms integrated changes in other aspects of corporation tax relevant to the innovative company, such as the Patent Box introduction and the general reduction in the mainstream rate of corporation tax. The current R&D package forms part of the reforms of the taxation policy upon corporate intangible reliefs which began to materialise in 2000.

SME incentives

1.4   Tax reliefs for UK SMEs are very valuable. As a rule of thumb, the SME company can obtain cash incentivisation worth around £32,000 per £100,000 of eligible spend from 1 April 2014.

The SME scheme reduces an organisation's corporation tax bill by allowing it to reduce its profits subject to corporation tax by 225% of qualifying spending on R&D. An SME that has no tax bill to reduce can either enhance its trading losses to be carried forward or back, or surrender part or all of the loss as a cash payment known as a 'tax credit'. The scheme is open to all SMEs which HMRC define as organisations with fewer than 500 employees and one or more of the following: annual turnover not exceeding €100 million, or a balance sheet not exceeding €86 million.

If the SME subcontracts R&D activity from a third party or exceeds the EC State Aid cap on a project, the relief may be restricted to the large company rate. Subcontracting activity is difficult to identify in practice and is listed by HMRC as a common reason for claims being rejected. **Chapter 4** reviews the approach necessary to consider this important issue.

HMRC statistics show that an extraordinarily high number of SME claims are incorrect or inadequate. The informed claimant needs to take a multidisciplined approach to comply with the relief framework and avoid costly errors. The following Chapters show that a thorough understanding of the nature of the company's R&D is critical.

Incentives for large companies

1.5   The large company scheme allows larger companies to reduce profits subject to corporation tax by 130% of qualifying spending on R&D. Losses enhanced by the R&D relief can be carried forward or back, or surrendered as group relief, in the same way as the SME scheme. From 1 April 2013, the 'R&D expenditure credit' enables companies to claim a tax credit to the value of 10% of their qualifying spend. The payment of this credit is based on draft legislation. It is subject to complex administration and aligns itself to what are effectively 'real time' corporation tax (CT) liabilities. The company must be completely up to date with CT and PAYE duties on a group-wide basis for a credit to be applied.

Until the changes in *FA 2012*, no cash credit was possible. This made the R&D relief almost irrelevant for loss-making companies or groups. In response to significant pressure, an 'above the line' credit was envisaged in *FA 2010* and materialised as the 'R&D expenditure credit' (RDEC) which will be legislated at *CTA 2009, Pt 3, Ch 6A*. The introduction of the credit has gone some way to respond to the criticism that little tax incentivisation was available for large company R&D activity. The adoption of the credit will be mandatory from 1 April 2016. For the time being it runs in tandem with the 'legacy' enhancement relief unless the company opts into the scheme before that date. RDEC has also introduced some complexities to the Accounting Standard by which it should be recognised. As the relief develops, the recognition of above the line profits (EBITDA) will require consideration of a range of factors. As this is resolved, the advantage of the RDEC for external investors in R&D companies is that the presence of R&D activity becomes more visible.

In determining whether a company is 'large', it is necessary to amalgamate the data of 'linked' and 'partner' enterprises' in some circumstances. The rules are outlined at **Chapter 5**.

WHAT IS R&D?

The R&D claim

1.6   Tax relief for R&D activity is based on a much narrower definition than those used in industry and by other EU tax codes such as the Frascati model. Only revenue expenditure is within the scope of the relief, although special rules apply to expenditure brought into the value of capitalised intangible assets. Is this significant? The Office of National Statistics data for 2011 shows that UK capital R&D expenditure was around £1.01 billion (6%)

of the total R&D expenditure. Additionally, research development allowances (RDAs) are available for some capital expenditure.

Costs incurred by the company for broader development activity such as marketing, intellectual property (IP) protection, legal or financial issues are also prohibited from obtaining any relief. The relief relies heavily upon Guidelines which were first published by the BIS (then Department for Trade & Industry) in 2000. The Guidelines define 'when' R&D takes place for tax purposes. These guidelines were updated in 2004 and 2010, but have remained fundamentally consistent in meaning.

relies heavily on the guidelines

Chapter 3 explains how to confirm whether or not an activity is 'R&D'. The hallmark of R&D work is established by two 'Gateway' tests. These require the company to seek an **advance** in a field of science or technology through the **resolution of scientific or technological uncertainty.**

These terms are not easily appreciated either by high-tech companies or advisers. The Guidelines go on to give a number of examples of an 'advance'. Work that fits within one of the following strategies is potentially R&D, and, of course, other scenarios will fit provided technical uncertainty is demonstrable:

- extending overall knowledge or capability in a science or technology;

- creating a product, process or system etc that demonstrates an extension of knowledge or capability;

- making appreciable improvements to existing processes, materials or devices etc through fundamentally changing its technical characteristics.

Experience has shown that the Guidelines are sufficiently broadly written to encompass most technical activity. The degree of 'advance' therefore needs to show that this goes beyond simply extending the company's knowledge.

However, a number of further activities are also potential R&D and are often overlooked, such as:

- technical planning work contributing to the identification of project uncertainties, such as high level scientific or technological feasibility studies (BIS Guidelines, para 36, 37);

- the design construction and testing of prototypes (para 39);

- design work with inherent scientific or technological uncertainty (para 40);

- producing aesthetic or cosmetic effects where scientific or technological complexity exists (para 42).

The R& D claim – who claims R&D tax relief and how?

1.7   R&D relief may only be claimed by companies which are liable to UK corporation tax. This can include:

- corporate members of limited liability partnerships;

- companies carrying on R&D in a joint venture;

- branches and permanent establishments of overseas companies;

- unincorporated bodies within the scope of UK corporation tax.

The claim is made through the corporation tax self-assessment system and subject to strict time limits. From April 2008, corporation tax returns were brought within the HMRC 'potential lost revenue' penalty system. As such, interest and penalties are chargeable where R&D claims are incorrect or where repayment claims are overstated. This may be up to 100% of the tax understated as a result of the error.

The R&D claim therefore has to be based upon a detailed and technical analysis of the R&D activity. Once the project objectives have been identified, it is possible to establish the start and end date of the technical issues involved in the company's work. These will start and end the collection of costs that the company may include in its claim to relief.

It is very common in R&D scenarios for fresh technical uncertainty to arise when a project draws to a conclusion. The extension of project work or the emergence of new project work will be included in the claim to relief, provided sufficient technical uncertainty and advancement of knowledge or capability is evident.

Once the R&D start and end points' 'envelope' is identified, tax legislation sets out a very precise code for costs which may or may not be included in the claim to relief.

The commercial circumstances of how the company performs the project will also impact upon the claim. For example, if the expenditure is subsidised through third parties or intra-group funding, the company will claim under *CTA 2009, Pt 13, Ch 4* at the large company rate. This would contrast to 'blue sky' R&D where an SME privately funds its project costs and where relief would be drawn from Ch 2 at the higher SME rate.

Chapter 3 of the book below explains the multiple scenarios. It is always possible that a claim may consist of both *CTA 2009, Pt 13, Ch 2* relief and *Ch 4* relief.

TAX RELIEF LEGISLATION

1.8 Tax legislation is only one part of the R&D tax relief framework. It is contained largely at *CTA 2009, Pt 13, Chs 1–6.*

Quantifying the R&D claim is a precise exercise. **Chapter 2** highlights the fact that tax legislation is just one of many piecemeal components of the relief. A strategy to navigate the framework is outlined here, which will assist the financial director or professional adviser to make a reliable foundation for the claim.

As the relief has evolved, it is evident that HMRC have added their own raft of additional 'requirements' and interpretations to the legislation, isolating a number of the terms within the BIS Guidelines and ascribing them special, if non-statutory, meanings. For example, the term 'subcontractor' has its ordinary meaning in the legislation at *Pt 13* and is absent from the BIS Guidance; yet the HMRC requirements and interpretations of the term run to four pages of the HMRC Corporate Intelligence Research & Development Manual (CIRD). Similarly, the 'competent professional' is a key term by which the 'advance' in a company's R&D work is theoretically demonstrable. Although the legislation does not recognise the term further, HMRC perceive such an extraordinarily high level of assumed peer knowledge that they advise in the CIRD Manual that the evidence of an independent industry professional could form part of the R&D records.

HMRC

1.9 HMRC are responsible for administering R&D tax relief. Seven specialist HMRC offices were established in 2007 to do this. They are staffed by technicians and tax inspectors with trained expertise in the subject. The units are tasked with examining and processing claims for relief and providing informed advice to taxpayers. Accounting specialists are attached to the R&D units to provide support upon technical issues, but there are no 'industry' professionals available to support HMRC.

Once filed through self-assessment, R&D tax relief claims are assigned to a unit according to the company's registered office postcode. The units were reorganised towards the end of 2013 to accommodate the setting up of the HMRC Patent Box Unit and the Creative Sector Unit. A list of R&D unit telephone numbers and the current postcode list are at **Appendix 8**.

The advisory function of the units has been formalised from time to time. At present, the latest 'advance assurance' service enabling companies to outline to HMRC, a summary of a claim for 'clearance'/approval has been withdrawn. In practice, the units set out to be informative and helpful and many interesting viewpoints can be looked up in the HMRC CIRD Manual, which is updated from time to time.

HMRC processed a little over 12,000 claims to relief in 2012 with an aggregate value of around £1,174 million. A little over 70% of the value of that amount was claimed under the large company scheme, although close to 10,000 of the claims made relate to SME activity.

R&D claim documentation, of course, forms part of the company's statutory tax and accounting records. Penalties for inadequate record keeping are available to HMRC, in addition to those for incorrect returns and understated quarterly instalment payments. R&D projects frequently lack adequate documentation and this difficulty is discussed in **Chapter 6** below with advice on key areas of records likely to be critical to the claim.

HMRC will not accept late claims for R&D tax relief without a 'reasonable excuse'. Although the claim can be referred to the courts, the statutory time limit is ordinarily two years from the end of the company's accounting period. The recent tax tribunal case of *Robins v HMRC* [2013] UKFTT 514 (TC) highlighted again the fact that for a claim to (any tax relief) to be effective, it must state the amounts of relief claimed by the taxpayer. A generic letter to HMRC stating that the company wishes to claim R&D tax relief is ineffective.

Substantive anti-avoidance regulations are available for HMRC to challenge synthetic claims to relief particularly in group situations.

'INGENIOUS BRITAIN' – THE DYSON REVIEW

1.10   Economic policy supporting R&D has been in place for a number of years. This follows the UK's policy belief that countries with growth patterns led by the export of technology sustain higher rates of economic growth.

Ten years after the introduction of the UK's tax relief schemes, James Dyson published a seminal review of the UK's R&D roadmap, 'Ingenious Britain – Making the UK a Leading High Tech Exporter in Europe'. A significant part of the report addresses the wider contexts for innovation, but the role and effectiveness of tax relief is carefully evaluated.

The Report publishes the following amongst a number of statistics:

World Intellectual Property Office
Patents filed in 2007

Japan	330,000
US	240,000
UK	17,000

The relatively poor performance of R&D gross domestic product (GDP) is also noted, with the UK lagging behind the EU R&D investment averages at an average of 1.79% GDP. **Chapter 8** explores the reality behind the statistic.

A fivefold support strategy for R&D was envisaged in the Dyson review. The ethos includes changing cultural and educational approaches to the development of technology as well as focusing upon exploiting and transferring knowledge bases from leading UK universities. Financing and supporting high tech through tax reliefs was already well established by 2010. The report therefore highlights the fact that tax reliefs are but one of a number of fundamental stimuli to UK R&D.

The report provided a number of key recommendations. The *Finance Acts of 2011, 2012, 2013* and *2014* that followed its publication quickly adopted these. Indeed the recommended uplift in the rate of SME relief to 200% was exceeded.

Sadly the report heavily criticises the role of HMRC in administering UK R&D tax reliefs, finding the approach 'lack lustre' and 'poorly informed', referring to a 'profound lack of understanding of how R&D takes place in industry. Dyson would possibly still find little change to the statistic published by the CBI, that 42% of companies eligible to claim the relief are prohibited by its complexity and do not do so.

Three years after the publication of the Dyson Review, the National Audit Office published a further landmark study into UK R&D, including its responsiveness to tax and non-fiscal incentivisation. Although little upturn for SME activity or any real uplift in the tempo of R&D claims can be gained from the NAO report, at the same time, UK large companies featured prominently on the EU 2013 R&D Scoreboard for large company R&D investment, being placed second behind Germany as the highest spender on high level R&D.

UK R&D FUNDING INITIATIVES

1.11   Tax relief is not always appropriate or even available for UK companies. R&D activity can receive a range of subsidies both from UK and EU sources. Tax incentives are only one part of a network of support tools. SME and large company tax relief provided around £1.09 billion for UK R&D in 2012. Funding from the EU sixth and seventh Framework programmes provided relief of around £4.02 billion during the period from 2007 to 2013. Non-tax support often relaxes the 'entity' rules which feature in the tax relief schemes, making them widely available to *unincorporated* businesses carrying on R&D.

Alternative funding sources for project work, such as grants and subsidies are outlined in **Chapter 7**. These can be a vital part of the innovative company's R&D strategy. As no 'handbook' exists to navigate through fiscal and alternative funding, a key part of the work of this book has been to pick out the funding methods currently available and relevant for the SME and larger company considering R&D incentives.

The functionality and effectiveness of incentivisation for R&D is a diverse topic with many publications drawn from the wider OECD and Frascati definitions of the term. The topic is well beyond the scope of this book, but a critical consideration when reviewing the wider tax relief opportunity.

2014 UPDATE

1.12   The R&D landscape has improved significantly following the Budget changes from 2011 to 2014. The innovative company performing R&D in 2014 can now take advantage of:

- 225% tax relief for R&D costs within the SME schemes;

- 150% tax relief for R&D costs within the large company schemes; *or*

- 10%/14.5% repayable tax credit for costs eligible under the large company and SME schemes;

- relaxed rules for externally provided workers such as employees using service companies or employed by group companies;

- the lifting of the restriction to PAYE liabilities of tax credit claims; and

- the abolition of the £10,000 project threshold.

When added to the Patent Box reliefs and wide availability of grants and other incentives, the UK now provides a comprehensive level of R&D support in addition to a low mainstream rate of corporation tax.

Hopefully the responsiveness of the tax relief programme will continue to keep up with the pace of the UK's emerging technologies.

As can be seen, the scope of UK R&D tax relief is valuable and extensive. The innovative company can choose from a range of tax incentives. Alternative funding and business support strategies can supplement the tax reliefs, and are widely available through both UK and EU agencies.

However, without complexity within the current UK R&D tax legislation, there would be no book. With this in mind, the following Chapters provide an experienced insight to understand and simplify the tax relief opportunity.

Chapter 2

The research and development tax relief framework

Contents

SIGNPOSTS

- **Basis** – The UK's research and development (R&D) tax relief framework is based upon five separate strands of legislation. It is necessary the company's project meets each aspect of this 'code' as no 'partial' relief is available (see **2.1–2.6**).

- **Scope** – The code applies to both small and medium enterprises (SMEs) and large companies. Further additional rules in *CTA 2009, Pt 13* apply to each R&D scheme (see **2.6**).

- **'Accounting' definition of R&D** – The accounting definition of R&D provides a starting point for a claim to relief. These principles are tailored by the Department of Business, Innovation & Skills (BIS) definition of R&D. Many further accounting issues are common in R&D companies, including the identification of 'capital' expenditure (see **2.1–2.3**).

- **'Tax purposes' definition of R&D** – The BIS Guidelines provide the foundation definition of 'when' R&D takes place. These supplement but do not override the tax legislation at *CTA 2009* and contain a number of detailed terms which must also be considered (see **2.1–2.5**).

- **Amount** – The amount of R&D relief depends upon identifying the 'boundaries' of eligible activity; the rules of *CTA 2009, Pt 13* are then applied to this 'envelope' (see **2.6–2.7**).

- **Influencing factors** – Commercial factors influencing the project may impact upon the relief due. This is particularly relevant for SMEs where activity is 'subcontracted' but also affects large company reliefs (see **2.7**).

- **Effect of grants and subsidies** – Grants and subsidies can affect the reliefs due – this is especially relevant for SMEs (see **2.6**).

- **Code to be followed strictly** – R&D case law shows that unless the code is followed meticulously, no relief at all may be due. Meeting the definition of R&D for tax purposes alone will not guarantee relief is due (see **5.10**).

- **'Frascati' model** – The R&D 'Frascati' model is adopted by the EC/OECD and is based upon a broader definition of activity and eligible costs than the UK. This model is also used for many grant framework programmes, meaning there is no assumption of tax relief from viable grant applications (see **5.9**).

SUMMARY/KEY POINTS

2.1   Claiming R&D tax relief (RDTR) in the UK involves the consideration of five different strands of legislation which effectively make up a 'code' for the relief. The company must comply with each of these statutory requirements, and the claim process can fail at any point. Following the changes in *FA 2013*, the UK R&D Scheme comprises six schemes of relief which are codified at *CTA 2009, Pt 13, Chs 1–9*. A successful claim under any scheme will depend upon each of these requirements being met.

This Chapter considers each of the milestones which make up the relief's framework. A competent claim will need to follow and document this methodology. The BIS Guidelines' definition of R&D for tax purposes is separately discussed, both because of its importance and because of its extensive nature. Clearly, the definition of R&D for tax purposes is at the heart of a claim to relief and the identification of the eligible project work and its related costs. But meeting this definition alone is insufficient and it will not necessarily follow that any tax relief will be due. The definition of R&D for tax purposes is discussed separately at **Chapter 3** below.

The first condition for relief is that the company's accounts fulfil the generally accepted accounting principles (GAAP) definitions of R&D. The UK Accounting standards were written in 1989 and continue to change and impact upon R&D accounting policies. Following a move towards the adoption of International Accounting Standards (IAS), the UK followed the EU and introduced special legislation to remove any barriers to companies claiming RDTR for eligible R&D expenditure that has been capitalised in accordance with IAS or other accounting policies.

RDTR is limited to revenue expenditure. Capital expenditure has no special definition for R&D tax purposes other than the prevalent 'enduring benefit' tests established through the courts over the past 120 years. Enhanced capital allowances are available for plant and equipment used in R&D activity. These are called 'Research Development Allowances' (RDAs) and an outline is at **Chapter 8** below.

Assuming GAAP compliant accounts are in place, the definition of R&D for tax purposes, published in the BIS Guidelines, should then be considered. This is much narrower than the Accounting Standards' definition of R&D. Two 'Gateway' tests must be met. This requires both a scientific or technological advance and technical uncertainty to be present in the company's project work. The nature of a technical 'advance' is extensive and can include most R&D activity irrespective of the type of company or its size.

The company must then identify activity 'directly contributing' to the technical advances and uncertainties within the project work. Whilst this fourth requirement is strictly part of the BIS Guidelines framework, it is drawn out as a separate part of the framework to reflect both its importance and because case law shows that without documentation of the R&D boundaries, a claim will not be competent.

The specific rules of the scheme of relief to be claimed can then be considered. Different rates of relief apply to the SME and large company schemes. Six

15

different relief schemes are available in the legislation, depending upon company size and whether or not the R&D is performed on behalf of others or is subsidised.

The schemes' rules focus upon the identification of costs which are eligible for relief. These apply equally to both the SME and large scheme reliefs. Further detail on each scheme is discussed at **Chapters 4** and **5** below. A project can potentially include claims to relief under more than one scheme.

HMRC's approach to the legislative framework is published in their Corporate Intelligence Research & Development Manual (CIRD). Tax cases relevant to R&D have shown that the relief framework must be followed 'meticulously'. For example, the cases of both *BE Studios Ltd v Smith & Williamson Ltd* [2005] EWHC 1506 (Ch) and *Gripple Ltd v HMRC* [2010] EWHC 1609 (Ch) show no purposive construction of the legislation is possible.

HMRC have overall responsibility for administering the R&D claim framework. The long-term statistic is that fewer than 25% of eligible UK companies receive the R&D relief to which they may be entitled. There are a number of reasons for this statistic, but the complexity of the relief is a common criticism. This Chapter and **Chapters 3** and **4** try to navigate the legislation providing an accurate and competent methodology for a claim.

The international R&D environment, where the Organisation for Economic Co-operation and Development (OECD) follows the Frascati Model for R&D activity, provides some context to the UK framework. R&D is often an international activity with variant definitions. Similarly grants and alternative funding for R&D use differing definitions of R&D and relevant costs.

BACKGROUND: THE R&D TAX RELIEF FRAMEWORK

Post-FA 2014

2.2 The UK R&D framework is complex and requires the satisfaction of a number of definitions in addition to the mainstream tax legislation. Some of these apply equally to both SME and 'large' scheme claimants. Others depend upon the rules of the relevant scheme through which relief is claimed. It is useful to approach R&D as a 'multi-discipline' analysis and to bear in mind its international context.

The current day SME and large company schemes were introduced by *FA 2000,Sch 20* and *FA 2003,Schs 1–6* and *11–20*. The Vaccine Research Relief Scheme (VRR) was introduced by *FA 2002, Schs 13* and *14*, coming into effect from 22 April 2002. The VRR Scheme is discussed briefly at **Chapter 5** below. The mainstream SME and large schemes are the subject of this and subsequent Chapters.

The current R&D legislation is contained within *CTA 2009, Pt 13*. The CTA provisions account for only one of the five statutory requirements making up the UK relief framework and take precedence over their counterparts. The CTA provisions provide for R&D relief to be given under more than one Chapter of *Pt 13*. Following the enactment of *FA 2013*, the R&D tax relief schemes now available are as follows:

SME relief upon in-house direct R&D and contracted out R&D	Chapter 2
SME relief for R&D work subcontracted to the SME	Chapter 3
SME relief for subsidised and capped R&D expenditure	Chapter 4
Large companies relief	Chapter 5
R&D expenditure credits*	[New Chapter 6A]
(*Available to both SME and large companies) mandatory from 1 April 2016	
Relief for SME and large companies conducting vaccine research	Chapter 7
Supplementary provisions and key definitions for all schemes	Chapter 9

Company requirements

2.3   R&D tax relief applies only to companies within the scope of UK corporation tax which meet the following additional conditions:

- The company is a going concern (SME scheme only).

- Total aid to the project is below €7.5 million, and for SME companies, no notified State Aid has been received for the project concerned.

- For expenditure before 1 April 2012 the company's costs upon its project work exceed £10,000 and for accounting periods ending before 9 December 2009, that intellectual property vests with the claimant.

SME companies must also comply with EC 'State Aid' requirements which are discussed further in **Chapter 4**.

Relief framework – key conditions

2.4   The relief framework depends upon the company satisfying five key requirements. UK RDTR comprises these strands of legislation:

1   GAAP: *SSAP 13*: To arrive at the definition of R&D for tax purposes, the legislation looks first at those activities described as such within GAAP (*FA 2000, Sch 20, para 25(1)*). This mirrors the *Income and Corporation Taxes Act1988 (ICTA 1988), s 837A* which confirms that

the beginning point of an R&D claim is the identification of those activities that are treated as R&D in accordance with GAAP; the relevant UK accounting standard is *SSAP13*. For companies adopting International Accounting Standards, the relevant standard is *IAS 38*.

2   Revenue expenditure: R&D tax reliefs are only available for 'revenue' as opposed to 'capital' expenditure. This was expressly stated at *CTA 2009, s 87* but the requirement disappeared from the rewritten CTA provisions. The default position is that no trading deduction is possible for capital expenditure (*CTA 2009, s 53*). As the relief works by providing an enhanced deduction for revenue expenditure, it follows that capitalised expenditure is ineligible. As is customary with tax legislation, there is an exception available in some circumstances. Relief is still feasible for expenditure forming part of the value of the company's intangible assets, in accordance with a specific accounting standard.

Relief is also possible for costs representing deferred expenditure asset (expenditure). This is only available when the costs are released to profit and loss and derecognised from the company's balance sheet.

3   The company's project activity must meet the definition of R&D for tax purposes. The definition is set out in a publication issued by the BIS: Guidelines on the Meaning of Research and Development for Tax Purposes (March 2004, updated December 2010). Foremost, R&D must be arranged as a systematic project targeting technical uncertainty. The definition embraces a number of key requirements. The starting point is that the company's work meets the 'Gateway tests' of 'advance' and 'uncertainty'. This is distinct from simply improving the company's own technological competence.

The current Guidelines replace guidance issued by the Department of Trade and Industry (DTI) in 2000 and were published on 5 March 2004 (*Finance Act 2004, Section 53 (Commencement) Order 2004 (SI 2004/3268)*) and updated in December 2010.

4   R&D relief rewards only those project activities which 'directly contribute' to the technical advances and uncertainties within the company's project work. This requirement features both within the BIS Guidelines (para 6) and throughout the detailed terms of the relief schemes at *CTA 2013, Pt 13*. The R&D boundaries are identified by isolating those activities making a contribution to the resolution of technical uncertainty. The boundaries will confirm the start and end points for the collection of relevant project costs. It follows that once technical certainty is achieved, the cost collection will end. This can be a circuitous process, particularly in the forefront of R&D activity and it is common to see one set of uncertainties transpose into further difficulties. Those costs will form part of the same project or may migrate into a different separate project.

5   Finally, the detailed scheme rules of *CTA 2009, Pt 13* must be applied. Most companies will claim relief under one Chapter, but reliefs are

potentially available under more than one scheme. The extent of this will depend largely upon the commercial context of the project. This is often exploited by SME companies claiming relief for subcontracted activity, but can be relevant where the company cannot meet the 'going concern' test at *Ch 2* or has exceeded the project cap.

Finance Act (FA) 2013 introduced an 'above the line' R&D expenditure credit (RDEC) in response to long-running concerns with the usefulness of the tax relief scheme available to large companies. The rules of this scheme are stringent and detailed.

HMRC apply the above 'code' and detailed requirements of each scheme rigorously. The documentation supporting the relief claimed will need to demonstrate:

- eligible project activity and its boundaries and milestones;

- eligible project costs;

- commercial influences such as how the R&D is performed and whether it is independently funded or subsidised;

- the proper engagement of subcontractors, externally provided workers and other third parties.

CURRENT ACCOUNTING DEFINITIONS OF R&D

2.5   To qualify on a preliminary basis as R&D, the company's activities must fall to be accounted for as 'R&D' under GAAP. This is 'Condition 1' of the relief.

Condition 1: Accountancy definitions – UK GAAP

2.6   The UK accountancy definitions of R&D differ from the BIS Guidelines. As the latter is used to define eligible activity for tax purposes, it follows that the presentation of expenses in a company's accounts as R&D does not necessarily mean an automatic entitlement to relief.

The accountancy treatment differs in a number of key respects. For example, neither the *SSAP 13* definition of R&D nor the *IAS 38* principles requires an 'advance' in scientific or technological knowledge to be present. However, if no advance is sought from project work, the BIS Guidelines show that the work will not be regarded as R&D for tax purposes.

Equally, HMRC inspectors are encouraged not to regard the absence of an R&D disclosure in the company's accounts, as meaning an absence of qualifying R&D activities. The requirement is that the activities fall to be accounted for as R&D, whether or not they are actually disclosed as such in the company's accounts. *SSAP 2* enables a company to report accounting information in whichever way is appropriate for them. The move to 'above the line' tax credit will still leave the relief 'invisible' for most SMEs and companies using the legacy large scheme prior to April 2016.

UK GAAP

2.7   SSAP13 is the UK standard for accounting for R&D activity. It provides a preliminary outline of the meaning of the term 'R&D' for accounting (rather than tax) purposes. The standard also provides a useful introduction of key concepts which are given special meaning by the BIS Guidelines when formulating the tax definition. These terms include 'project', 'uncertainty', development and research.

The standard defines three categories of research and development costs – pure research, applied research and development. In this way the GAAP definition of R&D distinguishes between pure and applied research. Pure research being undertaken purely for its own sake, applied research being undertaken for a practical aim or to gain new technical knowledge.

Development is regarded as the practical use or exploitation of scientific or technical knowledge. This is usually undertaken to develop new products, processes, systems, or to fundamentally change existing products, processes or systems.

SSAP 13 introduces the presence of an 'appreciable element' of innovation in product development work. For a product to be regarded as R&D, it should depart significantly from routine improvement or enhancement to 'break new ground'. This would exclude from the definition of R&D, development work aimed at producing simple, readily deducible improvements. This theme is developed within the tax definition by the BIS Guidelines.

The GAAP definition is useful only as a preliminary to the definition of R&D for tax purposes which is contained within the BIS Guidelines. For example, para 4 of the UK standard gets at the hallmark of most R&D analysis:

> 'The dividing line between these categories (of research, applied research and development), is often indistinct, and particular expenditure may have characteristics of more than one category.'

(*SSAP 13*, para 4)

What qualifies as a suitable R&D activity?

2.8   *SSAP 13* lists the following activities as normally being included as R&D:

- experimental, theoretical or other work aimed at the advancement or discovery of new knowledge;

- searching for applications of that knowledge;

- formulation and design of possible applications for such work (product development);

- testing or evaluation of alternatives to products, processes and similar;

- design, construction and testing of pre-production prototypes;

- design of products, processes etc involving new or substantially improved technology.

Similarly, the following activities are usually excluded from R&D:

- testing analysis for the purposes of quality control;

- periodic or minor alterations with marginal improvements;

- operational research not linked to specific R&D activity;

- correcting mechanical breakdowns no matter how complex;

- legal, administrative work regarding patents;

- market research.

(*SSAP 13*, para 6)

Practical point 2.1

The inadequacy of relying upon the GAAP standard as a reliable definition for tax purposes is shown in a number of key aspects, including:

Innovation – appreciable improvement

Whilst para 6 of the BIS Guidelines requires the presence of innovation in development-based work to meet the *SSAP 13* definition of R&D work, the standard falls short of the BIS Guidelines test which requires innovation is also represented by an 'appreciable improvement'.

System uncertainty

The cost of system failure in commercial production is not recognised as R&D within the SSAP activity list. Yet this type of failure is very common in the R&D environment. Experience shows that R&D activity, aimed at attaining system certainty will run alongside failure in the commercial production process or development of new systems or devices.

SSAP 13 – Helpful features

2.9   *SSAP 13* begins a useful review of technical uncertainties within a project. This appraisal is good groundwork for considering the tax definition of R&D and, in particular, the presence of 'technical uncertainty' within the project, as required by the BIS Guidelines, paras 13–14.

2.10 *The research and development tax relief framework*

The concept of scientific and technological uncertainty is extended significantly by the BIS Guidelines definitions. The documentation of uncertainty is the foundation of the R&D relief framework. For the purposes of the accounting standard, however, it does no more than provide an overview as to the relevance of technical uncertainty and the organisation of a valid project.

SSAP 13 is also useful because the important concepts of 'subcontracted R&D activity' and 'production work' are considered. These terms, which are so significant within the tax definition, have their first airing in the *SSAP 13* standard. For example, should a long-term contract have significantly enough subcontracting benefits, this must be disclosed as 'contract works in progress' (*SSAP 13*, para 17).

SSAP 13 Cost recognition

2.10 Where R&D expenditure on pure and applied research can be regarded as part of the continuing trading activities, the standard requires costs should be written off as they are incurred.

This contrasts to development based R&D. The development of new products is distinguishable from pure and applied research. It is normally undertaken with a reasonable expectation of specific commercial success and of future benefits arising from the work, either from increased revenue and related profits or from reduced costs. It is permitted, but not obligatory, to defer development expenditure if certain criteria are met, for example, the existence of a clearly defined project with identifiable expenditure.

Deferred revenue expenditure is unlikely to attract relief until released to profit and loss account and aligned to the profits earned by the company in the year. This presents the possibility of 'futuristic' R&D claims based upon historic cost accounting.

Other accounting issues

R&D tax relief for intangible assets: CTA 2009, s 1308 (FA 2004, s 53)

2.11 Accounting for intangible asset expenditure can compromise R&D tax relief. This was eased slightly when *FA 2004* introduced a special adjustment in the company's tax computation for 'capitalised' expenditure otherwise ineligible for RDTR. '*Section 53* adjustments' can be applied to capitalised R&D expenditure for accounting periods beginning on or after 1 January 2005 in very specific circumstances.

The move in the EU towards IAS and, in particular, the use of IAS 38, had presented issues for R&D companies required to recognise certain types of intangible asset expenditure as 'capitalised' expenditure in pursuance of that or other accounting principles. The ability to make an adjustment prevented any disparity between non-EU and EU R&D companies, adopting IAS for the first time.

But the adjustment only applies where a company had simply complied with accounting principles in determining the 'value of' an intangible asset (*SI 2004/3268; FA 2004,s 53(1)*). A common misconception is that if a company has capitalised R&D expenditure, tax relief is still available, but the wording of the legislation does not support this.

The *s 53* provision was rewritten into *CTA 2009, s 1308* in 2012. No relief is possible for amortisation or for deductions made in a previous accounting period (*s 1308(5), (6)*). For tax purposes an 'intangible asset' is defined as including, but not being restricted to 'any intellectual property' (*s 1308(7)*).

Practical point 2.2

Companies often take the principle of *CTA 2009, s 1308 (FA 2004, s 53)* to mean that any expenditure capitalised in the balance sheet is potentially eligible for RDTR.

This is not correct, as *s 1308* only permits RDTR where the expenditure is brought into account in determining the value of an intangible asset (*s 1308(4)*).

Whilst the definition of an intangible asset for accounting purposes is extremely broad, no other type of capital expenditure is recognised for the purposes of the relief until aligned to the profits earned in the period of claim.

The above practical point is best illustrated by an example:

Example 2.1 – Deferred Expenditure Co (DEC)

DEC paid for various project costs in 2012. DEC's accountant regarded these as deferred expenditure assets in the company's balance sheet and capitalised £1 million accordingly.

Analysis

RDTR arises where revenue costs relate to the profits earned in the year. *CTA 2009, s 1308(4)* relaxes this rule but only where expenditure is brought into account for determining the value of an intangible asset.

There is no indication that the expense relates to intangible asset expenditure. Once DEC releases the expenditure to the profit and loss account it can correctly claim RDTR. No claim is feasible for 2012.

REVENUE V CAPITAL EXPENDITURE

Condition 2: Eligible R&D costs – capital or revenue

2.12 R&D tax relief schemes reward only revenue expenditure, which is allowable as a deduction in the company's profit and loss account for the period of claim (*CTA 2009, ss 53, 1044(5), 1063(4), 1068(4) and 1074(7)*).

But the accounting treatment of expenditure by a company is not necessarily conclusive. For example, the recognition of an asset on the balance sheet or the write-off of expenditure immediately to the profit and loss account may simply represent the rules of a particular accounting standard. This is not indicative of whether the expenditure is revenue or capital for tax purposes.

The characteristics of capital expenditure have frequently come before the courts. Helpful case law such as *Odeon Associated Theatres Ltd v Jones* (1972) 48 TC 257 and *Conn v Robins Bros* (1968) 43 TC 266 point to the 'progressive' interpretation of what is revenue as distinct from capital expenditure. In the ever-changing R&D environment, it sometimes seems remarkable that an 'enduring benefit' can ever really be perceived from innovation.

However, the argument is still a valid one for HMRC, and care is required, particularly with initial work upon software systems which have been set up for the very first time. In general, HMRC will regard an 'enduring benefit' as one which lasts beyond two years without major overhaul. It is also not unusual for a 20% cost to balance sheet ratio to be considered as an appropriate indicator of capital expenditure.

Advisers often mistake pioneering systems work as eligible R&D activity, emphasising that the more bespoke, one-off and unique the outcome is, the more relief it is likely to attract. This can overlook the capital characteristics of a project, which may require further consideration before relief can be claimed. This point is best discussed by way of an example.

Example 2.2 – Company setting up initial systems – capital v revenue R&D projects

Pay Co (PC) is establishing a pay day loan business and invests considerable sums in the development of its systems for credit referencing and encrypted client portals. Whilst a great deal of this work is routine, there has been distinguished R&D activity in the encryption work as a unique portal accessible only to secondary lenders is embedded within the applicant's data.

PC has spent around £1.2 million to date on its project work, it does not expect to revisit the system architecture until around 2016 but it sees the encryption work as a recurrent spend as there are constant malware threats to the integrity of the data. It wishes to claim relief upon the £1.2 million spent to date and a further claim of £2 million over the next three years.

Analysis

PC has some valid project activity, leaving the routine activity to one side. However, the initial spend upon the system has produced an 'enduring benefit' for the company. In the software field, a benchmark of two years is generally acceptable. As the company is not likely to revisit the platform until 2016, it has capitalised the cost and no further relief is due.

The work upon the encryption aspect of the system is 'revenue' in nature. There is a short shelf life for the expenditure and it needs constant evaluation and development. The extent of R&D relief will be determined by the advances and uncertainty inherent within that work. Assuming this is established, the recurrent R&D spend qualifies for relief.

Practical point 2.3

In looking for capital/revenue characteristics within a project, it is sometimes useful to look at the hire of project staff in further detail. Where personnel are hired for a short period to work upon singular elements of a project, it may be that this is an indication of capital expenditure. This would contrast with hire on a regular basis for ongoing development work upon a system.

In practice, most projects will contain a split of both revenue and capital expenditure. Experience shows that the apportionment of costs is much easier towards the final stages of the project work. Interestingly, experience has shown that HMRC are not inclined to deny relief for capital aspects of failed R&D work, regarding the whole of such expenditure as being eligible. This reflects the obvious fact that any perceived enduring benefit could not materialise; there is no 'motive' test within the R&D relief framework.

Capital allowances

2.13 A scheme of capital allowances, called research development allowances (RDAs), is available for project equipment and fixed assets, excluding land. The allowance replaced the scientific research allowance.

Two particular areas of caution are required. The allowance does not cover the deployment of equipment into ordinary commercial use. At this point, an adjustment may be required to apportion the R&D/non-R&D activity.

Secondly, the allowance specifically excludes land costs from the relief.

The usefulness of the allowance has relaxed a little for SME companies, as the annual investment allowance (AIA) increases from April 2013 to £250,000.

The practical use of RDAs is underclaimed in SME R&D claims. This is discussed further at **Chapter 8** below.

Practical point 2.4

Capital expenditure upon equipment used directly in the project activity can qualify for 100% RDAs.

This is discussed further at **Chapter 8**.

THE DEFINITION OF R&D FOR TAX PURPOSES: THE BIS GUIDELINES

Condition 3: The definition of R&D for tax purposes – BIS Guidelines 2010

2.14   The BIS Guidelines list two key 'Gateway' tests which must feature in the company's R&D activity. The tests apply universally to all types of R&D work irrespective of the company's size, stating:

That R&D takes place for tax purposes when a project seeks to   para 3
achieve an **advance** in science, or technology.

Also:

The activities directly contributing towards achieving the advance   para 4
through the resolution of **scientific or technological uncertainty** are
R&D.

The BIS Guidelines have applied this generic definition of when R&D takes place for tax purposes since the relief was introduced in 2000. This Guidance does not define what R&D activity actually 'is', or 'is not', but rather, 'when' it occurs.

Although this analysis appears opaque at first reading, the concept of activity and its linked project costs running in tandem to each other is extremely relevant in calculating the relief due. This is drawn out by paras 4 and 6 of the Guidelines and throughout the legislation at *CTA 2009, Pt 13*, which highlights that the relief is triggered only by 'directly contributing' project activity. It is then that cost collection may begin.

The claimant must provide strong evidence of the technical advances sought from project work and be able to identify the uncertainties involved. Key to an understanding of this will be the strategies formed by the company's 'competent professionals' within the project team. The baseline knowledge against which the advances were identified will also be a key consideration. For example, development-based R&D work upon product improvements will

26

only be R&D for tax purposes where knowledge or capability is extended. Where a product, process or system is improved, the R&D project must demonstrate an 'appreciable improvement' was sought. This is taken to mean that the scientific or technological characteristics of the product, process or system concerned must be fundamentally altered.

The BIS definition of R&D then goes on to provide a number of R&D scenarios and benchmarks. These are summarised usefully at para 9. This and subsequent paragraphs then detail a number of practical examples of R&D and develop the relevance of terms with special meaning for the purposes of the relief.

Finally, there are a number of activities generally accepted by the BIS Guidance to be R&D, including:

- The design, construction and testing of prototypes and pilot   para 39
  plants
- The achievement of design objectives through the resolution of   para 41
  technical uncertainty
- The design of cosmetic or aesthetic improvements to processes   para 42
  and products where the cosmetic effect is achieved through the
  application of science or technological advance
- Improvements in the scientific or technological means to create,   para 43
  manipulate and transfer information or content

Although it may appear anomalous that innovative companies are required to use a definition of innovation which is some 14 years old, the Guidelines have stood the test of time and are generic enough to embrace any type of technical activity undertaken by any company type or size.

Experience shows that HMRC have added their own enhancements to many of the defined BIS terms and, where terms have no legislative special meaning, added additional special meaning and interpretation.

THE R&D BOUNDARIES – DIRECTLY CONTRIBUTING ACTIVITY

Condition 4: Directly contributing project activity, the R&D boundary

2.15   When a company works upon an innovative project, it will often view the whole of the project work as eligible. This is not correct, and in the case of product development-based R&D, can grossly distort the size of the apparent claim. Legislation restricts relief purely to 'directly contributing activity' which will take place during the 'start and end' of the project, ie within the R&D boundary.

'The activities which directly contribute to achieving the advance in science or technology through the resolution of scientific or technological uncertainty will be R&D.'

(BIS Guidelines, para 4)

'To directly contribute to achieving an advance in science or technology, an activity ... must attempt to resolve an element of the scientific or technical uncertainty associated with achieving the advance.'

(BIS Guidelines, para 26)

To identify the boundary between R&D and non-R&D work, it is useful to discuss the company's project work with the company directors and technical staff as well as competent professionals within the industry. The SSAP definition is useful, if inadequate here.

This shows us that an activity is R&D if it is carried on in a technical field with a view to the 'extension of knowledge'. Whilst the BIS definitions extend the R&D scenarios to include product development and a range of other activities, the boundary common to each is that the company is yet to reach ordinary production capacity and routine productive work. This blockage arises because of scientific or technological uncertainty.

Example 2.3 – R&D boundaries, directly contributing activity

Engineering Co (E Co) has formulated a special design for new concrete structures suitable for motorway use as crash barriers. It has patented the technology reflecting substantial R&D upon impact dynamics, alternative materials and finishing processes.

The directors confirm the project has been ongoing for the last four years and as the company is beginning to look at new uses for the product, it may last a further two or three years. It believes it has around seven years of RDTR, which may impact significantly upon its requirement to pay quarterly instalments of corporation tax.

Analysis

An R&D project is defined by the BIS Guidelines as beginning when work to resolve scientific or technological uncertainty starts. The project work will end when that uncertainty is resolved or work upon it ceases (paras 33 and 34).

E Co seems to have been carrying on valid R&D work at some point over the last four years, and it is possible that this will continue over the years to come. It is likely that pre-project work is included in the directors' estimation

28

of R&D activity, including feasibility studies, marketing and financial studies, which are not R&D. Similarly, the alternative use of the product may simply be commercial research at this stage, again not R&D.

At the heart of deciding the R&D boundary for the project(s) is an understanding of what technical uncertainties were formulated and when work towards each took place.

It may be that two separate projects will be visible, depending upon the technical work involved upon the alternative use of the new concrete structures.

It is feasible that project two never gets beyond the commercial evaluation phase and as such is not R&D at all.

For R&D activity to be regarded as making a 'direct contribution' to achieving the advance in science or technology, it must attempt to resolve an element of technical uncertainty which can be linked to the advance sought (para 26). It follows that project costs align themselves to the resolution of that uncertainty, which until it 'exists' cannot begin the collection of project costs. The following examples of direct activity are included in the BIS Guidelines at para 27:

'(a) activities to create or adapt software, materials or equipment needed to resolve the scientific or technological uncertainty, provided that the software, material or equipment is created or adapted solely for use in R&D;

(b) scientific or technological planning activities; and

(c) scientific or technological design, testing and analysis undertaken to resolve the scientific or technological uncertainty.'

The direct contribution requirement is repeated in the CTA legislation. For example, *CTA 2009, s 1124* which states that for staffing costs to be considered eligible for relief, directors or employees must be 'actively engaged' in relevant research and development activity.

Establishing directly contributing activity – the R&D processes/ lifecycle

In practice, directly contributing activity breaks down into four core phases:

A   Pre-project work;

B   Core project work;

C   Establishing the technology;

D   Entering commercial production.

29

2.15 *The research and development tax relief framework*

A Pre-project work

This includes the following activities:

● Technical feasibility studies;

● Proof of concept;

● Commercial costing considerations, marketing and legal preliminaries.

The first two pre-project phases will be eligible for consideration as R&D. Commercially driven work will not. Work that falls between the two extremes, such as the hire of the project team may be eligible as indirectly contributing activity.

B Core project work

Core project work will be aimed at resolving the technical uncertainty and will usually begin after a substantial research phase. This phase will be the company's core project work including developing prototypes or pilot plants in an attempt to confirm the project results are technically competent.

C Establishing the technology

This vital phase of R & D is often overlooked when a viable technology is attained on paper. This part of the project work will include activity aimed at integrating the technology into its technical setting and attaining system certainty.

D Attaining commercial production

The final project stages are usually non-qualifying activity as technical certainty will have been attained at C (above). However this is not always the case, for example, technological certainty may fail at a certain level of production and fresh technical uncertainty can arise.

Once technical uncertainty has been resolved, the collection of project costs usually stops. The core R&D phases will exclude the last two activities and may exclude the third element of testing where no technical uncertainty is evident, although this does not prevent the beginning of new projects in fresh areas of technical uncertainty.

☐ Non-qualifying

▨ Eligible & Activity including Qualifying Indirect Activity

(A) Pre-Project Work

| Idea | Technical feasibility studies | Proof of concept | Commercial & Marketing Analysis | Legal/ Preliminary | Hire of work force |

(B) Core Project Work

| Core Research | Planning & Analysis | Development Work | Pre Prototype Work | Pilot Plants |

(C) Establishing the Technology

| System Integration | Establishing Viable Production Capacity | Sci/Tech Viability Testing |

(D) Entering Commercial Production

| Testing For Certification* | Producing Samples | Clinical Testing* | Registering IP |

* Producing modifications or cosmetic effects

* may involve R&D if technical uncertainty

Practical point 2.5

The core areas of technical uncertainty are usually identified by an involved discussion with the company's project team leader. The company's 'competent professional' will know the R&D process that has taken place, and the steps that lead to the formulation of technical uncertainty and the boundaries involved.

The competent professional will also know the activities directly related to the advance, having arranged the project work to target and resolve these. Similarly, the competent professional will know when these uncertainties had reached a conclusion.

> Once the uncertainties are formulated, project activity from that date can be targeted at 'directly contributing' to the advance sought, until they are resolved or abandoned.
>
> This matrix will set the R&D project boundary and the timeline for the collection of project costs.

Activities that do not directly contribute to the resolution of technical uncertainty

2.16 Paragraph 28 provides a defined list of activity precluded from being R&D. These show obvious non-scientific objectives, but a second category of 'qualifying indirect activity' requires careful review.

Non-technical activity includes the following:

- commercial and financial activity connected to the innovation, such as marketing, or finance arrangement;

- work upon non-scientific aspects of the innovation such as simple graphic design, work satisfying industry standards of safety beyond technical uncertainty;

- production and distribution of the innovative product;

- administration and support costs, including maintenance and security, transportation and repairs.

Practical point 2.6

It is often useful to review project staff's timesheets to gauge the extent of ineligible activity. This will vary according to the experience and qualifications of the team members. Performance pay and bonuses may also provide pointers towards R&D activity.

Qualifying indirect activity (QIA)

2.17 Not all project activity undertaken by project staff will be directly linked to technical work and a 'halfway house' allows some relief for these costs. QIA can be regarded as R&D where there is a close link to the project's technical activity. This type of work supports the R&D project work, but in itself will not be R&D.

Paragraph 31 of the Guidelines explains that activity forming part of the project either in a 'support' role or directed at ancillary research, feasibility studies or training for the R&D project team is QIA.

This is best shown by an example.

Example 2.4 – Day-to-day administrative work – ineligible activity

Telecom Co is in the midst of a project aimed at a multilingual 'speaking' yellow pages service. There is a dedicated scanning department working within Telecom Co. One of its key functions is to populate the database for the R&D project, the costs are around £100,000 out of a £500,000 department budget.

Analysis

R&D relief will be feasible for the staff costs of £100,000, the remaining £400,000 is not supporting the R&D project activity, but is relevant to the company's day–to-day administrative work.

Example 2.5 – Commercial or legal work – ineligible activity

Telecom Co requires further qualified personnel to work on the next phase of the project. The team leader spends time upon drafting job specifications and interviewing. He is supported by the company's administrative team and the HR department.

Analysis

The team leader's time spent upon the recruitment is QIA (BIS Guidelines, para 31(b)) and indirectly linked to the project tasks. The work of the administrative team is not 'directly' supporting the project work. Together with the HR department's work, its key objective is a commercial or legal one to help the smooth running of the recruitment process.

System uncertainty

2.18   R&D activities will normally require some sort of testing to prove technical competence. This takes many forms. For example, beta testing, prototyping or dry runs are common in manufacturing-linked project work. Usually this type of work often cannot achieve technical functionality in isolation as there will also be unknowns about how the results of the project integrate into existing systems, technologies or production methods.

Bringing a particular project to an end may begin a new R&D process of 'system uncertainty', where a new system is added into the existing architecture and the performance as a whole may be scientifically or technologically uncertain.

Work directed at resolving system uncertainty is usually R&D. But in some industries, especially those with significant safety regulations, a great deal of 'safe' further testing is required to attain certification. This will not necessarily be R&D if no technical uncertainties are involved, and the point is an enthusiastic one for HMRC.

By way of an example, many cosmetic and pharmaceutical companies will be required to load tests upon representative samples of end users irrespective of attaining a 'safe' product. This type of activity will not be R&D but the satisfaction of a commercial agreement or industry safety standard.

Practical point 2.7

Subprojects are a common hallmark of R&D project work. There is no specific guidance upon this area, and each project activity must simply be evaluated as such in its own right.

Should new advances and uncertainties become apparent during the course of the project, the legislation is not taken to mean these should be excluded, as only the primary project can be capable of relief. Separate projects or subprojects must be reviewed on their own merits as potential new projects if the presence of an advance and uncertainty seems possible.

Similarly, if a subproject/'shadow project' begins, it carries no 'automatic' assumption of eligibility to relief simply because the main project is eligible.

Example 2.6 – Parallel project

Hot Air Co (HAC) began a project to develop a hand drier for use in schools. Two important features needed to be present in the appliance: (1) a temperature control mechanism so the temperature outflow never exceeded 35 degrees; and (2) a cut-out mechanism should small fingers be poked into it. HAC knew that the existing products on the market had neither feature, and this involved sufficient technological uncertainty in the advances sought.

HAC carried out a successful project and then considered the use of the drier in high usage outlets such as restaurants and airports. HAC carried out a parallel project but needed to resolve fresh areas of uncertainty arising from the effect of the high demand, and 24/7 environment. Parallel Project 2 needed to design more robust safety features with enhanced capability and heat detection. It wants to claim R&D relief for both projects.

Analysis

HAC has identified technical uncertainty in its first project and has begun a parallel project after promising reviews of alternative, more intensive uses for the Project 1 design. The point at which this is begun is an important one. There are two scenarios. If Project 2 has commenced when the knowledge from Project 1 was not available or apparent, it is likely to qualify as part of the scope of Project 1. The activity will be R&D.

If Project 2 simply exploits the knowledge obtained from Project 1 in a new way with some added safety features, this will not be R&D. Part of project 2 may qualify if the new features represent a technological advance and uncertainty which can be documented. If these features involve no more than copycat technology from existing hand driers, then that part of the activity will not be regarded as part of the R&D project work (no uncertainty, new knowledge or new capability) and will not be R&D.

Summary

When does R&D begin and end?

2.19　The above shows that for tax relief purposes, R&D will begin when the scientific or technological uncertainties relevant to the technical activity can be formulated. This is distinct from the ordinary commercial and legal steps that will precede R&D project work. However, in practice, technical uncertainty can meander and costs may still be eligible under a wide variety of circumstances. Paragraphs 33 and 34 of the BIS Guidelines confirm that the cost collection will 'end' when knowledge or capability is available in a form usable by competent professionals, or when a viable prototype or similar is produced and no uncertainty remains.

Practical point 2.8

Creating a concept for a new product or system and carrying out the relevant marketing and financial studies is commonly regarded as the beginning of valid R&D activity. Companies will believe that substantial amounts of the director's time at this stage will qualify for RDTR. Legislation tells us that neither activity is regarded as R&D.

Similarly, at the end of a project, product testing in compliance with industry safety standards or regulatory practice will often be regarded as an extension of the R&D work. Paragraphs 33 and 34 tell us otherwise. R&D ends once a viable technology is formulated, irrespective of extraneous safety standards or non-technological issues with the new product.

In the automotive industry, there are very high safety standards for new technology. Testing will go far beyond the benchmark for viable production in new products and batches of thousand product runs will be required to attain the necessary safety standard. This marginal activity is unlikely to be R&D, satisfying commercial or safety standards, as distinct from resolving technological uncertainty.

ELIGIBLE R&D COSTS – CTA 2009, PT 13

Condition 5: Scheme rules, Ch 13 – Categories of qualifying expenditure

2.20   Once R&D activity encompasses points 1 to 4 of the framework, the provisions of Pt 13 must be applied to the project costs by reference to the company's accounting period.

Although the details of each individual scheme differ, there are a number of common points which are summarised below. The detailed rules of each individual scheme are discussed at **Chapters 4** and **5** below.

A number of caveats apply to the choice of scheme for relief. The commercial context in which R&D activities are undertaken is often a decisive factor. For example, where the SME does not meet its R&D costs independently, it must claim under the *Ch 3* scheme of relief at the reduced 'large company' rate, or the new *Ch 6A* RDEC scheme.

An overview of the most common R&D costs follows.

Categories of qualifying expenditure

Staffing costs

2.21   Personnel costs make up the bulk of R&D claims within the SME schemes. Not all staff are regarded by the legislation as eligible for relief. Separate cost categories apply to employees, subcontractors and 'externally provided workers' (EPWs) supplied through third parties or agencies. Large scheme reliefs do not permit subcontracting costs as an eligible category of expenditure.

Currently, three types of relief are possible for 'people costs' ie:

* costs relating to salaries and emoluments paid to directors or employees of the claimant company (*CTA 2009, ss 1123–1124*);

* costs relating to personnel engaged by the company as subcontractors within the project (*CTA 2009, s 1133–1136*);

* costs relating to personnel supplied to the claimant through third parties. This relief is known as expenditure upon 'externally provided workers'.

The term 'subcontractor' is given its ordinary meaning. HMRC expect a subcontractor to have responsibility for a project 'deliverable' and bear the risk and costs associated to this, as distinct from a 'freelance consultant'.

An EPW is one supplied through a third party and engaged in research or development activity which is relevant to and under the supervision of the claimant. A 'tripartite' arrangement needed to be demonstrable for expenditure incurred before 1 April 2012. After that date, the requirement is not as prescriptive, but there must still be at least three parties involved in the engagement.

Practical point 2.9

A common misconception is that all staff costs for personnel working upon a project will qualify for relief. The scheme rules prescribe only three types of 'people' cost which can be considered for relief:

- emoluments and similar paid to employees and directors of the claimant company;

- the cost of EPWs which is met by the company;

- the cost of subcontractors tasked with meeting the responsibility of supplying specific project deliverables. This cost is available only within the SME scheme.

This leaves a number of bona fide project personnel costs without relief. Common examples are:

- group employees seconded on to the claimant's project work;

- employees and directors who are not 'paid' but costed through an intercompany account (*Gripple Ltd v HMRC* [2010] EWHC 1609 (Ch));

- freelance consultants, who may, in fact, be either subcontractors or externally provided workers;

- fees etc invoiced by directors who supply their services to the claimant company through an umbrella company or other entity;

- secondees from other companies within the group, for whom costs are not directly met by the claimant company;

- employees with dual contract arrangements;

- employees for whom government funding has been provided;

- subcontracting costs incurred by large companies.

The legislation upon staffing costs has changed only very slightly since 2000. In 2004, the 80/20 rule was removed. But it took until April 2012 for the strict tripartite rules of the externally provided workers regulations to be relaxed. It is generally felt these did not go far enough to remove the disparity of some project workers qualifying for relief and others being ineligible purely because of the contractual engagement used.

In practice, HMRC take the case of *Nichols v Gibson* (1996) 68 TC 611 to mean that R&D relief cannot be applied to redundancy payments, and presumably golden handshakes and ex gratia payments which are motivated by commercial or legal considerations.

Practical point 2.10

Freelance consultants are very common in a number of 'high-tech' industries. This reflects both the scarcity of very skilled personnel in the UK and the fact that hirers are working in an uncertain, highly innovative space.

Freelance consultants do not qualify for any type of R&D relief under either the SME or large schemes. Where a third party is engaged by reference to weekly/hourly pay, it is unlikely that the engagement will represent a 'subcontracting' relationship.

Where a third party is engaged through their own company, or other third party, as an EPW, care was required prior to April 2012 that a 'tripartite' arrangement was demonstrable.

These points are developed further at **Chapter 4** below. In practice, a review of both the invoices and contracts for non-employee project personnel should identify the substance of the relationship.

Employees and directors – CTA 2009, s 1123–1124

2.22 For R&D tax relief purposes, the legislation states that a company's direct staffing costs are those paid to employees and directors employed by the claimant company. Only those costs reflected, and paid, in the profit and loss account for the year of claim from the list below attract relief (*CTA 2009, s 1123–1124*).

- emoluments of employees or directors of the company. This includes salaries, wages, bonuses and any type of cash payment;

- expenses incurred directly by employees or directors and reimbursed as money;

- Class 1 secondary National Insurance contributions paid by the employer;

- compulsory EEA 'National Insurance' contributions for internationally mobile employees (*Council Regulation 883/2004/EEC ([2004] OJ L166/1), Article 3*);

- pension contributions paid into a qualifying pension scheme.

Practical point 2.9 illustrates that a number of scenarios in which project staff are engaged will preclude tax relief. Case law and statute have also shown us that the definition of staffing costs cannot include the following types of staff 'payment' or award:

- dividend payments or waivers;

- benefits in kind – a loophole existed briefly in 2004 permitting relief on all benefits made available to employees;

- redundancy payments – HMRC cite the case of *Nichols v Gibson* (1996) 68 TC 611;

- commissions paid to recruitment agencies for the hire of project personnel;

- wages and salaries etc paid to employees of other companies within a group unless the payroll is run by that company purely out of administrative convenience. Whether an arrangement like this could be regarded as the provision of externally provided workers will depend upon the individual circumstances;

- reimbursed credit card expenses of employees or directors;

- share awards or the award of share options;

- opportunity costs or notional salaries.

Practical point 2.11

Some high-tech companies 'pay' staff by means of dividends, share options or deferred equity rights. In the case of *PA Holdings Ltd* [2011] EWCA Civ 1414, the company directors agreed that dividends upon preference shares would be awarded to them in lieu of cash bonuses.

This arrangement gave the company valuable cash flow savings, and the directors clear performance incentives. HMRC argued an income and National Insurance charge was exigible. Although a partial victory by the company followed, in an R&D situation, no relief would be feasible upon a 'deemed' payment within the scope of what is now the avoidance provisions of the *Income Tax (Earnings and Pensions) Act* 2003 (*ITEPA 2003*), *ss 413B–425*.

Analysis

Staffing costs are only eligible where paid as cash to employees or directors of the claimant company. This precludes RDTR from being available for most incentive 'payments' not paid as cash.

Externally provided workers (CTA 2009, s 1127–1134)

2.23 Frequently R&D activities will be undertaken by non-employees of the company. The cost of using individuals engaged by the company through a third party is expenditure on an EPW. This is not expenditure upon 'staffing costs', or 'subcontractors', but a separately identifiable head of expenditure.

The definition of an EPW is based upon the income tax rules for agency workers (*ITEPA 2003, s 44*). The EPW rules also apply where the worker is an employee of the staff provider.

Prior to 1 April 2013, the regulations on EPWs required the R&D company to have in place a tripartite arrangement for the engagement. The following conditions needed to be met:

- The worker must be an individual rather than a company.

- The worker must not be a director or employee of the company or companies within the trading group of the R&D claimant.

- The worker must personally provide, or be obliged to personally provide the services concerned.

- The worker is subject to supervision and control by the R&D company in respect of how the services are performed.

- The worker must provide his services through or by the staff provider, whether or not he is a director or employee of the providing company.

- The provision of the services did not constitute the carrying on of activity contracted out by the company.

These rules were modified very slightly for expenditure on EPWs incurred on or after 1 April 2013. The rules now admit expenditure for additional parties involved in supplying the worker. Staff may now be provided indirectly through more than one party. The revised definition simplify the rules de

Subcontractor payments

2.24   The question of what a 'subcontractor' is follows the ordinary meaning of the word. The HMRC approach is summarised in CIRD84250, which states:

> 'Where there is a contract between persons for R&D activities to be carried out by one for the other, then the R&D activities have been subcontracted. A contract to provide services rather than to undertake a specific part of the activities is not subcontracted R&D. Nor is a contract of personal employment.'

Relief for subcontracting costs is provided by *CTA 2009, ss 1133–1136* for the purposes of calculating expenditure upon contracted out R&D activity (*ss 1053(1), 1072* and *1102(2)*).

The amount of relief depends upon whether or not the parties are 'connected or unconnected', or elect to be so. For most R&D claimants, the unconnected treatment relieves a maximum of 65% of the subcontractor's costs paid by the claimant in the relevant accounting period.

Where a payment is to a connected party, the costs to be included are the lower of:

- 65% of the actual payment to the subcontractor; and

- the relevant expenditure of the subcontractor upon the project's R&D deliverable.

Personnel costs: connected persons

2.25   The amount of relief claimable is dependent upon whether or not the claimant is 'connected to the personnel involved'. The identification of 'connected persons' is relevant to the following categories of expenditure:

- externally provided workers;

- subcontracted R&D activities;

- contributions to independent research (large schemes only).

'Connection' follows the definition of *ICTA 1988, s 839.* Various elections are feasible for unconnected parties to be regarded as 'connected', which are considered in more detail at **Chapter 4** below.

Software and consumable items (ss 1125, 1126)

2.26   Relief is available for both large and SME companies incurring revenue upon 'computer software or consumable items'. The project costs must reflect software or consumable items employed directly in R&D activity. The definition specifically includes water, fuel and power (*CTA 2009, s 1125*).

Relief is limited to costs attributable to 'direct involvement' with the project activity. The example given by HMRC states that power used in a training facility would be included to the extent that the facility was providing training to directly support an R&D project' (BIS Guidelines, para 31(d)) but not for training that was required for more general purposes.

Materials which are 'transformed' are equally eligible for relief. In practice, HMRC are not progressive in regarding anything other than physical, traditional materials as being capable of being 'transformed'. Experience shows that this viewpoint excludes the consumption or transformation of digital imagery or electronic information from one state to another changed state. This is disappointing as there is no simple definition of 'consumed or transformed'. CIRD82400 states that a key aspect is that materials or consumables are 'no longer so useable in their original form'.

Software

2.27   Software is not a consumable item, as it is not consumed or transformed. The definition also usually excludes hardware purchased for the project. This can lead to a conflict where software or hardware is commissioned as part of the company's beta testing or prototype work. Here specific relief is permitted under para 41 of the BIS Guidelines. For the purposes of *s 1125* relief, it is useful to look only at analytical work for which specific software was licensed or used.

Care is also required to apportion software R&D costs once production commences or system certainty is attained and the R&D project is at an end.

Example 2.7 – Software costs – non R&D use

Fast PC Co (FPC) purchased a number of software licences for use in its ongoing R&D project. One of the licences expires in five years; the other three licences are renewed annually. FPC anticipates its project will end in 2014. Having now reached its final stages, it has spent around £80,000 per annum on its software licences from 2012.

Analysis

FPC has shown the expenditure in its accounts, and the licences are used in the project work.

Relief is due as the expenditure meets the *s 1125* requirements. The costs must be apportioned to exclude ordinary commercial use of the software once the R&D project stops. The cost of the five-year licence will not attract relief in its entirety.

Use other than directly in R&D

2.28   Only activity by employees and directors upon work directly contributing to the resolution of technical uncertainty can be claimed. This is developed further below. The 'direct contribution' can include qualifying indirect activity, such as feasibility studies, personnel and administrative functions performed by project staff during the course of reaching the projects' objectives.

Practical point 2.12 – Staffing costs – large schemes and SME scheme

Staffing costs are defined by HMRC Guidance as being relevant to personnel directly employed by the claimant. Grouped companies frequently have R&D performers in the UK and it is important that employment contracts are aligned to the claimant.

There is an exception to this where, purely for administrative convenience, one company runs the group payroll or the payroll for two or more members of the group.

To develop this point further, the case of *Gripple Ltd v HMRC* [2010] EWHC 1609 (Ch) shows us that 'paying' staffing costs through an intercompany account entry will not qualify for relief.

Eligible costs summary – SME scheme

2.29 The following costs are eligible for relief under the SME scheme:

- staffing costs for payments to directors and employees;
- expenditure upon EPWs;
- payments to subcontractors whether connected or unconnected;
- costs of computer software and materials;
- capital equipment used in the project which is eligible for RDA (**Chapter 7**).

Eligible costs summary – large company schemes

2.30 The following costs are eligible for relief under *CTA 2009, Ch 5, s 1077*:

- staffing costs for payments to directors and employees;
- expenditure upon EPWs;
- costs of computer software and materials;
- relevant payments for clinical trials;
- costs of contributions towards independent research activities;
- capital equipment used in the project which is eligible for RDA (**Chapter 8**).

GRANTS AND SUBSIDIES

Subsidised expenditure – SME scheme only

2.31 Grants and subsidies can impact upon the amount of R&D tax relief due. This impact is by reference to the project as a whole rather than the accounting period of claim. The impact arises because SME R&D tax relief is a 'notifiable State Aid'.

R&D tax relief is not available at the higher SME rate where project expenditure is subsidised. As an alternative, the SME may claim that part of the subsidised costs under one of the large schemes.

There are a number of ways in which expenditure might be regarded as 'subsidised'. The most obvious types are where a project has received any funding which is a notified State Aid. In that case, no expenditure on the whole of that project can qualify for the R&D tax relief under the SME scheme. This reflects the UK's participation in the European Community Treaty.

If a grant or subsidy is received by an SME, other than through notified State Aid, the expenditure is 'partially' subsidised. This is to the extent that it does not exceed the subsidy. This may result in the expenditure qualifying for R&D tax relief partly under the SME scheme and partly under one of the large company schemes (*CTA 2009, ss 1052(6), 1053(5) and 1138* – SME scheme only). The examples at **Chapter 7** highlight the interaction of grants and subsidies with SME reliefs.

Practical point 2.13 – Stage payment or subsidy?

HMRC frequently extend the definition of 'subsidies' to include 'stage payments' or 'up front' contractual payments where an R&D company has entered into a contract for eventual product development.

The argument then flows that the SME has received a 'subsidy' and should be denied R&D SME relief upon eligible project work. It is not unknown where stage payments are made to the SME in conjunction with project development work, for the whole of the project costs to be regarded as subsidised and denied relief.

The drafting of contracts involving production-based R&D activity is crucial to R&D relief, and it is important that stage payments are demonstrable as such.

CONTEXT OF THE UK R&D FRAMEWORK – THE FRASCATI MANUAL

2.32   The Frascati Manual is an internationally recognised methodology for collecting and using R&D statistics. It is important because R&D relief is available in other territories measuring R&D in a different way. For example, many of the EU grant schemes adopt this model, providing relief for commercially driven costs as part of the R&D project, in contrast to the UK tax model, which concentrates upon purely 'technical' costs. The Frascati model defines research as follows.

Research and experimental development (R&D) comprise creative work undertaken on a systematic basis in order to increase the stock of knowledge, including knowledge of man, culture and society, and the use of this stock of knowledge to devise new applications.

The Frascati term 'R&D' covers three activities: basic research, applied research and experimental development.

Basic research is experimental or theoretical work undertaken primarily to acquire new knowledge of the underlying foundation of phenomena and observable facts, without any particular application or use in view.

Applied research is also original investigation undertaken in order to acquire new knowledge. It is, however, directed primarily towards a specific practical aim or objective.

Experimental development is systematic work, drawing on existing knowledge gained from research and/or practical experience, which is directed to producing new materials, products or devices, to installing new processes, systems and services, or to improving substantially those already produced or installed. R&D covers both formal R&D in R&D Units and informal or occasional R&D in other units.

The Frascati Manual lists situations where certain activities are to be excluded from R&D except when carried out solely or primarily for the purposes of an R&D project. These include: routine testing and analysis of materials, components, products, processes etc; feasibility studies; routine software development; general purpose data collection. The later stages of some clinical drug trials may be more akin to routine testing, particularly in cases where the original research has been done by a drug company or other contractor.

Frascati was originally written by and for the experts in OECD member countries who collect and issue national data on R&D. Over the years, it has become the standard of conduct for R&D surveys and data collection not only in the OECD and the European Union, but also in several non-member economies, for example, through the science and technology surveys of the UNESCO Institute for Statistics (UIS).

The Frascati Model plays no direct part in UK R&D tax legislation, but is relevant to UK R&D performers interested in obtaining EEA funding or grants for project activity, or trying to establish international tax comparisons.

JUDICIAL GUIDANCE

2.33   Two contrasting R&D tax cases have come before the courts in recent years. The case of *Gripple Ltd v HMRC* [2010] EWHC 1609 (Ch) shows the 'micro' detail with which the claim must be constructed. Complementing this, the case of *BE Studios Ltd v Smith & Williamson Ltd* [2005] EWHC 1506 (Ch) highlights the relevance of documentation evidencing the above R&D framework is critical. That case shows that the wider 'macro' high-tech R&D environment in which the company found itself is almost an irrelevance.

Both cases show that the structure of the R&D relief framework forms a 'meticulously drafted code which must be 'followed to the letter'. If R&D work is not evidenced as a project following a systematic approach targeting technical uncertainty, no relief is possible.

This became very evident in the High Court during the appeal made by *BE Studios Ltd*. BE Studios Ltd was a software company, which described itself as 'innovative' and at the 'cutting edge' of computer software development, a leader in its technological environment. It filed a claim for R&D relief upon various computer game projects. In support it described the high-tech nature of its setting and the enhanced functionality resulting from its work. The claim was then rejected by HMRC.

The company pursued its R&D claim to the High Court, where Mr Justice Evans-Lombe confirmed that the company's approach, in assuming that all of its activities were R&D, and deducting specific disallowable activities such as marketing, and non-technical work, was an 'entirely inappropriate' approach to preparing the claim. The provisions of *SSAP 13* and the BIS Guidelines act as 'gateways' through which all claims must pass to be allowable.

Mr Justice Evans-Lombe stressed the need to follow the R&D framework. It was crucial to identify the scientific or technological uncertainties in its work and quantify the expenditure on seeking to resolve these. The correct approach to preparing the claim was to read the guidelines and the legislation, to refer to the documentation and to consult with the people undertaking the work.

Practical point 2.14

The R&D claim documentation

Any claim to relief must document, as a minimum, the following criteria:

Accounting requirements

- The expenditure is reflected in the company's profit and loss account or has been used to determine the value of intellectual property.

- The expenditure is recognised as R&D under GAAP, or equivalent standards.

Project requirements

Satisfaction of the 'Definition of R&D for tax purposes' BIS Guidelines 2004 – providing evidence of:

- the field of science or technology and correlating advance(s) sought by the project work;

- the scientific or technological uncertainties present in seeking the advance;

- what the R&D project set out to do and how;

- how the current state of technical knowledge or capability was to be extended;

- why this knowledge or capability was not available or readily deducible by a competent professional working in the field;

- which activities within the project fall within the GAAP definitions and BIS definitions of activity directly contributing to the advances in science or technology which are being sought;

- which of those activities represent 'qualifying indirect activity' by the project personnel;

- the arrangement of the activities as a systematic project;

- the strength of the technical evidence of 'advancement' and 'uncertainty' described by the company's competent professional;

- how ineligible activity was identified and excluded from the claim;

- the relevance of and commercial context for the R&D activity;

- that the rules of the specific scheme have been followed and any commercial circumstances of the company or the project work, have been adequately considered.

Eligible cost requirements

- Only those costs relevant to the R&D work itself are included in the relief.

- The eligible cost headings of staffing costs, subcontractor costs, software and consumables and project equipment are considered in the claim.

- These costs are not subsidised (SME scheme).

CONCLUSION

2.34 R&D tax relief follows a 'meticulously drafted' code, made up from piecemeal legislation. The UK framework begins with the presence of GAAP compliant R&D activity within the company's accounts. The expenditure must then be further evaluated to consider the definition of R&D for tax purposes set out in the BIS Guidelines (2004). Activity that 'directly contributes' to areas of technical uncertainty within the advance sought by the project work must be identified. Finally, the expenditure must be both relevant and drawn from the specific heads of costs following the specific SME or large scheme provisions at *Pt 13*.

In summary, the R&D tax relief framework prescribes that a number of complex conditions must be satisfied. Some are particular to the relevant scheme of claim (SME or large schemes), and some are generic to all.

Chapter 3

The BIS Guidelines: the definition of research and development for tax purposes

Contents

SIGNPOSTS

- **Definition of R&D** – The BIS Guidelines formulate the definition of R&D for tax purposes. These supplement and develop the accounting definitions of the terms 'research' and 'development' (see **3.1**).

- **Potentially eligible for relief** – The Guidelines are used for a variety of tax reliefs and will identify expenditure which is only potentially eligible for relief; the legislation at *CTA 2009, Pt 13* and a number of other considerations may limit the amount of relief due (see **3.1**).

- **Gateway tests** – The definition of R&D for tax purposes is based upon two 'Gateway tests' (see **3.3**).

- **Advance in science or technology** – A project will only qualify as R&D if it seeks an 'advance in science or technology'. An advance can take place in a wide variety of circumstances which are commonly met in industry (see **3.6–3.11**). The Guidelines develop these by way of examples.

- **Direct contribution** – A project must deploy resources making a 'direct contribution' toward the resolution of scientific/technological uncertainty relevant to the advance. The activity that makes a 'direct contribution' is R&D, but some indirectly contributing activity will also count (see **3.41**).

- **Systematic approach** – The project needs to be systematic in its methodology. Accidental or copycat R&D will not qualify for relief (see **3.34**).

- **Three key types** – R&D projects often split into three key types, directed at extending overall knowledge or capability, or seeking an appreciable improvement to existing processes, systems or products etc. Each represents an 'advance'. Seeking the advance is the key point; the project need not be successful (see **3.6–3.9**)

- **Uncertainty essential** – Uncertainty means that the knowledge path does not exist and is not easily deducible to a 'competent professional'. For any project to be regarded as R&D there must be uncertainty. The industry peer requirement underlines the definition of R&D for tax purposes but can be hard to establish (see **3.12–3.18**).

- **Eligible R&D activity** – The Guidelines provide a number of scenarios as examples of eligible R&D activity to establish the core meaning of R&D and the relevance of terms given a special meaning (see **3.19**).

- **SME and large companies** – The Guidelines apply universally to both SME and large companies and all types of R&D activity. There is no specific guidance upon the individual branches of science and technology. Social and 'soft' sciences are not eligible fields (see **3.9**).

- **Key terms** – A number of key terms are used in the BIS Guidelines, which do not reappear in the specific rules of the schemes in *CTA 2009, Pt 13*. The case of *Gripple Ltd v HMRC* [2010] EWHC 1609 (Ch) is taken to mean that no purposive construction of any terms is possible (see **3.34**).

- **Practical case studies** – The Guidelines summarise the principles of R&D as practical case studies, covering a range of technical activity (see **3.38–3.41**).

SUMMARY: KEY POINTS

3.1   This Chapter discusses the definition of research and development (R&D) for tax purposes. This definition relies upon the BIS Guidelines and the emphasis placed upon key terms within that guidance.

The Guidelines supplement and develop the accounting definitions of the terms 'research' and 'development'. Taken together, the definitions within the accounting principles and BIS Guidelines will establish whether a company's project work has any eligibility for relief under one of the R&D schemes at *CTA 2009, Pt 13*. Where there is a conflict between the UK GAAP principles and the BIS Guidelines, upon the nature of the R&D activity, the latter take precedence.

R&D takes place when a project seeks a scientific or technological advance. The activity targeted directly toward the resolution of technical uncertainty inherent in seeking the advance is R&D. The terms 'advance' and 'uncertainty' form a gateway to identify the substance of the company's R&D activity. These terms seem opaque, when encountered for the first time, but form the 'R&D boundaries', if any relief is to be due. The Guidelines are so broadly written that R&D can arise within almost any type of technical project work, and in any industry. An 'advance' is developed by the Guidelines into three types of R&D activity, although others are possible. An advance can focus upon specific knowledge or capability or represent project work seeking an 'appreciable improvement' through scientific or technological change. Many projects will have more than one of these key elements present.

Uncertainty means fundamental technical doubt. A common starting point in R&D work is that the company 'does not even know' if a solution exists. The Guidelines introduce the concept of 'theoretical knowledge', meaning the knowledge or capability must be neither available nor 'deducible' at the time the project uncertainties are formulated. This excepts expertise subject to trade secrecy or scenarios where several companies work in isolation upon new technologies. Commercial uncertainty or work to advance the company's own knowledge is not R&D.

Research or 'knowledge-based' R&D makes up around 9% of claims filed to HMRC. Capability- and improvement-based R&D makes up around 90% of SME activity. For either 'type' of activity, the project goals must demonstrate the advance sought goes beyond knowledge or capability that is either available or 'deducible'. This theoretical test is a very high standard and can be hard to establish.

R&D projects focusing upon appreciable improvement must also seek scientific or technological 'change'. This requirement is easily overlooked. Seeking an appreciable improvement means to fundamentally adapt or alter the technical characteristics to the point that it is 'better than the original'. This will ordinarily require a scientific or technological change. If the definition is correctly applied, it will disregard most functional changes to technology or minor/routine amendments. The 'test' of this type of R&D is comparative – the improvement would generally be agreed technically significant by industry peers, or 'competent professionals'.

A number of very specific terms are added in to the tax definition of R&D within the Guidelines, and these need to be considered fully if relief is to be due (see **3.34**).

This Chapter will establish whether or not project work described as R&D in the company's accounts is potentially eligible for tax relief. It considers in detail, the BIS 'Gateway' tests requiring a scientific or technological 'advance'. The demonstration of this cannot be understated. Without documenting the systematic project work focused upon this 'advance' and 'uncertainty', judicial guidance shows that no relief is possible, no matter how innovative the work may be, or how 'high-tech' the environment in which the company operates.

THE DEFINITION OF R&D FOR TAX PURPOSES

Context

3.2

1   R&D takes place when a project seeks a scientific or technological advance. The activity targeted directly toward the resolution of technical uncertainty inherent in seeking the advance is R&D. The key terms 'advance' and 'uncertainty' are so broadly defined that they apply universally to any branch of science or technology and can take place within almost any industry and size of company. These key terms form a 'Gateway' for any claim and the Guidelines provide a number of scenarios and examples to establish the full extent of their meaning.

2   The legislative basis of the definition of R&D begins in *CTA 2009, s 1041 (ICTA 1988, s 837A)*. This confirms that the starting point in identifying R&D activity is the costs identified as such under generally

accepted accounting practice (GAAP). Because this provides both a broader and narrower definition of R&D, the GAAP interpretation is then modified by the BIS Guidelines. These were published on 5 March 2004 and updated in 2010. The latest Guidelines replace those issued on 28 July 2000 and came into force for accounting periods ending on or after 1 April 2004.

3   In order for there to be R&D at all, there must be a systematic project environment. This does not need to be successful, but will show considered specific technical activity targeting a scientific or technological advance. Although the Guidelines are very broad, applying universally to all branches of science and technology, or any type of company and industry, *CTA 2009, Pt 13* inserts the requirement that the activity must be 'relevant' to the company's trade. The only exception to the 'relevant' condition is for contributions to independent research activity made by large companies.

4   The specific rules of the small and medium enterprise (SME) and large company tax schemes under which tax relief is claimed will restrict the amount of qualifying expenditure identified by the Guidelines.

The Guidelines are therefore one of many parts making up the relief. The EC Regulations have a similar effect for SME companies where project costs are subject to EC State Aid requirements.

5   Summary: BIS Guidelines – Context:

a   *CTA 2009, s 1126 (ICTA 1988, s 837A* – definition of eligible UK company).

b   GAPP or relevant IAS used in company's accounts.

c   Revenue (rather than capital) expenditure reflected in the accounting period.

d   BIS Guidelines and appropriate Treasury Orders.

e   EC Recommendation 361/EC/2003 ([2003] OJ L 124/36).

f   Specific SME or large scheme legacy or RDEC rules (*CTA 2009, Pt 13*).

g   Judicial and HMRC Guidance and Interpretations.

6   The context of R&D is broad. This sometimes means the full depth of a project can be overlooked. The Guidelines confirm that the R&D boundaries need to be fully reviewed to understand all related subprojects relevant to the uncertainty targeted by the project. 'All [technical] activities' collectively focused upon the project aim are within these boundaries. This is an area of important consideration for HMRC and the project boundaries need to be correctly drawn. The project start and end point is driven by the uncertainty within the project and will confirm when the collection of potentially eligible costs begins and ends (see **3.41**).

THE BIS 'GATEWAY' TESTS

Definition of R&D

3.3

'THE DEFINITION OF RESEARCH AND DEVELOPMENT

R&D for tax purposes takes place when a **project** seeks to achieve an **advance in science or technology**.

The activities which **directly contribute** to achieving this advance in science or technology through the resolution of **scientific or technological uncertainty** are R&D.'

BIS Guidelines (as updated December 2010, paras 3, 4)

The definition does not initially state 'what' R&D actually is, but rather 'when' it takes place. Writing in an abstract tense is at first sight an opaque and confusing way to define R&D. If this absentia can be put to one side for a moment, consideration of each term will help define when R&D activity first began. Once uncertainty and its relevant advance can be established, it is possible to begin to collect R&D costs targeted at their resolution. The definition therefore synchronises the R&D activities with the collection of potentially eligible expenditure from the company's accounting records.

Identifying the claim

3.4   To evaluate the terms 'advance' and 'uncertainty', the company's technical work must be discussed with the project director or company's competent professional(s) to identify the advances sought and the uncertainty attached to this. All types of R&D work must establish the aim of scientific or technological advancement and its uncertainty. This will include extended scientific or technological knowledge or capability as well as work which is aimed at appreciable improvement. Improvement R&D requires changes to the technical characteristics of existing products, systems or materials to the point where they are comparatively 'better than the original'. For any type of project to be regarded as R&D, the company must be able to comment on the baseline knowledge apparent or deducible at the time the project began. Uncertainty which is easily deducible will not count as R&D.

The R&D review

3.5   This will include a review of:

- what scientific or technological advances were sought from the project;

- what uncertainty was present;

- what the company has sought to achieve and how;

- the extent to which the company has advanced knowledge or technology, or sought to 'appreciably improve' an existing product, material or device;

- the granularity of the advance, whether this involved simply taking components apart in a routine way, or fundamentally rebuilding the characteristics of the original technology;

- which activities were routine, or without technical uncertainty and did not contribute to the overall project advances;

- the baseline knowledge available or deducible in the industry at the time of the project's conception to see if the uncertainty is fundamental;

- whether a peer–to–peer discussion could have easily resolved the uncertainty perceived in bringing the project about;

- what technical staff were hired or contributed to the project expertise, what qualifications and experience were pooled to attain the advance;

- the status of the company's competent professional and project team;

- the scientific or technological progression of the project ('milestones');

- the ultimate outcome.

ADVANCE IN SCIENCE OR TECHNOLOGY

Test One: Seeking an advance in science or technology

3.6

'R&D for tax purposes takes place when a project seeks to achieve an advance in science or technology.'

(BIS Guidelines 2004, para 3)

The term 'advance' is one of the two gateways which establish that R&D has taken place. What is meant by the term 'advance' is developed into a vast number of scenarios commonly met in industry by paras 6–12 of the Guidelines. Paragraph 9 (discussed below) is particularly helpful and sets out four key examples of R&D scenarios which represent a technical 'advance'.

An 'advance in science or technology' has the following permutations from paras 6–12. Each can be applied in a wide range of circumstances to any product, process, material, system, device or service etc:

- an extension to overall knowledge or capability in a field of science or technology, including the adaptation of technology from another field;

- the creation of a product, process or system representing an increase in overall knowledge or capability in a field of science or technology;

- an appreciable improvement to an existing product, process or system through scientific or technological change;

- using science or technology to duplicate the effect of an existing product, process or system in a new or appreciably improved way, where built in a fundamentally different manner.

Other activities can be regarded as R&D where significant technical uncertainty is apparent. These activities appear later in the Guidelines and include project prototype work and specific design work that advances scientific capability or knowledge, including work upon aesthetic effects.

Paragraph 6 focuses upon 'knowledge'-based R&D and 'capability'-based R&D:

> 'An advance in science or technology means an advance in **overall knowledge or capability** in a field of **science** or **technology**. This includes the adaptation of knowledge or capability from another field of science or technology in order to make such an advance where this adaptation was not readily deducible.'

(BIS Guidelines, para 6)

An advance in overall knowledge in a field of science or technology

Knowledge-based R&D

3.7   Knowledge-based R&D activity is usually arranged as a research project(s). These types of project are usually prominent and pronounced and will require little prompting by the adviser. Key tranches of research are likely to have taken place either as an R&D activity in itself or as a preliminary to the development of a new product, design or process etc. Hallmarks of this type of project work might be collaboration with higher education/independent research bodies. Significant feasibility studies and the recruitment of specialist staff or subcontractors to explore and corroborate the new knowledge will be evident. The management of the company's intellectual property (IP) rights will feature in this type of project. Alternatively, the knowledge may be in a field that is subject to perpetual change with inbuilt technical obsolescence and little commercial value. The usefulness of the 'Patent Box' tax regulations may be a consideration.

But there are many gaps in the theoretical studies of many scientific fields which impact upon R&D in industry as well as in 'pure science' environments. For example, manufacturing companies frequently engage in knowledge-based projects that aim to significantly expand technological expertise relevant to a particular product or process. This may be a forerunner to a specific project aiming to introduce a new product or production method or an expansion in the company's technological capability. This preliminary R&D is eligible for relief within the Guidelines as an extension to 'overall knowledge' in the technical field concerned.

This lack of awareness happens for a variety of reasons, perhaps because it is carried out frequently or because it does not come to fruition. The R&D activity will be undertaken by experienced staff in overalls on the production line, rather than 'white coated' personnel, but this does not detract from its eligibility within the BIS Guidelines as an 'overall advance in technological knowledge'.

Automotive and precision component manufacturers will also engage in substantial research phases as part of the evaluation of materials and components and their synchronicity and effectiveness in established large-scale production lines. This 'system certainty' can involve extensive knowledge-based R&D.

The pharmaceutical industry is commonly regarded as having substantial knowledge/research project activity. This is usually a preliminary to viable new products and ingredients. But this can be driven by regulatory rather than pure R&D issues. In an almost contradictory way, little R&D may be involved, despite the extensive 'knowledge' feature of the activity; the research may be substantively testing or comparative in nature. Around 9% of R&D claims are accounted for as 'pure research' activity, or directed at very technical knowledge areas such as predictive computer science, pharmaceutical, aerospace etc.

An advance in scientific knowledge is distinct from an advance in technological knowledge. Both can qualify for R&D relief but marginal advances in the latter category are more easily overlooked and taken as 'routine' activity.

For any type of advancement in 'overall knowledge or capability' to be regarded as R&D, the expertise must not be 'readily deducible' or comparative. Activity that simply enhances the company's own knowledge or know-how will not be R&D. This can except knowledge protected by copyright or similar, or where theoretical knowledge is put into practice. This is a key barrier to R&D in practice, and can be overlooked (BIS Guidelines, para 20–22).

Advance in overall capability in a field of science or technology

3.8 Capability-based R&D is not limited to a specific type of industry. 'Capability' within the BIS Guidelines has its ordinary meaning. The term means the technological or scientific limits of something or its relevant environment.

This excludes commercial capabilities or enhancing the 'capability' of a company to align itself to its competitors. The definition also excludes projects which seek minor or routine changes or deploy a technology from one field into another with little uncertainty involved. 'Capability' means the generic technological components of a product, process or system have been advanced, either in the way in which they integrate or in terms of their individual absolute capacities having been fundamentally altered.

Like knowledge-based R&D, the Guidelines specify that the capability must be genuinely and fundamentally advanced when compared to what was available or deducible at the time of the project. The definition also shares the added 'competent professional' benchmark test from para 23.

Summary – advances in scientific or technological knowledge and capability

3.9 The guidelines confirm that an advance can manifest itself in a number of ways. Once the project activity has been understood it will be characterised as either knowledge- or capability-based advancement, or work targeted at appreciable improvement or adaptation. Most R&D projects will simultaneously seek more than one type of advance.

A number of common features apply:

• The knowledge or capability relevant to the technical 'advance' must not be readily available or deducible to an experienced professional at the time when the project work starts.

• The project's advances may be abandoned, or the work need not come to fruition to qualify as R&D.

• Several companies can seek the same knowledge or capability (as often happens) but all can qualify provided bona fide research effort is involved.

• Simply 'using' science or technology is not an advance.

• Routine analysis and enhancements to the company's own knowledge or capability is not an advance.

• Adding in functionality is not an 'appreciable' improvement, as it will probably lack a fundamental change to the technology concerned.

• The adaptation of technical knowledge or capability from another field of science or technology can be an advance where the characteristics have been fundamentally altered.

Example 3.1 – Software company advancing knowledge and capability, competitors expertise

Fast Games Co (FGC) introduced a tennis application game to the android market. It contained a number of algorithms which were common knowledge in the gaming industry, but had done extensive development work upon a real time graphic user interface. It knew that its major competitor, Top Games Co (TGC) had this technology. TGC's development work was highly secretive. Both companies enforce security and IP clauses on their staff and subcontractors. Most of the work has to be carried out in a white box room.

Analysis

FGC has undertaken R&D project work relevant to its trade. It is not clear whether FGC is seeking an advance in 'knowledge' (computer science) or technical capability (front end logistics). Either activity would qualify (BIS Guidelines, para 6) as an advance to the extent that:

(a)   the expertise was not available or readily deducible; and

(b)   the project work contained fundamental uncertainty linked to the advances sought.

As regards (a), TGC's expertise and intellectual property can probably be disregarded (para 21).

As regards (b), the area of R&D is an emerging one and there is likely to be significant uncertainty linked to the advance sought.

TGC is seeking an 'advance' within the BIS Guidelines – an advance in the technological capability of systems relevant to computer games. It is also seeking to advance overall knowledge in the field of computer science.

Any routine analysis, copying or minor adaptation within the project work will not be eligible activity (para 22).

Adapting existing technology

3.10   Companies do not always seek *new* knowledge or capability. The adaptation of existing capability or knowledge into new fields is a perpetual R&D activity. Similarly, the appreciable improvement of existing products, processes or systems will be R&D where this moves through scientific or technological change (see **3.20**).

Adaptation which transposes existing technical knowledge or capability from one field of science or technology into another is R&D. This is so where the technology underlying the transition was not 'readily deducible' (BIS Guidelines, para 6).

Recent examples of adaptation-based R&D activity include the development of laser technology into fields as diverse as medicine, cosmetics and opthalmology. Where this adaptation involves technological uncertainty and 'new' areas of science or technology, there is likely to be a case for further R&D analysis.

Adaptation of science or technology is common in all walks of industry focusing upon 'greener' or 'cheaper' product development as a commercial objective. It is common in manufacturing industries, and can be understood by an example.

Example 3.2 – Manufacturing industry: product improvement as R&D

New Chair Co had previously followed the industry technology in applying plastic backing with metal spring structures into its chairs. It now wishes to use plastic rather than metal springs; the plastic springs had been successful in mattress technologies and were useful because they were both cheaper and lighter than traditional metal springs.

New Chair Co trialled the plastic spring on a series of prototypes. For a period of around eight months it tried various combinations and weight loads but was unclear as to the pressure and stress factors within the new assembly. Eventually the combinations were successful and commercial production will begin next year. The design is applying for patent protection.

Analysis

The existing bed technology is being adapted into a completely new form of technology. The chair company can show fundamental technological uncertainty in the new design and there are also gaps in the theoretical knowledge about stress and load bearings which are apparent from the technological adaptation.

The company has shown a clear cut methodology towards resolving this. The knowledge around the new combination of components was not easily deducible. Both technological knowledge and capability have been extended through the project's resolution of linked uncertainty.

The project activities are R&D.

Other adaptation work may focus upon the 'end' result rather than cheaper or variant ingredients. This might demand a new scientific or technological path is found. The automotive industry has provided many examples of this type of R&D activity. The 'advance' must be able to demonstrate that it is not based upon deducible knowledge or capability but targeting fundamental uncertainty linked to the adaptation. This adds an additional layer of 'proof' for the adviser, which is made more difficult as gaps in the existing knowledge must be demonstrable.

Example 3.3 – Manufacturing company: adapting established technology for alternative uses as R&D

Smarter Car Co is a market leader in compact car technology. Its cars were traditional petrol emission vehicles, but the company has won a number of 'green' awards over the last ten years because of their reduced CO_2 emissions and the company's efficient production line. Smarter Car Co developed the commercial production of an identical car with 'hybrid' emissions and then went on to develop the commercial production of an identical 'electric' vehicle.

Adapting the existing technology meant that the production line had to undergo substantial technological changes to fit the new engine variants because of temperature control issues and scalability problems arising from the engine's different specifications. A competent professional confirmed the adaptation of the existing petrol and hybrid technologies was an area of fundamental uncertainty in four specific technical areas.

Analysis

Smarter Car Co is a car manufacturer that appears to be actively engaged in technology-based product development relevant to its trade. Using primarily the 'same' technology to run the production of vehicles in fundamentally 'different' ways has presented a number of technological uncertainties. The project seeks to resolve these to attain the technical advances that the adaptation requires. Knowledge of the underlying technology involved in the car production has been advanced and was not readily deducible.

The work is R&D.

Advance in science or technology: appreciable improvement

3.11   Where a project seeks to make an appreciable improvement to a product, process or system etc, the work will be R&D, but this must be achieved through scientific or technological change. 'Appreciable improvement' is a defined term in the Guidelines and requires the scientific or technological composition of the product is changed or adapted so significantly that it is 'better than the original'. Additionally, a peer in the industry would regard the transformation as non-trivial and genuine.

R&D characterised as an 'appreciable improvement' is common in SME companies (see **3.20**).

RESOLUTION OF SCIENTIFIC OR TECHNOLOGICAL UNCERTAINTY

Test Two: The resolution of scientific or technological uncertainty

3.12

'The activities which **directly contribute** to achieving the advance in science or technology through the resolution of **scientific or technological uncertainty** are R&D.'

(BIS Guidelines, para 4)

What is uncertainty?

3.13   Scientific or technological uncertainty is defined at paras 13 and 14 of the BIS Guidelines and a common starting point is that the company may not even know if a solution exists. Scientific or technological uncertainty that can be easily worked out is not R&D. Upgrading or adapting knowledge or capability in a trivial way will not be R&D. Significant technical work that does not result in an extension of science or technology through the resolution of project-linked uncertainties will similarly not be regarded as R&D.

Uncertainty for R&D tax relief purposes means that the absolute knowledge of whether something is technically feasible or achievable is not within the grasp of a competent professional. The added leg of this test, that the knowledge concerned is not 'deducible', is an area of difficulty in practice. The Guidelines require the uncertainty is not 'readily' resolvable by a professional in the industry, for example from a peer-to-peer discussion. Uncertainty means the absence of a knowledge path; the R&D work might leave know-how available for the benefit of the technical community concerned. In practice it is unlikely that a project's intellectual property will be made available after the project.

To establish all areas of technical uncertainty, both the breadth and depth of the R&D project must be considered. One area of uncertainty may link directly into a fresh technical area and activity directly contributing towards both should be included in the R&D review. This is commonly overlooked after commercial production begins.

Uncertainty linked to the relevant advances sought is therefore the start and end point for the project's cost collection. It will set the boundaries of activity that does or does not contribute to the goals sought. R&D activity begins when the competent professional is able to formulate the uncertainties involved.

How does technical uncertainty come about?

3.14

'...uncertainty exists when knowledge of whether something is scientifically possible or technologically feasible ... is not readily available or deducible by a competent professional working in the field.'

(BIS Guidelines, para 13)

The Guidelines do not provide a 'scale' for uncertainty. This can vary from 'marginal' to completely 'ground breaking' uncertainty but the common thread is that this will not be discernible. For example, the introduction of the hybrid engine would have involved 'ground breaking' technical uncertainty at inception. Yet fundamental R&D work continues on hybrid engine technology 11 years later, with complete 'uncertainty' about comparatively 'marginal' advances sought in carbon complex emissions.

The resolution of uncertainty manifests into R&D advances in two logical ways:

- pure research uncertainty 'gaps' which will be relevant to advances in scientific or technological knowledge – *knowledge-based uncertainty*; and/or

- capability-based uncertainty linked to advances in technological capability, which will be particularly relevant to new technological development – *capability-based uncertainty*.

Manufacturing, engineering and construction companies are emerging onto the R&D scoreboards as they become aware of the significance of the work they carry out resolving technological uncertainty and attaining new capability as R&D. Traditional R&D industries such as ICT producers and ICT service providers can work almost permanently on capability-based uncertainties.

System uncertainty

3.15   System uncertainty is common in R&D projects. This takes place where feasible knowledge or capability is put into practice (BIS Guidelines, para 13). System uncertainty will feature as an end point of R&D or may be an R&D project in its own right. Many companies overlook this important area of R&D and will omit potentially eligible project costs. This is particularly common in manufacturing industries.

Inferior technology

3.16   Fundamental uncertainty can exist when technology that already exists is 'scaled down' into an inferior product for, perhaps, a much wider consumer market.

This type of uncertainty will be based upon migrating an existing technology into a new fundamentally different product.

This can be understood by an example.

Example 3.4 – ICT hardware company producing inferior products as R&D

Windows Phone Co produces top-of-the-range smartphones. It has not tapped into emerging African and third world markets but now wishes to do so. It knows that there are key technologies within its phone technology which are highly relevant to the market, such as long-range GPS locators and instant messaging but there is little use for the raft of ancillary technology in its current technical formation of the product.

It wishes to produce an inferior phone for the new market which will have three functions: calls, MMS and GPS in areas of scarce population.

Analysis

Significant technological uncertainty can exist in producing an 'inferior' technology. Examples may be the 'what/if' attached to removing key components and functionality etc. Although there are a number of 'simple' phones on the market, none have the processor speeds of the new 'Smart Africa' phone and the knowledge and technical capability is not deducible.

Given the above uncertainty, the new phone represents an advance in technological capability, although an inferior product results.

The project is R&D.

Origin of uncertainty – commercial context

3.17 An R&D project may be either premeditated or speculative in its origin. This can influence the relief due. Suppose a petrochemical company decides to target development in the field of CO_2 emissions with obvious commercial benefits. It may not even know if a technical solution is feasible and begins to carry out feasibility studies upon relevant nitrate compounds to establish the parameters of its project. This technical 'uncertainty' is clear and should be capable of documentation through the company's project strategy documents or board meetings.

This would contrast with the company that performs 'blue sky' project work without specific target markets in the pursuit of know-how, which may be in too early a stage of infancy to be commercially viable or technically predictable. Blue sky R&D is common in R&D intensive industries. For example, in an IT environment it would not be unusual for a company to ask its developers to dedicate a day a month on speculative or trial coding development for future knowledge bases. There is no set market for this R&D effort at present but the intrinsic knowledge and capability it will build will be regarded as 'blue sky' R&D work in the specific field of language development.

Both market led and 'blue sky' R&D can demonstrate scientific or technological uncertainty, but it is the degree to which this can be evidenced by reference to the company's methodology that will determine whether or not any tax relief is due.

Example 3.5 – Uncertainty: systematic v coincidental R&D activity (software company)

True Believer Co (TBC) believes it has carried out a number of R&D projects. It believes this because it is a high-tech company and regularly wins awards for its software development. Lately it has been involved in malware development. It sees this area as being highly valid for R&D purposes. It cannot really put a finger on when this project began. Staff have been looking at exploratory fields of data encryption from time to time but there is no budget and little actual direction for their work. TBC feels it is about to break into the market and turnover will be up by £5 million if its contracts are won. TBC would like to claim R&D upon the last 24 months' activity on £300,000 of time costs.

Analysis

TBC has deployed engineers into a field of uncertainty and innovation. There is no doubt that in the future it will be seeking both scientific and technological advances and the work is 'relevant' to its trade.

At present, TBC has no tangible 'start point' or specific advances in mind as a basis for identifying the 'uncertainty' required at para 4 of the BIS Guidelines. It has carried out some pre-project activity. There is little to document the requirement that the company is not even sure a solution may exist. There is no target for the project work and without relevant R&D boundaries, uncertainty is not identifiable. There is little 'methodology' evident and the areas of uncertainty and advances sought are not discernible.

There is no project evident; the activity is not R&D.

Summary – scientific or technological uncertainty

3.18   The 'Gateway tests' of advance and uncertainty apply equally to all branches of science or technology and all types of R&D, and in a variety of circumstances. The BIS Guidelines confirm:

- The definition of R&D does not state a particular field of scientific or technological project work relevant to the uncertainty.

- No requirement is made regarding the degree of uncertainty provided a change in technical knowledge or capability is established.

- The size of the uncertainty involved in a project is not prescribed by the Guidelines, although a project cap applies to State Aid for SMEs.

- Uncertainty can relate as much to a service or material as it can to a process, system or product.

- The location in which the R&D activities targeting uncertainty should take place is not prescribed.

- New knowledge is not required; extensions and advances in the knowledge base currently available or discernible will qualify.

- Knowledge and/or capability can be transposed from one field to another and be regarded as R&D although an established technology already exists elsewhere.

- Several companies can each carry out (non-collaborative) R&D at the same time upon the same area of technology or science.

The R&D case studies published from time to time by the DTI (now BIS) have gradually shown that advance and uncertainty can take on many guises. The variety of potential R&D scenarios is therefore very broad.

BIS GUIDELINES – R&D SCENARIOS

Practical examples of R & D (para 9)

3.19   The BIS Guidelines highlight a number of examples of eligible R&D project work at paras 9, 41, 42 and 43. These cover a number of commonly met R&D scenarios and can apply universally to any industry or scale of activity. The Guidelines contain a number of specially defined terms, the significance of which is drawn out by these examples (see **3.34**).

Paragraph 9 makes up the bulk of SME R&D claims which are filed to HMRC. It provides four examples of R&D in practice. Project work will be regarded as R&D where it seeks any, or all, of the following objectives:

'9. A project which seeks to, for example,

(a)   extend overall knowledge or capability in a field of science or technology; or

(b)   create a process, material, device, product or service which incorporates or represents an increase in overall knowledge or capability in a field of science or technology; or

(c)   make an appreciable improvement to an existing process, material, device, product or service through scientific or technological changes; or

(d)   use science or technology to duplicate the effect of an existing process, material, device, product or service in a new or appreciably improved way (e.g. a product which has exactly the same performance characteristics as existing models, but is built in a fundamentally different manner)

will therefore be R&D.'

(BIS Guidelines, para 9)

Knowledge- and capability-based R&D work will fall within the scope of paras 9(a) and 9(b) and has been discussed above. Much SME activity will come within paras 9(c) and 9(d), targeting an 'appreciable improvement' in products, processes or systems etc or replicating existing technologies in a way that is technically fundamentally different to the original. Examples of this would be synthetic materials, or materials and technologies which are cheaper, greener or less wasteful.

Advance in science or technology: R&D involving an 'appreciable improvement' (para 9(c))

3.20   Appreciable improvement is a defined term but it must also demonstrate scientific or technological 'change' which can be difficult to establish. R&D seeking an 'appreciably improved' product etc. will need to pass these secondary tiers of criteria for expenditure linked to it to be regarded as eligible for tax relief:

- '[a]ppreciable improvement means to change or adapt the scientific or technological characteristics of [the product] to the point where it is 'better than the original', and

- 'acknowledged by a competent professional working in the field as a genuine and non-trivial improvement.'

(BIS Guidelines, para 23)

'Appreciable improvement' projects often seek tangible and fundamental improvements to products, processes, materials or devices. These projects will be focused on visible outcomes such as a better, cheaper, more efficient or 'safer' product. But other projects will be more marginal in their effect.

Green technology has been one of the biggest examples of para 9c work in recent years. The obvious improvement is the enhanced environmental impact of the product; the technical complexities in attaining this are often so significant that a 'competent professional' would regard the technical work involved as bona fide and incapable of easy resolution.

Appreciable improvement characteristics of R&D

3.21

- Companies may be clear about the commercial use of the improved product/system/process but the start point of the technical activity may be blurred. A common error is to consider the commercial evaluation of appreciably improved products and the market place for them as R&D work but this does not 'directly contribute' to the resolution of scientific or technological uncertainty as the objective is not 'technical'.

- Companies find the demonstration of an 'appreciably improved' product relatively straightforward. Many companies carrying out product development will find it less easy to demonstrate how the product's technical characteristics were made to be 'fundamentally different'.

- There is often a lengthy 'end' phase of the R&D activity with significant prototype development. Industry safety standards often impose significant testing in this phase, which will qualify for R&D tax reliefs if technical uncertainty is still present. The R&D boundary needs to be properly drawn to include this activity appropriately.

- IP protection is sought at a mature stage of development.

3.22   A fair degree of granularity is needed in the R&D analysis of what is an 'appreciable improvement', to establish both the scientific or technological changes and the extent to which the new product is 'better' than the original. This can be shown in the example below.

Example 3.6 – Level of technical detail constituting a 'scientific' or technological change

(BIS Guidelines, paras 23, 25 – non trivial product improvement)

Red Paint Co needed to produce a low odour, fast drying paint for use in commercial kitchens. The benefit would be that businesses would have less 'down time' during maintenance and renovation. It perceived a high demand for the product.

Red Paint Co undertook a development-based R&D project focused upon changing the molecular structure of its paint products to dry more quickly. This involved the interaction of the paint ingredients with a substance that increased evaporation and so drying. In effect the usual scientific reaction of the ingredients needed to fundamentally change through scientific change to synthesise the drying effect.

During the course of manufacture, Red Paint found that the colour pigments lost quality as a result of Phase I of the project which brought about the scientific change. This was due to the speed of the manufacturing line which did not allow 'settling' time for the paint. The production engineers experimented with the manufacturing technology by devising an adaption to the production line to slow down the run for 'quick paint'. This involved much experimentation and analysis of the product compounds etc during the course of manufacture. It eventually found a bridging mechanism that was effective. This solution was not 'generally available knowledge'. Speaking to other competent professionals in the field, Red Paint Co had been able to find the solution without the project work on the bridging equipment.

Analysis

Red Paint Co's project is 'relevant' to its trade. The end product is an 'appreciable improvement'. Both the scientific and technological characteristics of the product have been fundamentally changed or adapted to the point where they are 'better' than the original. The improvements are neither 'minor' nor routine changes; a competent professional working in the field would regard the work as a genuine and 'non-trivial' improvement (para 23).

The development of the pigment solution involved scientific change and there has been an 'appreciable improvement' sought. The scientific change can be documented by the pigment and compound experimentation. Taken alone, that part of Red Paint Co's project is within the definition of an 'advance in science or technology' at para 9(c).

Red Paint Co put the appreciably improved product into commercial production and had to conduct further experimentation to resolve the technological improvement to its manufacturing equipment for this to happen. The related project work is again 'relevant' to its trade.

The technological change can be documented by the bridging equipment experimentation. This technology was not readily available technological knowledge to competent professionals in Red Paint Co's industry. The project work sought to make an appreciable improvement to an existing product and process through technological change (para 9(c)). The correlating definitions of 'appreciable improvement' are also met (para 23).

The project work is R&D.

The para 9(c) test envisages only technological 'change' and does not specify a degree of alteration. The degree of change is not defined but in reality the mechanics of effecting a technological 'change' will not be trivial, they will usually involve substantial R&D work.

It is feasible, but harder to document, that at the end of the project work, Red Paint Co may have extended overall knowledge and capability in both scientific and technological fields. If so, Red Paint Co meets the 'extended knowledge' definitions at para 9(a) and (b). The overall evidence points more towards 9(c) or (d) R&D activity. There is no extra relief for satisfying more than one definition.

Appreciably improved technologies must be regarded as technically 'non trivial' by industry peers. This can be difficult in practice but is an area of frequent HMRC review (see **3.33**)

Advance in science or technology – R&D projects duplicating scientific or technological effects

(BIS Guidelines, para 9(d))

3.23   Where a project seeks new, cheaper and simpler models of existing technologies or materials, the activity may be R&D depending upon the degree of scientific or technological alteration (para 9(d)).

> 'A project which ... use[s] science or technology to duplicate the effect of an existing process, material, device, product or service in a new or appreciably improved way (e.g. a product which has exactly the same will be R&D (the product may have exactly the same performance characteristics as existing models, but is built in a fundamentally different manner will therefore be R&D'.

(BIS Guidelines, para 9(d))

Note the possibility of duplication. A product which has exactly the same performance characteristics of an existing model, but is based upon technology being applied in a fundamentally different manner is characteristic of this type of R&D.

An example of this type of R&D would be work on synthetic materials which is common in a range of industries, from manufacturing to pharmaceutical to construction and engineering companies.

A pre-requisite of the activity is that the product, process or system is fundamentally different in the way in which it is built, and represents an 'appreciable improvement'.

Routine extensions to existing product lines will not show sufficient alteration to be regarded as be R&D because it will not demonstrate the necessary 'appreciable improvement' or fundamentally different build.

Example 3.7 – Shoe and clothing manufacturer: product design and improvement as R&D

Laboutin Heels Co (LHC) is a high-end [sic] shoe manufacturer. It makes seasonal changes to its shoe designs depending upon heel height and shoe colours. The shoes are dramatically different from the preceding season but the manufacturing process is largely duplicated. The arrival of the new season will always involve a period of project work where new designs are prototyped and adapted and eventually put into commercial production. The company's production process is still largely labour-based with hand stitching and finishing of the end product accounting for around 85% of the shoe.

Analysis

LHC's project work seeks the 'appreciable improvement' of para 9(c) and the duplication of production processes which is highlighted at para 9(d). But it is unlikely that the appreciable improvements are the result of fundamental scientific or technological changes. The project work will not meet the definition of para 9(c).

It is also difficult to evidence that the seasonal variations use science or technology in a new or appreciably improved way, to the extent that they are produced in a way that represents 'a fundamentally different manner' (para 9(d)).

The projects are not R&D.

Functionality

3.24   Enhanced functionality (the end product of many R&D projects) is not featured in the BIS Guidelines and is not usually R&D work. A very common perception is that if a company undertakes work, the results of which appear to the directors to represent a greatly improved product or end user experience, then the project will be eligible for R&D. The directors will go on to emphasise how the improved outcome is highly functioning and award winning.

This is a common pitfall for software claims focused upon functionality. This type of work, despite its apparent complexity, attains only superficial technological or scientific change. Such work often uses very standardised methodology and readily available programming or language tools. These types of 'projects' are often improvements in the company's own capability. Once dissected, there is often little advancement that outstrips the knowledge or capabilities available or discernible to the technical community behind the industry at large. HMRC will point out that this type of work has probably simply involved the 'use of' science or technology with no correlating advancement in either knowledge or capability in the field concerned. Paragraph 6 of the Guidelines prohibits extensions to the company's own knowledge, or the superficial use of science or technology as being R&D.

BIS Guidelines – additional points

3.25   To a large extent the project's 'end product' is almost irrelevant; it is the advances in science or technology sought to attain this and the degree of knowledge or capability sought, which will attain the relief.

This prevents R&D relief being available where science or technology is simply 'used' rather than furthered (para 8).

Example 3.8 – Any industry type using science or technology in development work unlikely to be R&D

Magic Media Company Ltd (MMC) found that most of its competitors were using customer relationship management (CRM) software and media in a more effective way than they were. MMC employed a team of specialist consultants, which they termed 'subcontractors', to analyse and increase the offering of its data systems. The work was regarded by the company as specialist and technical and resulted in a greatly improved CRM system capable of multichannel client interfaces and providing real time communication strategy reports at the push of a button. To some extent this outstripped the systems of key competitors and there was already a noted increase in customer satisfaction. MMC won numerous awards for its system, and it is now widely acknowledged to be amongst the market leaders in terms of its CRM status.

The costs for the work reached £1 million and MMC wishes to claim R&D tax relief if it can, highlighting the bespoke nature of the system and its pioneering awards.

Analysis

The project undertaken by MMC is relevant to its trade, depending upon the durability of its benefit it may be regarded as 'revenue' expenditure, although the possibility of capital expenditure would also need to be reviewed.

Little is known about the areas of technological advancement or if this simply represented an increase in the company's own state of knowledge and competence. It seems as though specialist knowledge has simply been used in developing the system; the project team may simply have used standard software models and algorithms in the build, and little by way of an 'advance in science or technology' seems demonstrable.

The end result is an enhanced functionality but all that seems to have happened is the 'use' of science in the new system – the company has purchased a high-tech extension to its system. The company would need to review the planning activity involved in the project, which is likely to show industry standard methodologies.

Additionally, CRM in itself is not a scientific field, but a 'soft science' relating to consumer behaviour.

It is unlikely that R&D has taken place.

BIS Guidelines – Distinction between capital and revenue project work

3.26   Care is required when analysing R&D project work, particularly internal R&D projects, to consider the durability of the end product. The BIS definitions make no reference to capital expenditure, drawing no distinction between capital and revenue costs. Capital expenditure producing an enduring benefit to the company will not qualify as R&D but will be capitalised over the course of the development. HMRC frequently regard substantial aspects of software projects as representing capital expenditure.

BIS Guidelines: start and end of R&D

3.27   The collection of potentially eligible project costs can begin once work to resolve technical uncertainty starts. The R&D ends when knowledge or capability becomes 'useable' or functional.

'33. R&D begins when work to resolve the scientific or technological uncertainty starts, and ends when that uncertainty is resolved or work to resolve it ceases.'

34. R&D ends when knowledge is codified in a form usable by a competent professional working in the field, or when a prototype or pilot plant with all the functional characteristics of the final process, material, device, product or service is produced.'

(BIS Guidelines, paras 33, 34)

FURTHER R&D SCENARIOS

Paragraph 39 prototypes

3.28   Paragraph 39 confirms the development of prototype and experimental technologies usually fall within the scope of R&D for tax purposes. This is upon the proviso that the prototype 'is an original model on which something new or appreciably improved is patterned … It is a basic experimental model possessing the essential characteristics of the intended process, material, device, product or service'.

Paragraph 39 is a useful and often overlooked route to R&D tax relief. The key factor to document is the degree of technical uncertainty associated with the commissioning of the prototype. Simple 'upgrading' or minor cosmetic adjustments in product development will not have the degree of technological uncertainty present to be regarded as 'functionality' prototypes. The amount of time the prototype has taken to build, test and design will be helpful in deciding the degree of 'change' involved.

The presence of extraneous factors such as 'safety' and industry standards often demand significant pre-production/prototype activity. This can be routine, and activity during this phase will only be R&D where technical uncertainty is evident.

The fact that a project is rejected for commercial use after prototype development will not prevent the costs from obtaining R&D tax relief.

Design work (para 41)

3.29 Paragraph 41 provides for design work to be R&D where the resolution of scientific or technological uncertainty is a fundamental part of the company's work.

Paragraph 41 is often helpful to construction, engineering and architectural companies working to bespoke design specifications. Computer-aided design (CAD) is a common tool within this sector, but this will not adequately resolve the scientific or technical uncertainty involved. The steps taken by the company after the basic design plan is passed will be the area for review.

Design activity that is routine or standard in its approach will not be R&D even if a major change in the design of a product is attained.

Cosmetic/aesthetic product improvement (para 42)

3.30

'[Attaining a specific] cosmetic or aesthetic effect through the application of science or technology ... resolving the scientific or technological uncertainty associated with such a project would therefore be R&D.'

(BIS Guidelines, para 42)

This area of product improvement is an important aspect of R&D activity that is easily overlooked. Manufacturing companies invest significant 'point of purchase' R&D work in how a product first appears or feels to the consumer. This 'eye appeal' can involve significant technical input such as the performance of materials or the durability/pliability of key ingredients when first handled.

Frequently such development is outsourced, but provided the company can show an R&D 'environment' it may be possible to claim for such work where subcontracted to, or commissioned from third parties.

Content delivered through science or technology

3.31   Paragraph 43 highlights the potential for improvements in technology to create, manipulate or transfer information to be regarded as R&D activity. This requires evidence of both technical advance and the resolution of uncertainty associated with the improvements sought. The advances and uncertainty definitions follow the requirements of paras 6–12 and 13–14. This is a highly relevant scenario for 'software' development. The fact that this is the last scenario perhaps belies the age of the Guidelines.

Summary: R&D scenarios – BIS Guidance

3.32   The Gateway tests of advance and uncertainty at paras 3 and 4 will indicate when R&D activity has taken place.

Project work can span a number of different 'advance' scenarios as highlighted in paras 6–12, particularly in the case of SME activity. The paragraphs at 39, 41, 42 and 43 should also be reviewed for relevance. Meeting more than one definition will not affect the extent of relief available and will not require separate calculations for each phase but will extend the project boundaries.

Scientific or technological uncertainty takes on a very broad range of characteristics but will exclude commercial and non-R&D factors. The uncertainty must be 'relevant' to the advances targeted by the project work. It is not uncommon for uncertainty to branch into new 'subprojects' which may in turn extend into new knowledge where capability had been targeted and vice versa.

The Guidelines state that an advance in both the baseline and hypothetically deducible knowledge underlines any type of R&D work. This is a high standard and a difficult test to document, and distinguishes the UK's definition of R&D from other territories.

The definition of an 'advance in science or technology' then contains a number of further defined terms which must be read in conjunction with the key project advances and uncertainties. Additional documentation will be needed to confirm the project's compliance with these terms, listed as a Glossary below.

BIS GLOSSARY OF DEFINITIONS

3.33   The following terms are considered below:

- Advance in science or technology
- Scientific or technological uncertainty

- System uncertainty
- Science
- Technology
- Project
- Overall knowledge or capability
- Appreciable improvement
- Directly-contributing activity

Paragraph 1 states that a number of key terms in the Guidelines have a special meaning for the purposes of providing R&D relief. It is also important to note that a correlating number of terms, such as 'competent professional', do not. They retain their ordinary, generic meaning, but additional inferences are made in HMRC's Corporate Intangibles Research & Development (CIRD) Manual, which ascribes special meanings to a number of the terms and interpretations within the BIS Guidelines.

Purposive construction of terms

3.34   HMRC take the judgment in *Gripple Ltd v HMRC* [2010] EWHC 1609 (Ch) to mean that any purposive interpretation of the R&D legislation is not permissible. Put succinctly, this case focused upon staffing costs as 'payment' of the director's remuneration. The case examined the 'payment' of the costs and entries on the director's tax return. The reality was that the 'costs' were, in fact, intercompany recharges. The judgment favoured HMRC's viewpoint that no purposive construction of *CTA 2009, Pt 13* is possible. As the remuneration was not 'paid' but cross-charged, the amounts were not costs eligible for R&D relief as no 'payment' for staffing costs (or externally provided workers) was made. The significance of the case is discussed further in **Chapter 2** above.

Advance in science or technology

This important term is discussed at **3.6** above.

Scientific or technological uncertainty

This important term is discussed at **3.13** above.

System uncertainty

'System uncertainty is scientific or technological uncertainty that results from the complexity of a system rather than uncertainty about how its individual components behave.

(BIS Guidelines, para 29)

System uncertainty is a common starting point for R&D activity, or may feature towards the end of the project work when prototyping begins. This type of uncertainty is distinct from assembling a number of components, in a standard way using a methodology that is in common use in the industry.

At first sight, this is a promising R&D scenario, but there are two dangers with system uncertainty work. Firstly, if the uncertainty is so great, the character of any investigation may be capital in nature and secure an enduring benefit from its resolution. R&D relief rewards revenue expenditure and care will be required in these circumstances.

Secondly, in documenting 'what the company did next', there is the danger that the extent of system uncertainty is so complex, one project merges into another and the company may lose sight of the original project boundaries whilst a new separate project begins.

Science

What is science? The BIS Guidelines define science as encompassing any study of the nature and behaviour of the physical universe and its interactions at paras 15 and 16. Any other studies directed at, for example, social sciences are ineligible as R&D.

> 'Science is the systematic study of the nature and behaviour of the physical and material universe. Work in the arts, humanities and social sciences, including economics, is not science for the purpose of these guidelines. Mathematical techniques are frequently used in science, but mathematical advances in and of themselves are not science unless they are advances in representing the nature and behaviour of the physical and material universe.
>
> These guidelines apply equally to work in any branch or field of science.'

(BIS Guidelines, paras 15, 16)

Technology

What is technology? In practice, the border between science and technology can be hard to define. The BIS Guidelines' definition of technology at paras 17 and 18 is broad, and seen as embracing potentially all areas of practical work following scientific principles and theorems.

> '17. Technology is the practical application of scientific principles and knowledge, where "scientific" is based on the definition of science above.

18. These Guidelines apply equally to work in any branch or field of technology.'

(BIS Guidelines, paras 17, 18)

Project

The organisation of a project is fundamental to an R&D claim. The project will provide evidence of the company's R&D methodology and the key 'advance' objectives. This should show a systematic approach to resolving uncertainty.

HMRC often ask for evidence of a company's project strategy. Without a project-based approach, no evidence of advancement or uncertainty is readily available. The judicial guidance made in *BE Studios Ltd v Smith Williamson Ltd* [2005] EWHC 1506 (Ch) refers.

R&D record keeping is a statutory requirement and is discussed at **Chapter 6** below. Direct evidence of project work may include:

- the project budget documents;
- notes from the company's competent professional about the fundamental uncertainties and their extent;
- board meetings concerning the funding of the project particularly at key milestone stages;
- the recruitment of a team of project staff or at least the appointment of a project leader;
- appropriate training of the project personnel;
- the appointment of specialists or subcontractors to assist with specific parts of the project;
- IP valuations and discussions about the commercial benefits of the project work and when these might become available.

In reality a project, particularly one spanning a large technical area and a number of accounting periods will probably involve many subprojects.

'A project consists of a number of activities conducted to a method or plan in order to achieve an advance in science or technology ... It should encompass all the activities which collectively serve to resolve the scientific or technological uncertainty associated with achieving the advance...'

(BIS Guidelines, para 19)

Overall knowledge and capability

'Overall knowledge or capability in a field of science or technology means the knowledge ... which is publicly available or is readily deducible ... by a competent professional working in the field. Work which seeks an advance relative to this overall knowledge or capability is R&D.'

(BIS Guidelines, para 20)

Some types of R&D project work must be referable to an advance in overall knowledge or capability in a field of science or technology. The advance goes beyond baseline knowledge then 'available or deducible to a competent professional working in the field' (paras 20 and 23 (see under heading 'Competent professional' below). The reference to a 'competent industry professional' working in the relevant field is a specific gateway test for R&D work. The test is a difficult one. Many companies conducting 'good' R&D work see this as a barrier to claiming RDTRs, assuming that an industry awareness of a technical complexity pre-empts a qualifying advance in the field.

Although the Guidelines make an exception for knowledge or capability being available or deducible on the grounds of trade secrecy or independence, HMRC inspectors require good documentation or the use of an independent expert to document the extension in overall knowledge or capability at the start of the company's work.

Analysis of the extension of overall knowledge or capability may focus upon the company's approach to registering intellectual property. This will be informative, but not necessarily decisive. For example, some start-up companies are only too keen to assign their intellectual property to a 'big fish' for the first lucrative contract. IP registration usually has a time lag of at least 12–24 months behind the R&D project work and can only really be regarded as a subjective indication of the advance of knowledge or capability.

A starting point is that knowledge advancement takes place where expertise could, in theory, be 'left on the table' for the benefit of the scientific or technological community as a whole, or at least the industry in which the company operates. Of course, the company has no obligation to make its expertise or information generally available, and indeed it will often take key steps to protect or license this. The acid test is that there is an advance in overall knowledge in a particular field of science or technology which will either be retained by the company or become common knowledge in due course.

As para 6 of the Guidelines shows, the apparent extension in overall knowledge or capability must be more than an improvement in the company's own 'know-how'. This would cover the situation where one company had successfully mastered a production process or system but registered a patent protecting its 'secrecy'. The second company would not be precluded from claiming RDTR on a similar process it had mastered itself despite the availability of the knowledge in the industry or previous success of perhaps an overseas competitor.

Example 3.9 – Overall knowledge or capability: significance of existing expertise

4WD Co developed a steering system for partially sighted drivers that detected erratic steering patterns at speeds above 50mph and sounded an alarm. It spent £2 million on relevant project work over five years and patented the design in the UK and EEA. 2WD Co (unconnected) was aware of the technology which had won numerous industry awards and considered the idea highly useful to motorway safety in fog, rain or adverse weather. It set about developing a steering option on Beta car that would alert the driver of steering errors in adverse weather. It claimed RDTR on the development costs of £3 million over the past two years and anticipates a further spend of £1 million in the next 18 months. The work represents an extension to overall knowledge and capability in a field of technology.

Analysis

It is likely that both 4WD Co and 2 WD Co are large scheme claimants. The same 'advance' requirements are common to both the SME and large scheme frameworks. The same technological advancement has been sought, to some extent, by both companies but for different end users.

The automobile industry is heavily patented and prone to trade secrecy; it is highly likely that despite the base technology being 'available' in theory, the design work is not 'common knowledge' or readily deducible without the need for project work.

2WD Co meets the BIS Guidelines, para 20 in respect of the overall knowledge available and deducible.

The work is R&D.

The usefulness of knowledge is not a factor in deciding whether or not it has been 'advanced' and is 'eligible' as R&D activity. Indeed the advancement may be abandoned as not being commercially viable, but this will not detract from the 'quality' of the R&D project and its potential for relief. **Chapter 13** contains a 'relevant' requirement confirming the R&D must fit with the company's trading activity but no 'success' requirement is found in either the BIS or CTA legislation.

For example, if 2 WD Co found the new knowledge was not really that useful in its way into this market, because of further design flaws such as the impact of rain or temperature, it could still claim relief.

An advancement in the company's own knowledge or capability alone is unlikely to be R&D. Purchasing high-tech products or solutions will not be R&D. The R&D needs to have an 'environment' in which the company has sought to make an advance. In turn this must be relevant to the company's trade or intended trade.

This context is often overlooked by company directors looking at the enhanced functionality of a high tech tool now used in the business. The perceived complexity displaces the fact that the company has simply followed a trend or improved its own technical knowledge.

Appreciable improvement

'Appreciable improvement means to change or adapt the scientific or technological characteristics of something to the point where it is "better" than the original.'

(BIS Guidelines, para 23)

This term is discussed above (see **3.11**) and is the benchmark for project work which seeks to make an advance through an 'appreciable improvement' to an existing process, material, device or product etc through scientific or technological change. It is also relevant to project work that seeks to duplicate the effect of a product, process or system in a new or 'appreciably improved' way.

The advance must be regarded as fundamental and non-trivial by (hypothetical) industry peers. It is important to remember that this should not be documented with hindsight, but when the improvement is first sought, i.e. at the time the project commences.

'[It should] be acknowledged by a competent professional working in the field as a genuine and non-trivial improvement.'

(BIS Guidelines, para 23)

The correct analysis of 'genuine and non-trivial improvement' should not focus upon the tangible outcome of the project. The methodology by which it has been attained is the relevant criteria to establish (or not) the R&D activity.

The industry or nature of the innovation itself may be very dynamic and it is important to consider without hindsight the scale of improvement sought from the project. This can be difficult as knowledge paths can enhance significantly during the course of a project and uncertainty is quickly forgotten.

Clearly, in setting so many 'grey areas' of scale and complexity, the Guidelines are almost unhelpful. However, where substantial sums depend upon the proof of this, the number of days spent by the project personnel upon 'hard research' at the beginning of the project may be helpful.

Directly contributing activity

'Directly contributing activity' targets technical uncertainties. The term will direct which costs are eligible for R&D relief which is discussed at **Chapter 2** above. Indirectly contributing activity can also qualify as R&D where specifically linked to the project work (BIS Guidelines, para 5). The Case Study at **3.41** demonstrates how directly contributing activity is established in practice.

Competent professional

As above, this term is not a defined term, but is relevant to all R&D situations.

However, HMRC Guidance has given the term significant meaning which is heavily focused upon the state of play in theoretical knowledge. The professional is expected to:

● be knowledgeable about the relevant scientific and technological principles involved;

● be aware of the current state of knowledge; and

● have accumulated experience and be recognised as having a successful track record.

CIRD81300 states:

'To enable an opinion to be properly assessed as to its contents and reasoning, an opinion offered by the company as being that of a competent professional would need to explain clearly, without the use of jargon, what the advance in science or technology being sought is, and why it an advance in the overall knowledge or capability in a field of science or technology, rather than just in the a company's own state of knowledge or capability, and so should objectively review the current state of knowledge, and the work carried out. A simple assertion as to the R&D nature of the project is unlikely to be satisfactory.

While due weight will be given to an opinion offered by the company's competent professional as to whether there is an advance in science or technology being sought, it will not necessarily be conclusive of the issue, and further enquiry may still be needed.'

BIS GUIDELINES: PRACTICAL EXPERIENCE

Production costs

3.35 Most innovative companies will know that R&D activities can continue well into the production process. This does not fit well with para

28(c) of the Guidelines which excludes the 'production and distribution of goods and services' from being R&D for tax purposes. The Guidelines do not define 'production and distribution'. This presented a conflict as HMRC examined claims and expected expenditure to be reduced by the possibility of 'production costs' being present. This argument gains further traction towards the end of research phases or once commercial production begins. This is also a very common argument where there is a client interface present in the project work.

The confusion arose because para 34 of the Guidelines defines when an R&D project ends as follows:

> 'R&D ends when knowledge is codified in a form usable by a competent professional working in the field, or when a prototype or pilot plant with all the functional characteristics of the final process, material, device, product or service is produced.'

To try to resolve the problem, guidance was published by HMRC to encourage inspectors to bear in mind that there can be circumstances where production and R&D activity can take place simultaneously. This goes on to provide a number of examples. In such circumstances the test in para 34 of the Guidelines is ineffective, because new uncertainty can arise at any time despite the end of a particular tranche of uncertainty.

Extension of overall knowledge and capability

3.36   Although this is a very high technical standard for R&D, other R&D regimes are not as demanding. In setting the benchmark so high, claims for R&D tax relief have faltered. The pace of innovation in the 'Tiger economies' owes a fair amount of its momentum to 'copycat' rather than unique knowledge. By virtue of its sheer volume, the drive has resulted in whole countries being labelled 'high-tech'. The correlating export drive and explosion in worldwide consumer demand for innovative copycat technologies was perhaps the intended result. The Guidelines therefore set a very high standard for the UK's innovation strategy.

The 'competent professional'

3.37   The UK's focus upon an individual's theoretical knowledge, conclusions and competence, rather than the state of play of baseline knowledge in an industry is unusual. An industry-based approach would perhaps enable more effective commercial parameters to be used in judging both the relevance and technological content of R&D work. This would provide relief based upon the absolute 'tech spend' by innovative companies, rather than work seeking an academic advance.

BIS GUIDELINES: PRACTICAL EXAMPLES OF R&D

R&D case study – the R&D process

3.38   The following example reproduced from the BIS Guidelines is an illustration of the R&D process:

'A1. A company conducts extensive market research to learn what technical and design characteristics a new DVD player should have in order to be an appealing product. This work is not R&D (paragraph 37). However, it does identify a potential project to create a DVD player incorporating a number of technological improvements which the company's R&D staff (who are competent professionals) regard as genuine and non-trivial. This project would be seeking to develop an appreciably improved DVD player (paragraphs 23–25) and would therefore be seeking to achieve an advance in science or technology (paragraph 9(c)).

A2. The company then decides on a detailed specification for the desired new product, and devises a plan for developing it. Some elements of this plan involve planning of activities which directly contribute to resolving the project's scientific or technological uncertainties (such as the system uncertainty associated with an improved control mechanism for the laser that "reads" the DVD). This element of planning is R&D (paragraph 36), as are the activities themselves (paragraph 4). Other elements of the plan focus on obtaining intellectual property protection or cosmetic design decisions, for example, which do not directly contribute to resolving the project's scientific or technological uncertainties and are not qualifying indirect activities (paragraph 31) and are therefore not R&D. Neither this planning (paragraph 37) nor these activities (paragraph 28) are R&D.

A3. The scientific or technological work culminates in the creation of a series of prototype DVD players, and ultimately a "final" prototype is produced and tested which possesses the essential characteristics of the intended product (circuit board design, performance characteristics, etc.). All the activities which directly contributed to resolving the scientific or technological uncertainty of creating the DVD player up to this point (such as the testing of successive prototypes) are R&D (paragraphs 34 and 39).

A4. Several copies of this prototype are made (not R&D; paragraphs 4–5 and 26–28) and distributed to a group of consumers to test their reactions (not R&D; paragraph 28((a)). Some of these consumers report concerns about the noise level of the DVD player in operation. Additional work is done to resolve this problem. If this involves a routine adjustment of the existing prototype (i.e. no scientific or technological uncertainty) then it will not be R&D (paragraph 14); if it involves more substantial changes (i.e. there is scientific or technological uncertainty to resolve) then it will be R&D.'

R&D case study – advance in science or technology

3.39   The following example reproduced from the BIS Guidelines is an illustration of 'advance in science or technology':

> 'D1. Searching for the molecular structures of possible new drugs would be an advance in science or technology, because it applies existing knowledge of science (which compounds are known to cause particular physiological effects) in search of new or improved active compounds (paragraph 9(b)). This is true even if the method used to search for those molecular structures (e.g. running a computer programme on a particular set of data) is itself entirely routine; the activity directly contributes to the resolution of scientific or technological uncertainty (paragraph 27(c)) and so would be R&D (paragraph4). Work to identify new uses of existing compounds would also be creative work in science or technology, because it seeks new scientific knowledge about those molecules (paragraph 9(a)).

> D2. However, the development of software intended for the analysis of market research data (which is not scientific or technological knowledge; paragraphs 15–18) which was not expected to result in the development of a scientific or technological advance in the field of software as a whole (such as an algorithm which extends overall knowledge or capability in the field of software) would not be R&D (paragraph 8). Work to adapt such software to analyse, say, customer spending patterns would also not be R&D.

> D3. An advance in science or technology need not imply an absolute improvement in the performance of a process, material, device, product or service. For example, the existence of high-fidelity audio equipment does not prevent a project to create lower-performance equipment from being an advance in science or technology (for instance, if it incorporated technological improvements leading to lower cost through more efficient circuit design or speaker construction) (paragraph 9(d)).'

R&D case study – scientific or technological uncertainty

3.40   The following example reproduced from the BIS Guidelines is an illustration of 'scientific or technological uncertainty':

> 'E1. A firm's project involves finding a new active ingredient for weed-killer (an advance in overall knowledge or capability in the particular field of science or technology; paragraphs 6, 20), and developing a formula incorporating the new active ingredient for use in a commercial product (paragraph 9(b) or (c)). Both of these would constitute an advance in science or technology.

E2. In order to achieve this advance, a programme of investigation by computer to pick likely ingredients and the systematic testing of possible ingredients and products based on those 'trial' ingredients is undertaken. The work involves the adaptation of existing software to tackle the specific problem, and product formulation and testing using established methods. This investigation and testing evaluates the weed-killing performance and other relevant characteristics of the formulations (for example, toxicity to humans and wildlife, water solubility, adhesion to weeds, damage done to other plants). All of these activities would therefore be R&D (paragraphs 4, 26, 27).

E3. The company also does work to assess what characteristics a new weed-killing product should have in order to appeal to consumers. This activity does not directly contribute to the resolution of scientific or technological uncertainty (paragraph 28(a)) and is not a qualifying indirect activity (paragraph 31), and is therefore not R&D (paragraph 4).'

R&D case study – directly contributing activity

3.41   The following example reproduced from the BIS Guidelines is an illustration of 'directly contributing activity':

'F1. Work to compare the effectiveness of two possible designs for controlling part of a new manufacturing process would directly contribute to resolving the scientific or technological uncertainty inherent in the new process, and hence the activity would be R&D (paragraphs 4, 26). But work to raise finance for the project, while indirectly contributing to the resolution of scientific or technological uncertainty (e.g. by paying for work) does not of itself help resolve the uncertainty, and hence is not R&D (paragraph 28(a)). Human Resources work to support the R&D is a qualifying indirect activity (paragraph 31) and hence is also R&D (paragraph 5), though it does not directly contribute to the resolution of scientific or technological uncertainty (paragraph 28(e) and (f)).'

Summary – practical points

3.42

- The BIS Guidelines are just one of a number of strands of legislation giving effect to R&D tax relief. They provide the fundamental definition of when R&D takes place. The Guidelines take precedence over the GAAP definitions of the terms 'research' and 'development'.

- R&D takes place when a project seeks to achieve an advance in a field of science or technology. This will have inherent technical uncertainty and those activities relevant to the resolution of this are R&D.

- Documenting the areas of scientific or technological advance and uncertainty is vital. Without evidence of the 'Gateway' tests at paras 3 and 4 no claim is possible, and no starting point for the cost accounting exercise is found.

- The R&D review (see **3.5**) will confirm the company's technical aims and objectives, what they have set out to do and how they did this. The methodology used to resolve the uncertainties and its 'deducibility' will need to be appraised. The project boundaries and timeline will need to be drawn up alongside a list of key project personnel. The project's competent professionals need to be identified; their evidence will be crucial in identifying the inherent uncertainties.

- The term 'scientific or technological advance' is defined through a number of examples at paras 6–12. These scenarios focus upon the advance of knowledge or capability, which includes hypothetical knowledge deducible to an experienced professional and excludes improvements to the company's own knowledge base. Similarly, appreciable improvement work must be represented by scientific or technological change. Appreciable improvement is a defined term meaning 'better than the original' and representing a product that may have been built in a fundamentally different manner.

- The R&D 'advance' scenarios at para 9, have stood the test of time and typify both SME and large company activity. Separate scenarios at paras 39, 41 and 42 show that work on prototypes, design work and cosmetic improvement work can also qualify as R&D.

- 'Scientific or technological uncertainty' is a prescribed term (paras 13, 14). If this is evaluated with hindsight rather than from contemporary R&D project records, it can be quickly obscured by the pace of innovation in the industry or technology concerned.

- Provided the Gateway tests of advance and uncertainty are evident, failed or abandoned projects are eligible for relief. Inferior and cheaper products are equally eligible. Development taking place in tandem to similar projects carried out by other companies will qualify if the knowledge is not generally available or deducible.

- The Guidelines do not discuss the nature of capital or revenue expenditure. Neither do they indicate the amount of relief possible. The amount of qualifying expenditure relevant to a project is governed entirely by the legislation in *CTA 2009, Pt 13*.

- The Guidelines apply equally to both the SME and large company scheme reliefs. There is equal applicability to any field of science or technology. Social sciences, pure mathematics and 'soft' sciences are not within the scope of the definition of R&D.

- Activity identified as R&D by the Guidelines may be conducted anywhere in the world.

Chapter 4

Research and development tax relief – small and medium-sized companies

Contents

SIGNPOSTS

- **Tax relief legislation** – The detailed tax relief legislation applying to the SME schemes and large company scheme is consolidated at *CTA 2009, Pt 13* which sets out four detailed relief schemes for SME companies (see **4.3**).

- **RDEC effective date** – Large companies and SMEs claiming at the large company rate of relief can access the RDEC from 1 April 2013 (see **4.1**).

- **SME status** – The claimant company must establish that it is an SME by reference to the EC Recommendation 361/EC/2003. This requires the aggregation of the accounting data of linked and partner enterprises which can include non-corporate entities (see **4.4, 4.6**). Not all shareholdings or voting rights affect the status of the company as an SME, institutional and business angel investment is exempted in some circumstances (see **4.8**).

- **Impact on SME status** – Group reorganisations such as demergers or hive downs can impact upon the R&D company's status as an SME. Transitional rules can preserve SME status for a limited period in some circumstances (see **4.15**).

- **Subcontracted activity** – Where the SME engages in 'subcontracted' activity, the SME rate of relief will not be available. This can be difficult to identify in practice and is a 'grey' area of the legislation. The issue will have a significant impact upon the RDTR due (see **4.25**).

- **Connected parties** – The discussion of eligible R&D project costs is developed to consider the impact and identification of 'connected parties' and to review the impact of the *FA 2012* changes upon payments made to externally provided workers (see **4.31**).

- **Maximising the benefit of the RDTR** – This will require a detailed review of the company/group's tax position across three years. The relief can be taken by SMEs in a number of ways, including a repayable R&D tax credit, but this will lower the cash value of the claim (see **4.41**). Start-up SMEs can obtain a repayable R&D tax credit for pre-trading expenditure subject to detailed rules (see **4.41(4)**).

- **Practical examples** – The Chapter outlines the benefit of the SME reliefs in a number of practical examples (see **4.43**).

OUTLINE – RELIEFS AVAILABLE

4.1

1   The original R&D scheme, introduced in 2000, was aimed entirely for the benefit of companies that were small or medium-sized enterprises. The scheme has changed almost annually since then. In 2009 a number of these changes were consolidated into *CTA 2009*, where most of the rules affecting the SME (and large company scheme) can be found.

2   But the changes continued. The most recent raft of changes to the SME scheme were made in *FA 2013* and *FA 2014*, following lengthy consultation on aspects of the R&D relief and the wider aspects of the taxation of corporate intangible assets. The backdrop to the changes is the decreasing rate of UK mainstream corporation tax, from 30% when the schemes were first introduced, to 20% by financial year (FY) 2014.

3   From 1 April 2012, an SME company (now called 'an SME'), performing eligible R&D activity has four schemes of tax reliefs available. The maximum relief under the SME scheme is obtained through a super deduction of 125%, in computing its profits. This can result in a reduction of the company's tax liability or where a loss results, a repayable tax credit of 11% in exchange for the surrendered R&D loss.

4   SME start-up companies may claim a similar tax credit for costs relating to the period before trading begins – 'pre-trading expenditure'. The claim, like all R&D tax relief claims, needs to be filed within two years of the end of the accounting period concerned.

5   The changes introduced in *FA 2013* considerably help SMEs performing subcontracted R&D. These SMEs may now claim the new 'R&D expenditure credit' (RDEC) for work performed as a subcontractor, claiming relief at 10% of the eligible R&D spend.

6   An SME obtaining a subsidy for project work, usually as a result of obtaining notifiable State Aid can claim R&D tax relief at the reduced large company rate. This obtains an enhanced deduction of 130% or, from April 2013, access to the RDEC. As SME tax relief is a notifiable State Aid under European Community (EC) rules, the definition of an SME follows EC guidelines. These are set out in *EC Recommendation 361/2003/EC* and apply to accounting periods ending on or after 1 April 2004. The definition of an SME requires the accounting data of linked and partner enterprises to be aggregated in certain circumstances. Complicated rules apply to equity held by venture capital stakeholders.

7   An SME exceeding the project 'cap' on State Aid can similarly claim relief at the large company rate upon the excess project costs. An overall project cap of €7.5 million in State Aid has applied since 1 April 2008.

8   In its current state, the SME scheme now provides the opportunity for a small or medium company to obtain a very significant tax relief worth up to £25,000 per £100,000 of the R&D spend. The SME reliefs are detailed at *CTA 2009, Pt 13*, and determined by whether or not the

company performs R&D independently, or on behalf of third parties; and whether the relief is subsidised or exceeds the overall project cap for State Aid. The qualifying SME costs will be formulated from both the commercial arrangements through which project staff are hired and the broader definition of 'directly contributing R&D activity' (see **3.3**).

9   An understanding of the commercial context in which the R&D takes place is essential to determine the amount of SME relief available and which Chapter(s) of the relief schemes are relevant to the company's claim to relief.

LEGISLATION

4.2   Once eligible R&D activity has been established (see *CTA 2009, Chs 2 and 3*), the relief schemes for SME companies are generous. The amount of qualifying expenditure available as R&D tax reliefs to the SME is established by the rules in *CTA 2009, Pt 13, Chs 2, 3, 4* and *6A* and depend upon the commercial context in which the R&D work is undertaken.

Chapters 2, 3 and *4* of *Pt 13* provide for three specific types of activity to be eligible for SME relief. These are influenced by the commercial arrangements involved in the project work. For example, if the SME performs R&D work which has been subcontracted to it, it will claim under *Ch 3* and will not be able to claim the SME rate of relief available in *Ch 2*, and no repayable tax credit was available before 1 April 2013.

SME rates of relief

Activity	CTA 2009, Pt 13	Rate of relief	Repayable Credit*	Comments
In house R & D	Ch 2	225%	SME rate	
R & D activity contracted out by the SME	Chr 2	225%	SME rate	Costs limited to 65%
R & D activity contracted to the SME performed directly or contracted out	Ch 3	130%	No SME credit From 1 April 2013 – RDEC	Legacy scheme available until 2016
Subsidised R & D expenditure performed directly or contracted out	Ch 4	130%	No SME Credit From 1 April 2013 – RDEC	Legacy scheme available until 2016

*Company must be a going concern

92

The SME company may claim relief in an accounting period, under more than one Chapter (*CTA 2009, s 1040*). This reflects the commercial conditions in which the company engages in R&D and the availability of a 'subsidy' or the application of a project cap in the period of claim.

An overall cap on aid for SME companies was set by the EC. This reflects the fact that the relief is regarded as State Aid and is subject to EC Regulations. The maximum assistance is capped at a limit of €7.5 million per project (*s 1113(2)*).

SME relief under *Ch 3* (subcontracted R&D), or *Ch 4* (capped or subsidised R&D) is given at the large company rate. For both Chapters, R&D, which is not performed in-house but contracted to third parties, carries the large company requirement that the entity to whom the R&D is contracted must be carried out directly by an individual, qualifying body or partnership. This precludes relief where further contracting out by the third party takes place.

Many SMEs carry out subcontracted R&D activity, subsidised and capped R&D is seen less often. For SMEs in this position, *FA 2013* introduced the new RDEC as an alternative to the 'super deduction'. This becomes mandatory from April 2016. The choice is therefore a repayable credit of 10% or an additional enhancement of 30% of the eligible project costs. An election into the RDEC scheme is irrevocable.

The definition of an 'SME' for the purposes of R&D tax relief originates from various EC Directives, but is not regarded as 'tax legislation' per se, by HMRC, although their published viewpoint is that the Recommendations are acceptable for UK corporation tax purposes. Although the thresholds relevant to the SME are similar to the thresholds used for transfer pricing purposes, there is no 'read across' from conventional definitions used for other UK corporation tax purposes. This can set a number of issues in play. For example, what are in other corporation tax contexts, regarded as 'minority' shareholdings, can become extremely relevant to the potential status of the company as an SME for R&D purposes, and the amount of relief available.

WHAT IS AN SME?

Accounting periods ending on or after 1 January 2005

4.3   Companies are regarded as 'SMEs through a series of 'thresholds'. If the company's published accounting data for the period of claim shows the employee headcount is below 500 and the annual turnover or balance sheet value is below €100 million/€86 million, the company will be an SME. This adopts the EC Recommendation 361/2003/EC ([2003] OJ L 124/36) on the definition of micro, small and medium-sized enterprises because RDTR is regarded as a State Aid.

Summary: SME thresholds:

The following thresholds were introduced by *CTA 2009, s 1119–1120* for expenditure incurred on or after 1 August 2008.

Headcount below 500, plus

- Turnover below €100 million/balance sheet below €86 million
- If the headcount exceeds 500 the entity cannot be an SME.

The EC Recommendation states that the SME must also consider the shareholdings of other 'enterprises', described in the Recommendation as 'linked', or 'partner' enterprises, to identify if the accounting data of other entities which should be aggregated.

The EC Recommendation provides a number of considerations to establish that the company is an SME.

EC Recommendation 2003/361/EC

4.4   The *Finance Acts* of *2000* and *2002* stated that the definition of what is a small or medium-sized enterprise follows the *EC Recommendations 1996* and *2003*. The *Recommendation 2003/361/EC* was introduced in 2005 by the *Finance Act 2000, Schedule 20 (Definition of Small or Medium-sized Enterprise) Order (SI 2004/3267)* because of difficulties in interpreting the *1996 Recommendation*.

The current definition of an SME came into effect for accounting periods ending on or after 1 January 2005. It replaced the EC Recommendation of 1996 which had been in force at the time the R&D reliefs were introduced in 2000.

The definition of an SME revolves around the concept of a maximum number of employees but this excludes certain absentees and includes trainees on vocational courses. The company must then consider its annual turnover or balance sheet data. Linked or partner enterprises must be considered, but 'enterprise' is a much broader term than 'associated companies'. Special exceptions apply to institutional investors, but the rules are complex. Where it is established that there is a 'linked' or 'partnered' enterprise, the accounting data is aggregated either on an absolute basis or in proportion to the relevant shareholding or voting rights of the entity concerned.

The 2003 EC Recommendation is reproduced at **Appendix 3**. The detail of the 2003 Recommendation is contained within seven Articles which prescribe:

Article 1:   What is meant by an 'enterprise'

Article 2:   Staff headcount and financial thresholds

Article 3:   Types of enterprises relevant to the thresholds

Article 4:   Alignment of data used for the headcount and thresholds to the accounting period

Article 5:   Staff headcount – employees included/excluded

Article 6:   Methods of data aggregation

Article 7–9:   Sundry provisions

The Statutory Instruments introducing the 2003 Recommendation contained qualifications impacting upon the transition of companies between the SME and large scheme reliefs (see **Chapter 5**).

What is an enterprise?

4.5   An 'enterprise' is not necessarily a company. The term used in the European Recommendation is much broader. It covers any entity carrying on an 'economic activity' (trade).

The R&D claimant must consider the equity held by non-corporates and the extent of their control. This would include:

- self-employed individuals;

- partnerships;

- charities;

- not for profit organisations etc.

Aggregation – linked and partner enterprises

4.6   In establishing the EC SME thresholds (see **Appendix 10** 'SME flowchart'), the accounting data may need to be aggregated with 'partner' or 'linked' enterprises.

The three types of 'enterprise' categorisation for the purposes of RDTR are therefore possible.

Autonomous enterprise

4.7   An autonomous enterprise has no linked or partner enterprises. The threshold tests are applied to its accounting data only for the accounting period of claim.

This can be established if either:

- the enterprise has a holding of less than 25% of the capital or voting rights in one or more enterprises; and/or

- other enterprises do not have a stake of 25% or more of the capital or voting rights in it.

This can include the scenario where the enterprise has investors each with a stake of under 25% provided the investors are not linked. If the investors are linked the enterprise may be regarded as a linked enterprise or partner enterprise (see **4.9**, **4.10**).

Exceptions – specified investment enterprises

4.8   The following types of enterprise can be excluded from the test where not more than 50% of the voting rights or capital is held. The enterprise should also not be linked individually or jointly with the enterprise whose status is being considered.

a   public investment corporations;

b   institutional investors;

c   regional development funds;

d   venture capital companies;

e   individual or grouped 'business angels' – provided their total investment does not exceed €1.25 million;

f   universities and non-profit research centres;

g   local authorities with an annual budget of less than €10 million and fewer than 5,000 inhabitants.

These exceptions can be subject to further complicated rules and exceptions. The HMRC guidance at CIRD 91700 should be reviewed in cases of difficulty or doubt.

Partner enterprises

4.9   An enterprise will be a 'partner' enterprise if it is not a linked enterprise and a relationship exists whereby one holds 25% or more of the capital or voting rights in another.

An enterprise cannot be regarded as an SME if 25% or more of an enterprise's capital or voting rights is held by a public body other than a university.

For this purpose, ownership is taken to mean both direct and indirect methods asserted over the control of voting rights or capital (see **4.13**) in the enterprise concerned.

Once partner enterprises are identified, the accounting data for the relevant periods are then aggregated in proportion to the interest held.

Example 4.1 – Establishing SME tax relief

Partner enterprises aggregating data in proportion to capital and voting rights

Up co own 40% of Down Co's capital and 30% of its voting rights. Up Co has 450 employees and Down Co 200 employees in the accounting period.

Analysis

The companies are partner enterprises because Up Co holds more than 25% of the voting rights and capital of Down Co. The accounting data must be aggregated pro rata to the ownership at 40%.

The employee headcount is 400 plus the aggregated partner enterprise data of 80 (200 × 40%).

Up Co is not an SME and will be regarded as a large company for the purposes of RDTR.

Linked enterprises

4.10   A linked enterprise is defined by EC Recommendation 361/EC/2003 to exist where:

- it controls another enterprise; or
- is controlled by another enterprise.

Grouped companies will usually be linked enterprises.

The definition of control can be extensive and will include, but is not limited to, situations where:

- a majority of shareholdings or voting rights is held;
- the power to appoint or remove the majority of board members is exigible.

If the link is established because of an individual's shareholdings or influence, it is limited to companies in similar or adjacent markets (Article 3). This definition can become complex as the Recommendation defines 'market' in very broad terms. It can be defined as either a 'geographical' market, or a 'product' market. HMRC Guidance provides the assurance of a 'direct upstream/downstream' limitation at CIRD 91400, but the issue has been aired in the EC courts.

Example 4.2 – Establishing SME tax relief: linked enterprises

In an accounting period Chalk Co owned 51% of the voting rights and capital in Cheese Co. Both employ 251 employees in the year.

Analysis

The consolidated accounts should be aggregated for the accounting period. Neither company can be regarded as an SME for R&D purposes.

Linked and partner enterprises: summary of enterprise types

4.11

EC Recommendation 2003/361/EC

Enterprise type*

Autonomous	Holding of no more than 25% of voting rights or capital, held in or by other enterprises	Exclusions for venture capitalists. Ceiling of 50% for external investor	
Linked	One enterprise can exercise control (50%+) over the other	Control direct or indirect Groups always linked Exceptions for companies linked through individuals.	Accounting data amalgamated for threshold tests
Partner	Enterprises not linked but one holds 25%+ of other's voting rights or capital	Exceptions for institutional investors and business angels	Pro rata accounting data amalgamated for threshold tests

*A declaration of status can be made in good faith where an enterprise cannot determine with certainty that it is not owned 25% or more by another enterprise or jointly by linked enterprises.

What accounting data is used?

4.12   For each of the threshold tests, turnover and balance sheet data is regarded as that in the company's published accounts and is taken as the 'gross' amount of the balance sheet but 'net' amount of the entity's turnover.

Data will be converted according to the year-end exchange rate and applied to the figures published in the entity's consolidated accounts.

Headcount

Headcount is derived from the entity's employees, owner managers, secondees and partners. These can be located in the UK, EC, or elsewhere. The following personnel are excluded:

- apprentices and students engaged on vocational training or apprenticeship contracts;

- maternity/paternity leavers.

Annual turnover

The annual turnover figure is taken from the company's published accounts, annualised where appropriate. This excludes VAT or indirect taxes.

Turnover and balance sheet total

The balance sheet total is the gross amount of assets shown in the accounts. Normally the balance sheet totals are taken from conventional year-end accounting data. But where this produces an unjust result, HMRC are able to consider the relevant circumstances.

Where accounts have not been drawn up in euros it is necessary to convert the figures of turnover and balance sheet totals for the purposes of the tests.

Voting rights and capital

4.13   Voting rights and capital are not defined by the EC Recommendation. The HMRC Guidance is extensive and can apply to methods establishing indirect control or to contrived situations as if they were transparent. The viewpoint encompasses all the traditional exertions of control (*ICTA 1988, s 416*).

Changes to SME thresholds

4.14   Some anomalies arose when the thresholds establishing SME relief were increased for R&D expenditure incurred on or after 1 August 2008 (*CTA 2009, ss 1119–1120*).As a company's status as an SME in one period may be affected by its status in earlier periods, the higher thresholds were deemed, for the purpose, only, of determining the correct treatment of expenditure on or after 1 August 2008, to have always applied.

This meant some companies which exceeded the 250 headcount in the old threshold were deemed to be large companies and became SMEs. This led to potential difficulties arising because of the intellectual property requirement until its abolition in December 2009. Here, companies claiming under the large scheme prior to August 2008, but becoming SMEs may have not have been entitled to relief at all under the SME scheme rules as the intellectual property requirement may not have been met (*CTA 2009, ss 1052(4), 1053(3)*). In such a case the company would not be entitled, as an SME, to additional *Ch 3* or *4* relief for large companies (*CTA 2009, ss1070–1072; 1134–1136*) because that relief is only available where the SME fails to qualify because its expenditure is subsidised or exceeds the €7.5 million cap.

Transitional provisions were therefore introduced for large companies becoming SMEs, allowing the retention of status for two whole years.

Transition to and from SME scheme

Special situations: demergers

4.15   But the effect of the transition rules can work in an adverse way. For example, in a demerger situation, it may take a further whole year for an entity to access SME reliefs because of the way in which the transitional provisions of the EC Recommendation apply.

This can be understood by an example.

Example 4.3 – Transition of large company to SME scheme

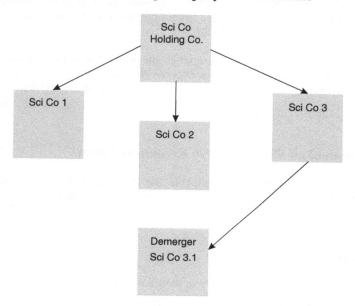

In this example, Sci Co 3 had to aggregate its data with Sci Co 1 and Sci Co 2 as the entities were 'linked' for the purposes of RDTR. Sci Co 3 has claimed RDTR under the large scheme for year 1 and demerges from the group in year 2. It will only be able to access the SME scheme if it attains the thresholds for two successive years and the earliest date of SME relief will be year 3.

Transition to large company: SME becoming a large company

4.16 The *2003 EC Recommendation* is affected by Statutory Instruments implementing the transition from the *1996 EC Recommendation. Statutory Instrument 3267/2004* contains qualifications which apply an instant transition to large company status where this occurs as a result of the aggregation of linked or partner enterprises.

Example 4.4 – Impact of EC 2003 Recommendation qualification

Large company takeover of SME

Small Enterprise R&D Co employs 450 people in year 1, and is so successful it is taken over halfway through year 2.

Analysis

SME Co will be regarded as an SME only until the time of the takeover. It will be regarded as large from the accounting period of change (unless this happened before 1 December 2008).

Qualification 2: *SI 3267/2004* disapplies the transition period of the 2003 Recommendation, if an enterprise exceeds the staff headcount or financial ceiling as a result of the aggregation of partner or linked enterprises.

Definition of an SME: the 1996 Recommendation

4.17   Although now rarely applicable, the 1996 Recommendation defining an SME was based upon two tests, a quantitative test and an independence test:

Quantitative test

A company is an SME if it has fewer than 250 employees and has either:

- an annual turnover not exceeding €40 million or

- an annual balance sheet total not exceeding €27 million;

then it was regarded as an SME so long as it satisfied the independence test.

Independence test

A company could not be regarded as an SME if it was owned, singly or jointly (25% or more of the capital or voting rights) by enterprises that were not SMEs.

This excluded most scenarios involving specified investment enterprises such as venture capital companies, institutional investors and public investment corporations, so long as individually or jointly they could not exercise control over the company.

1996 Aggregation rules

These differed from the 2003 Recommendation. The effect was to aggregate the entity's figures with those of all the enterprises, which it directly or indirectly controls through possession of 25% or more of the capital or of the voting rights.

The text of the 1996 Recommendation is reproduced at **Appendix 11**.

RELIEFS AVAILABLE TO THE SME

In-house R&D; R&D contracted out by the SME (CTA 2009, Ch 2)

4.18   Most SMEs claim R&D tax relief under *CTA 2009, Ch 2*. This scheme of relief represents the majority of SME claims filed to HMRC. It provides a supplementary deduction for R&D revenue costs in calculating the profits of the SME. This is in addition to any ordinary deductions for expenditure under *s 87*, and is reflected in the SME's tax computation as a 'below the line' adjustment.

Chapter 2 relief is available for R&D costs incurred by the SME for project work carried out upon:

- 'in-house' R&D (*s 1052*); or

- contracted-out R&D activity (*s 1053*).

The relief provides five scenarios to utilise the additional corporation tax deduction:

- absorption of the tax relief to reduce profits chargeable to corporation tax in the accounting period;

- the carry back or carry forward of the trading loss as enhanced by the R&D tax relief to other accounting periods;

- the surrender of the enhanced trading loss as group relief;

- the surrender of the loss in exchange for a repayable tax credit if the entity is a going concern (*s 1046*);

- where the R&D has been carried out in a 'pre-income' company, the enhanced R&D expenditure can be treated as a deemed trading loss which can be surrendered as a repayable tax credit immediately after the company's first accounting period (*s 1045*).

Qualifying expenditure

4.19   CTA 2009, Ch 2 relief rewards relevant revenue expenditure for either in-house R&D activity or contracted-out work. In the case of in-house activity, the costs eligible for relief are those incurred upon:

- staffing costs and the costs of externally provided workers (*ss 1123,1127*);

- software and consumable materials (*s 1125*).

Research development allowances (RDAs) may be claimed for relevant capital expenditure.

Where R&D is subcontracted to third parties ('contracted out'), the SME can also claim relief for unsubsidised subcontractor costs (*s 1134–1136*).

The subcontractor, when viewed in isolation, may not be performing R&D from their perspective but the R&D will be relevant to the claimant's project work.

If the subcontractor is unconnected to the company a maximum of 65% of the costs are eligible for tax relief. If the subcontractor is connected to the company, its own 'relevant cost' provides a ceiling for the expenditure eligible for relief.

Conditions

4.20   The *CTA 2009, Ch 2* relief scheme is subject to a number of conditions and features:

- The company must be an SME for the accounting period concerned and carrying on, or preparing to do so, a trade.

- The company should incur qualifying R&D expenditure which is 'relevant' to that trade.

- The R&D should not have been contracted to the SME by third parties.

- Unlike the large company scheme, there is no requirement in the SME scheme for the subcontractor to carry out the work itself without the involvement of further third parties.

- Qualifying R&D expenditure must reach a minimum of £10,000 in the accounting period. *Section 1050* provides for this to be reduced proportionately for accounting periods of less than 12 months. This requirement was removed by *FA 2012* for expenditure incurred on or after 1 April 2012.

- The expenditure must not be subsidised; if it is, limited relief is available at the large company rate of relief through *CTA 2009, Pt 13, Ch 3*.

- Loss making companies must not be reliant upon R&D tax credits and should meet the 'going concern' conditions at *CTA 2009, s 1046*.

It is also feasible that the subcontractor payment includes a payment for software or consumables, in which case the payment will need to be analysed to identify the payment relating to the assigned R&D project work itself.

SME: Going concern condition

4.21   Purely for the purposes of SME claims under *Ch 2*, the claimant company must be a 'going concern' based upon its published accounts. This requirement applies to:

The additional deduction in respect of R&D expenditure   *CTA 2009, s 1044*

Pre-trading expenditure involving R&D   *CTA 2009, s 1045*

The surrender of enhanced losses for repayable tax   *CTA 2009, s 1054*
credits

FA 2012 introduced clarity to the definition of 'going concern'. This confirmed that companies in administration or liquidation are not regarded as 'going concerns' and are unable to claim any of the above reliefs after 1 April 2012.

As the going concern condition applies purely to *Ch 2* claims, it is possible for SMEs not meeting the 'going concern' condition to obtain R&D tax relief under the reduced rates of either *Ch 3* (relief for R&D work contracted out to the SME) or *Ch 4* (relief for subsidised R&D expenditure or costs subject to the State Aid cap set out within *s 1113*). In practice, the ability to make such an alternative claim under either *Ch 3* or *4* is likely to be extremely limited.

R&D SUBCONTRACTED TO THE SME

4.22   The full rate of SME relief in *Ch 2* is not available for subcontracted R&D. Where the SME acts as a subcontractor for third parties (*s 1052(5)*, *1053(4)*), relief is available at the large scheme rate.

This can cause problems because the expenditure eligible for relief at the large scheme rate of R&D excludes the costs for further subcontracting of the work. Subcontracting is common in the R&D environment, reflecting the fact that it is not economical or even technically feasible for many companies to undertake all of the steps in a development project themselves. The increased regulation of many innovative industries has also encouraged the use of subcontracting arrangements with bona fide expertise from third parties.

In a scenario where the SME subcontracts R&D activity, *Ch 3* provides relief at the much lower 'large company' rate of 130%. The changes made by *FA 2012* introduced the RD expenditure credit (RDEC) for eligible expenditure incurred on or after 1 April 2012. Prior to this, no repayment credit was available to the SME for subcontracted-in activity. The new RDEC will run in tandem with the 'legacy' large company scheme until it becomes mandatory in April 2016.

The area can be contentious and involve significant amounts of tax relief. The nature of subcontracting is that the R&D performer can usually demonstrate:

- economic risk; and

- autonomy as to how the project deliverables are achieved.

There is no commentary on 'subcontracting' in the BIS Guidelines. The commentary at *CTA 2009* is limited to highlighting the 'deliverable' objective (see **4.25**).

Chapter 3 relief: conditions

4.23   The relief is available for subcontracted R&D undertaken either in-house, or where contracted in a limited number of circumstances. A number of detailed conditions apply to this relief, including from whom the work is contracted and to whom any work is subcontracted:

- The claimant company must qualify as an SME for the accounting period.

- The contracted-out expenditure is deductible in calculating its trading profits of the period for corporation tax purposes; including allowable pre-trading expenses.

- The subcontracted R&D work must be contracted from:

  o   a large company; or

  o   a person otherwise than in the course of carrying on a chargeable UK trade. This might include, for example, a charity, government agency or a person resident overseas. A chargeable trade is defined at *CTA 2009, s 1065* as one carried on wholly or partly in the UK, the profits of which are subject to income or corporation tax as representing 'trading profits'.

Eligible costs – in-house and subcontracted activity

4.24   Where the subcontracted activity is undertaken by the SME 'in-house', it must be directly performed and relevant to the SME trade.

The SME may claim the usual R&D costs incurred upon:

- staffing costs, including externally provided workers;

- software and consumable items.

Where the SME contracts out some of the subcontracted activity, a number of further conditions apply, narrowing the relief considerably (*CTA 2009, s 1067*). These include the requirements that:

- the costs incurred reflect payments to a qualifying body, an individual, or a firm of individuals;

- the R&D is directly performed and not then contracted on again to another person; and

- the expenditure is attributable to relevant R&D in relation to the SME claimant.

These requirements similarly feature in the large company scheme, aligning the *Ch 3* relief to the *Ch 5* (large company) relief.

What is subcontracted R&D activity?

4.25   Experience shows that subcontracted R&D activity is not always clear, particularly where an SME has production contracts involving large companies. Subcontracting activity will not always be apparent from a review of the company's accounts and balance sheet. The commercial context of R&D is frequently a grey area for both claimants and inspectors reviewing potential claims to relief.

Subcontracting is listed by HMRC as a 'common error' in SME claims for relief. To compound matters, HMRC give a special meaning to subcontracted activity and often infer that any 'peer to peer' activity or involvement with a large company or third party prohibits the company from claiming R&D tax relief under the SME scheme.

In an ideal situation, the contracts between the contractor and subcontractor company will specify whether or not R&D activity is allocated by one to the other. But many SME claims show that a deliverable is bound into the contract, with the 'subcontractor' being responsible for the delivery of a tangible aspect of the development work. In this situation the SME may bear the risk and autonomy of its own R&D costs incumbent upon it to provide the contract deliverable.

This contrasts with the R&D performer scenario where there is a key R&D deliverable but no responsibility to deliver a finished product. However many cases are not clear cut in either direction and what may be clear from a contract from the outset may be the subject of change and alteration as the contract is carried out.

Practical point 4.1 – Is the R&D subcontracted?

A useful test fitting with the legislative definition of R&D for tax purposes is therefore to consider:

Does the subcontracted activity contribute directly to the resolution of uncertainty within the contractor company's R&D project work?

Further areas of consideration will include:

- the control of intellectual property;
- risk management strategies;
- the status of the subcontractor as an expert;
- the clientele of the subcontractor and track record in the field;
- the indemnity offered by the subcontractor and its nature.

Examples 4.5 and **4.6** show differing scenarios commonly met in practice:

Example 4.5 – R&D performed by the SME as a subcontractor

Trial Co (TC) has a specialised laboratory in the UK and India. It undertakes chemical testing of various trial products on behalf of Bigger Cos and will complete the final stages of many of these companies' experimental work at their premises.

Analysis

TC is an SME engaged to perform R&D as a subcontractor. It has subcontracted R&D activity on behalf of third parties which are large companies and will be able to claim an additional deduction of 30% of any expenditure involved under *Ch 3*. It will not be able to claim relief under *Ch 2*.

It can carry on this activity anywhere in the world.

Example 4.6 – SME performing R&D freely

Trial Co 2 (TC2) has a specialised laboratory in the UK with testing facilities in India. It has used its laboratory to develop specialised chemical finishes for optic cable for use in the aerospace industry. It has been able to sell this finished product to a number of Bigger Cos (BCs) and has a number of contracts to produce the cable for worldwide markets.

BCs sometimes make payments in advance to TC2 for these products.

Analysis

Bigger Co (BC) has ordered a number of products from TC2. In contrast to the scenario in **Example 4.5**, the SME has not been engaged to perform R&D but has a client relationship with BC.

TC2 has undertaken substantial R&D activity at its own expense and economic risk, independently of the demands of BC, although both are commercially intertwined.

TC2 has undertaken relevant R&D eligible for relief under *Ch 2*, although it has various contracts with BC, it is performing autonomous R&D and can use this expertise outside of the relationship it has with BC.

The stage payments are not related to the performance of R&D but the commercial contracts between the companies; the R&D is undertaken freely by TC2.

SUBSIDISED AND CAPPED EXPENDITURE

4.26　The usual rule is that an SME may not claim RDTR upon any expenditure which is subsidised; this rule does not apply to large companies. However, in some circumstances the SME can claim RDTR under the provisions of *Ch 4* on subsidised R&D activity.

To establish whether a project has received a subsidy, it is important to look at the nature of any third party funding for R&D work as the tax treatment differs depending upon whether or not the funds count as State Aid.

State Aid funding

4.27　The UK is subject to the EC rules upon State Aid, which impacts the amount of relief the SME may claim. EC Rules prescribe that SME companies cannot claim both State Aid and SME tax relief (*Ch 2*) upon the same project work.

Where a project has received **any** funding which is a notified State Aid (usually through an enterprise board or government grant), then no expenditure on that project can qualify for the R&D tax relief under the SME scheme. Experience shows that HMRC enforce this prohibition vigorously. Were a grant to be repaid in the hope of receiving RDTR, this would not circumvent the requirement that no State Aid funding has been **claimed** for the project. The topic is considered in more detail in the Chapter 'Grants and Alternative Funding' below.

Subsidies

4.28　Where State Aid is not in question, *Ch 4* enables the SME to claim an additional tax deduction at the large scheme rate upon:

- subsidised expenditure upon in-house direct R&D work; and/or

- subsidised expenditure upon contracted out R&D activity (*CTA 2009, s 1070*).

R&D costs are subsidised to the extent that the costs do not exceed the subsidy. This analysis is then applied to the R&D costs resulting in claims which may be made partly under the *Ch 2* SME scheme and partly under *Ch 4* at the large company scheme rate.

Example 4.7 – Subsidised R & D projects: inter-company funding

Sub Co has run an in-house project with costs of £1 million in the 2012 accounting period. A sister company in the group has provided some funding for the project, advancing £500,000 in the same period.

Analysis

Sub Co has not received State Aid but has received a subsidy in respect of its project work. It can consider relief under *Ch 4*. One-half its R&D costs are subsidised and the other half are borne autonomously.

RDTR is due at £500,000 × 130%   Ch 4

RDTR is due at £500,000 × 225%   Ch 2

SME SCHEMES – WHICH COSTS CAN BE CLAIMED?

4.29   *Chapters 2–5* of *CTA 2009* provide relief for relevant R&D expenditure incurred by the SME upon:

● staffing costs, including the costs of externally provided workers (EPWs);

● software and consumable items relevant to the project;

● subcontractor costs – restricted where the SME performs subcontracted R&D or where R&D is subsidised or exceeds the project cap for State Aid.

Detailed provisions apply to each cost category, which are summarised mainly in *Pt 13, Ch 9*. Any relief claimed within *Ch 2–5* must be formulated from these detailed conditions.

Staffing costs

4.30   As above (**Chapter 3**), the costs eligible for relief are those in the company's accounts for the accounting period of the claim. These will come from personnel costs for staff directly contributing to the resolution of uncertainties fundamental to the R&D project activity. Activity that is indirectly relevant to the project or which indirectly supports the project work will also be eligible for relief (*ss 1123, 1124*). **Chapter 3** provides a list of eligible payments to personnel eligible as 'staffing costs'.

The SME and large company reliefs use the same definition of staffing costs.

The legislation does not recognise 'book entries' for staffing costs, or indeed any further R&D cost headings; where workers are supplied through group company arrangements, relief may be available through the EPW Regulations only. Crucially the EPW Regulations restrict relief to 65% of the costs incurred.

Externally provided workers

4.31   EPWs are workers engaged by the company through third parties, for example, agency workers supplied on a temporary or one-off basis. The legislation provides a number of general conditions. The final two conditions arise from very detailed regulations originally intended for use in 'status' tax cases. The conditions for valid EPW costs are that:

- the worker is an individual;

- the worker is not a director or employee of the claimant company;

- the worker is providing the services concerned personally to the claimant company, under the terms of a contract between him and a person other than the company (the 'staff controller'). For expenditure incurred before 1 April 2012, the legislation referred to a tripartite contract between the person and a 'staff provider' (see below);

- the provision of those services does not constitute the carrying on of activities contracted out by the company;

- the worker is subject to (or to the right of) supervision, direction or control by the company as to the manner in which those services are provided;

- the worker's services are supplied to the company by or through the staff provider (whether or not he is a director or employee of the staff provider or of any other person).

When the R&D legislation was first drafted, only directly employed staff costs were included in the relief. Yet many R&D performers hire staff in a variety of circumstances for short-term or highly skilled hire. The Government recognised this was unfair and introduced legislation recognising the costs of EPWs as eligible 'staffing costs' in *FA 2003*. However, these changes spanned six separate pieces of legislation based upon the PAYE Regulations formula. The practical effect was a confusing and detailed process for any costs to be eligible for relief. Common labour hire vehicles such as umbrella companies and *IR 35* companies hired through an agency remained ineligible for relief. The legislation prevented the costs of many bona fide R&D personnel from being included in the R&D relief computation.

Prior to the 2012 changes, a 'tripartite' arrangement was essential to any EPW engagement. This required project workers to be hired from a 'staff provider' and subject to the personal supervision by the company in respect of their work. The contractual and payment terms of the engagement needed to demonstrate that the claimant company had made a payment 'staff provision payment' to a 'staff provider' in respect of the supply of personal services of the project workers concerned.

The tripartite arrangement could fail on a number of aspects. Common examples were where:

- the staff provider used a personal service company as an intermediary bringing four, rather than three, parties into the arrangement;

- the staff provider used an umbrella company, similarly failing the 'three' test;

- the staff provider did not provide the R&D services 'personally';

- the staff provider used an intermediary between itself and the claimant;

- the staff provider and claimant were grouped companies and the staff provider in turn hired staff from a third party.

The claimant did not personally control or supervise the personnel.

FA 2012 introduced some changes for expenditure incurred on or after 1 April 2012, recognising primarily that provided an arrangement satisfies 'at least three' criteria, costs are eligible EPW expenditure.

The benefit is best understood by way of an example:

Example 4.8 – Failed EPW payments

Big Group Co A (BGC A) has carried out R&D for a number of years spending around £1 million per annum on personnel it regards as EPW costs. The arrangement is that BGC A uses staff hired from the management company, Group Co B, for its project work. Group Co B uses agency staff hired from a third party and supplies the workers to BGC A after contracting with the agency.

Prior to the 2012 changes BGC A could not claim the costs of the EPW expenditure.

Analysis

A has paid for the provision of workers by B, the 'staff provider'. However, the worker has no direct link to the staff provider as the contract is between the individual and the agency rather than the staff provider.

Prior to April 2012, the fact that there are four parties to the engagement, rather than three, would prevent the EPW costs from being eligible for relief.

For expenditure incurred after April 2012, the relevant part of the legislation, *CTA 2009, s 1128(7)* simply requires the services are provided through an arrangement with a 'staff controller', ie between 'the worker and a person other than the claimant'. This removes the strict requirement that the contract lies between the worker and staff provider. Similarly, the staff provider and the staff controller could be the same person. Indeed, there could even be multiple staff controllers (although there can only be one staff provider in any arrangement).

Freelance consultants can sometimes be regarded as EPWs particularly where a consultant supplies his services through a personal service company. This may not reflect the requirements of the legislation and may come under attack from HMRC as payments to freelance consultants are not an eligible R&D cost. The operation of PAYE is usually demonstrable within an EPW relationship and is one of the key tests applied in cases of difficulty by HMRC. This can apply even where the staff controller or staff provider are not based in the UK, when the obligation to operate PAYE may shift to the claimant company.

The definition of EPWs is discussed at **Chapter 3** above and applies equally to SME and large companies.

Connected parties

4.32   *CTA 2009, s 1129* applies special rules where the parties are connected. Here, the claimant's qualifying expenditure on EPWs is prescribed *by CTA 2009, s 1129(2)* as the lower of:

- the entire staff provision payment; and

- the aggregate of the relevant expenditure of each staff controller.

The 'relevant expenditure' in this context is defined by *CTA 2009, s 1129(3)* and is essentially the staff costs or agency workers' remuneration incurred by the appropriate company in providing the EPWs.

Where the staff provider and (if different) the staff controller (or controllers) are not all connected (*CTA 2009, s 1130*) provides that the companies may jointly elect for the provisions of *CTA 2009, s 1129* to apply. Such an election is irrevocable and means that the claimant will be dependent upon the other parties providing details of their relevant expenditure for the duration of the arrangement.

In all other cases, *CTA 2009, s 1131* provides that the qualifying expenditure on EPWs is restricted to 65% of the staff provision payment.

The legislation on EPW payments applies equally to any R&D scenario, ie for relief claimed throughout *Ch 2–5*.

Subcontractor payments by the SME

4.33   An SME might engage subcontractors to assist with its own 'in-house' R&D, or upon work that has been contracted to it – where the SME acts as a subcontractor itself.

For in-house R&D, the SME may take the gross payment made to the subcontractor in the accounting period and claim either:

- 65% of the costs incurred in the accounting period where the parties are unconnected (see **4.19**); or

- 100% of the 'relevant cost' of the subcontractor itself if the parties are connected or elect to be so (see **4.32**).

Where the SME acts as a subcontractor, there is only very limited scope for relief upon subcontracting costs. The costs are only allowable if they are payments to:

- a qualifying body;

- an individual; or

- a partnership of individuals.

However, a number of positive factors also apply to subcontractor costs:

- Subcontractors can carry out their activity anywhere in the world.

- The expenditure follows the accounting treatment.

- Subcontractors' work need not be R&D when taken in isolation; but will be referable by the part they play in the claimant's R&D project work.

Large companies

4.34   Large companies subcontracting out R&D work have to follow a similar code prescribing which payments are eligible for relief. This is discussed at **Chapter 5** below and is limited to payments made to qualifying bodies, individuals and partnerships for work directly undertaken on behalf of the claimant.

SME subcontractor payments – connected parties

4.35   The concept of what a subcontractor **is** has been discussed above at **4.33**. Once eligible subcontractor costs are identified, the amount of relief available is determined by whether or not the parties are 'connected' or elect to be regarded as such.

The amount of relief due for subcontractor payment costs is determined by whether or not the parties are regarded as 'connected' persons, or make an irrevocable election to be regarded as such.

Connected parties

The definition of connected parties is based upon tax legislation which can be very widely drawn, and care is required that a full review of any potential 'connection' is made. The definition of connection applies to:

- payments to subcontractors;

- payments to EPWs;

- contributions to independent research (large company schemes).

Detail – what is a connected party for R&D purposes?

Connected parties can exist on many levels; common scenarios are at A, B and C below.

A. Examples of companies being connected are where:

- the same person has control of both, or a person has control of one and persons connected with him, or he and persons connected with him, have control of the other; or

- a group of two or more persons has control of each company, and the groups either consist of the same persons or could be regarded as consisting of the same persons by treating (in one or more cases) a member of either group as replaced by a person with whom he is connected.

B. A company is connected with another person if that person has control of it or if that person and persons connected with him together have control of it.

C. Individuals:

- Any two or more persons acting together to secure or exercise control of a company are treated in relation to that company as connected with one another and with any person acting on the directions of any of them to secure or exercise control of the company.

A person is connected with:

- an individual if that person is the individual's spouse or civil partner, or is a relative, or the spouse or civil partner of a relative, of the individual or of the individual's spouse or civil partner;

- any person with whom he is in partnership, and with the spouse or civil partner or relative of any individual with whom he is in partnership.

It is also possible to be connected via settlements and trusts (*ICTA 1988, s 839(3)*).

Transfer pricing issues

4.36   Where connected companies engage in transactions between themselves UK/UK or otherwise, transfer pricing implications often arise. But any advance pricing agreements for subcontractor costs or wider application of UK or other territorial transfer pricing rules do not displace the limits on expenditure for subcontracted R&D between connected persons.

The term 'connected' therefore follows the meaning given in *ICTA 1988, s 839*.

Unconnected/connected subcontractors: tax relief available

4.37 Where the parties are unconnected, a maximum of 65% of the relevant expenditure is available for relief (*CTA 2009, s 1133–1136*).

Where the subcontractor and claimant are connected or choose to be so, the special rules at *s 1132(2)* state that the amount of relief is the lower of:

● the entire payment; or

● if less, an amount equal to the subcontractor's relevant expenditure.

This will require a disclosure by the subcontractor of his expenditure upon R&D costs, ie staffing costs, including the costs of EPWs and software and consumable items. This examination by the claimant of the subcontractor's accounting data may be one of the reasons why elections for connected party treatment are rare.

Software and consumable items

4.38 SME companies often underestimate the amounts spent upon software and consumable items in R&D work (see **Chapter 2**).

Materials used in building prototypes or pilot plants are eligible for relief where these are constructed as feasibility models.

Similarly, routine heat, light and power costs may be apportioned to include the R&D costs pro rata. The basis of apportionment is not prescriptive but should sensibly reflect the occupation of the R&D project within the company's premises.

The costs of software and consumable items incurred by the SME are the same whether computed as part of a claim at either the SME or large company rate.

Research development allowances

4.39 This important area of relief is discussed at **Chapter 9** below. Many SMEs find the annual investment allowance sufficient to cover the cost of capital expenditure relevant to the project work. There is no possibility of a 'double allowance' upon the same costs.

Artificially inflated claims for relief or tax credit

4.40 HMRC have the power to disregard claims for relief arising 'arrangements' entered into purely for the purposes of obtaining RDTR under *Chs 2–5*. This avoidance legislation is widely drawn and applies to both SME and large company claims however construed (*CTA 2009, s 1084*).

VALUE OF RDTR – HOW SME RELIEF IS GIVEN

4.41 As above, there are a wide variety of factors influencing the amount of R&D expenditure eligible for relief. The scheme under which relief is claimed should aim to maximise the amount of corporation tax relief available in the accounting period, which will be applied as a 'super deduction' in the company's corporation tax computation. The tax 'relief' is shown as an 'enhanced deduction, *CTA 2009, Pt 13*' in the corporation tax computation, unless the RDEC is claimed (*Ch 5*).

How the SME chooses to use the relief will further affect the 'cash value' of the claim.

To obtain the maximum benefit from the relief, the corporation tax computations from the current, past and anticipated future accounting periods will need to be considered.

Any loss arising from the R&D super deduction is regarded as an ordinary trading loss in the accounting period, and no special conditions apply to its utilisation, unless it is surrendered for a repayable R&D tax credit.

The practical examples below show the various options available and how the relief can be best utilised. Five permutations are available to SMEs as follows:

(1) R&D relief – reduction in corporation tax liability

For most established SMEs RDTR is simply taken as a reduction in the corporation tax liability for the accounting period of claim. Two points arise:

i)   The enquiry window operates in the normal way and the claim and its documentation can be reviewed at any time within that, despite the company's self-assessment being processed by HMRC (see **Chapter 6**).

ii)   The R&D super deduction can result in a trading loss (see **5.23**).

For an SME with a 20% corporation tax rate, the relief is therefore worth 25% of the R&D expenditure in the accounting period (20% × 125%) for accounting periods ending on or after 1 April 2012.

Where lowered corporation tax liabilities for quarterly instalment purposes are established through RDTR, the following year's corporation tax instalments can be reduced accordingly. This contrasts with the RDEC scheme which does not permit a reduction in quarterly instalments in advance of R&D costs being finalised.

(2) R&D relief – set off of trading losses

R&D expenditure can be exceptional and result in the company just about breaking even for the accounting periods of project activity, or recording a loss. The effect of the R&D enhancement can be to produce/enhance a trading loss for the accounting period.

This is relievable as either:

- carry back to previous accounting periods and set against previous corporation tax liabilities;

- carry forward into the next accounting period and set against future corporation tax liabilities if the same trade is continued;

- surrendered as group relief;

- surrendered to other SME members in a consortium;

- surrendered in full or part, in exchange for a repayable tax credit.

Subject to the marginal rate of corporation tax payable, if the R&D company is within a group, the SME in this scenario will benefit as in (1) above, at a 20% corporation tax rate, i.e. the loss relief is worth 25% of the R&D expenditure in the accounting period (20% × 125%).

If a company changes ownership, the carry forward tax losses are subject to detailed rules and may not be available. In these circumstances, it can be prudent to carry back any current year loss or surrender the R&D loss in exchange for a repayable tax credit. The detailed conditions affecting terminal loss relief claims are outlined at **Chapter 6**.

Group relief

Subject to the usual consent and surrender notices, the SME is free to surrender all or part of its trading loss for the accounting period to group members.

Consortium relief

The rules for consortium relief restrict the surrender to other consortia members to SME members only.

(3) R&D tax relief – the R&D tax credit

Where the application of RDTR results in a trading loss, the SME will have a 'surrenderable loss' which, if not utilised as above, can be exchanged for a repayable RD tax credit (RDTC) (see **4.42**).

The maximum surrender rate is set at 11% for FY 2014. This is calculated upon the lower of:

- the R&D expenditure as enhanced; or
- the company's adjusted losses in the accounting period.

This is subject to:

- the absorption of the R&D enhancement against any current year profits;
- a reduction for any part of the loss carried back against prior accounting periods;
- a reduction for any part of the loss surrendered as group or consortium relief.

Once surrendered, the company's trading loss for the accounting period is accordingly reduced. A company does not have to surrender all of the losses concerned; if it makes a partial surrender it must reduce the loss carried forward in proportion.

PAYE/NIC liabilities

For accounting periods ending before 1 April 2012, the RDTC relief was subject to a 'PAYE cap'. The maximum tax credit available was subject to an additional limit of the total amount of the company's PAYE and NIC liabilities for the payment period ending in the accounting period of claim.

Unlike the RDEC, the PAYE and NIC limit applied to all staff employed by the company in the accounting period, rather than just the R&D staff.

A payment period was defined as ending on the fifth day of a month for which the company is liable to account to HMRC for PAYE and NIC. The total amount of the company's PAYE liabilities for a payment period was the total amount which it was required to account to HMRC for in that period. This excluded certain statutory payments.

Repayment of the tax credit is always subject to the company having no outstanding PAYE or NIC liabilities. Repayments through the RDEC are subject to group-wide liabilities being up to date.

The R&D tax credit is paid through the CT self-assessment system and HRMC aim to process tax credit repayments within 28 days. The claim for the tax credit forms part of the company's corporation tax return for the accounting period and is subject to the enquiry window, and liable to interest and penalties should the amount be incorrect (see **Chapter 6**). Unlike the RDEC credit, the tax credit is not regarded as income for the company whether claimed as a mainstream credit as above or as a 'pre-trading' tax credit (see below).

SME companies claiming the RDTC must be a going concern at the time of the claim.

(4) R&D tax relief – pre-trading tax credit

The SME scheme enables a start-up company to obtain RDTR as if the resultant loss from the R&D costs were a 'deemed trading loss' in the pre-trading accounting period. To achieve this, the expenditure must be allowable as revenue expenditure for tax purposes and 'relevant' to the company's intended trade.

The credit is then given by application to HMRC through the company's tax return in the same way as the RDTC above. Any amount surrendered in exchange for the credit is not available to carry forward against the company's future accounting periods or to be surrendered as group or consortium relief.

R&D relief benefit

RDEC (from 1 April 2013)

Not all SME activity will attract relief at the SME 125% rate. These types of activity do not carry the repayable SME tax credit, although medium enterprises (MEs) are able to claim the RDEC for expenditure incurred on or after 1 April 2013. Prior to these changes, no credit was available where the SME:

- acted as a subcontractor and claimed relief under *Ch 3* (see **5.11**);

- had subsidised R&D expenditure and claimed relief under *Ch 4*;

- had exceeded the project cap and claimed relief under *Ch* 4.

The RDEC relief is explained with examples, below, at **Chapter 5**.

SUMMARY AND PRACTICAL POINTS

4.42

- A number of EC Regulations impact upon the SME, including the prohibition of R&D tax relief if State Aid has been claimed for any project costs in the past.

- An SME is defined by EC Regulation. It is necessary to consider the accounting data of linked or partner enterprises. This can present difficulties in its own right and further complexities where the SME changes status to or from a large company.

- The SME scheme provides a valid alternative to grant funding and other funding opportunities which may be regarded as State Aid. In particular, the SME may claim a repayable tax credit for R&D costs incurred during the company's start-up phase.

- *CTA 2009, Pt 13, Chs 2–4* outline a number of reliefs available for the SME. The choice of relief is driven by the commercial circumstances in which the company carries out the development activity, for example, if the SME subcontracts the R&D work from a third party, or its project costs are subsidised.

- An SME may claim under more than one Chapter of relief. A project may include activities which are subsidised or allocated to the company by third parties. This would involve claims for both the *Ch 2* SME rate of relief and the large company rate of relief.

- A repayable tax credit can be claimed by loss making SMEs and start-ups. This provides relief of around 22% of the eligible R&D expenditure and is not taxable in the hands of the company.

- R&D relief is always given as a super deduction. The company/group's tax computation will need to be reviewed for the preceding and forward year if the most is to be made of the enhanced deduction.

- SMEs are now able to benefit from the RDEC for costs incurred on or after 1 April 2013.

PRACTICAL EXAMPLES

R&D tax relief for SMEs

4.43   Where the SME carries out in-house direct R&D or subcontracts R&D activity to third parties, it may claim an enhanced revenue expenditure deduction upon its eligible costs, as in **Example 4.9** below.

Example 4.9 – Profitable SME: effect of RDTR, enhanced expenditure

SME 2 Co carries out in house R&D work developing specialist tooling for its cake manufacturing arm. Costs of £80,000 are included in the 2012 accounts. The company subcontracts the food allergy testing relevant to the new production methods to a third party who in turn subcontracts part of the work to further third parties. A figure of £20,000 for costs on allergy development work is reflected in the company's accounts.

Analysis

SME 2 Co has carried out R&D work eligible entirely under *Ch 2*. In-house activity amounts to £80,000. As the company is not connected to the subcontractor it can claim 65% of these costs of £20,000.

The company's total eligible R&D spend is:

In-house costs	£80,000
Subcontractor costs	£20,000 × 65% = £13,000

In computing the deductible expenditure, the company can claim:

£93,000 × 225% = £209,250

The benefit of the tax relief is:

£93,000 × 125% at the company's marginal rate of corporation tax.

Practical point 2: Start-up SMEs – the pre-trading RDEC

Many innovative companies incur substantial development costs during start up. The usual corporation tax rule is that this expenditure is captured in the company's first accounting period, delaying tax relief until some nine months afterwards.

CTA 2009, s 1045 permits the SME to elect to claim relief in the accounting period in which the expenses are incurred. This provides a valuable cash flow opportunity for the claimant. The election needs to be filed within two years of the end of the relevant accounting period.

In practice, most SMEs claim a repayable credit in respect of this type of expenditure but the loss is relievable in the usual way. There is no facility for the loss to be carried back unless the company was eligible to claim relief in that period.

This credit is not available for activity subcontracted to the SME, or for subsidised expenditure.

Example 4.10 – Pre-trading development costs: tax credit claims

Start Up Co (SUC) undertook eligible R&D development project work whilst preparing to commence a software development trade. Its project work began in 2010 but because of the long tender process, its first client contract was only anticipated to commence in June 2012. It has chosen a December year-end for accounting and corporation tax reporting purposes.

In the ordinary scheme of things, *the company* would recognise the R&D costs in the accounting period ended 31 December 2012. This would delay any relief due for at least two years after the costs were incurred.

Analysis

As SUC is an SME, during the 2010, 2011 and 2012 accounting periods, it may claim the repayable RDTC relief for three accounting periods provided the 'going concern' condition was met and the costs were 'relevant' to the start-up trade (*CTA 2009, s 1045*).

If SUC incurred pre-trading development costs of £100,000, it could elect to claim relief upon £225,000 as a repayable cash credit.

This would provide a repayment of £225,000 × 11%, subject to the PAYE/NIC cap for expenditure incurred before the removal of that cap in April 2012. If the loss of £225,000 is surrendered it is not available for carry forward.

SUC must file its elections within two years of the end of the relevant accounting periods of claim – December 2010 and 2011 (*CTA 2009, s 1047*).

Practical point 3: Loss making SMEs

SME relief: the RDTC

Claiming RDTR under *Ch 2* enables the SME to obtain a repayable tax credit of 11% of the loss surrendered. The repayable tax credit is a useful source of funding for start-up companies and a valid alternative to grant funding, which may compromise later R&D claims for the project. Similarly, where there is likely to be uncertainty regarding the company's future, or the prospect of a long loss 'window', the claimant may prefer to capture the benefit of the relief in cash.

The loss can represent either ordinary trading losses arising as a result of R&D activity or losses arising before trading commences. The pre-trading credit is discussed above. The entitlement to and conditions of the repayable tax credit are set out at *CTA 2009, ss 1054, 1062*.

Calculation – repayable tax credit

The rate of repayable tax credit has reduced each year from 2008, in line with the reduction in corporation tax rates; from 16% at its inception in *FA 2008*, to its current level of 11% (*FA 2012*). The amount of loss that may be surrendered for a cash credit is limited to the lower of:

- the SMEs adjusted unrelieved trading loss for the accounting period; or

- R&D expenditure as enhanced for the accounting period (ss *1058– 1062*).

The company's unrelieved trading loss is the amount of the year's trading loss as reduced by:

- any relief the company may have received by setting the loss against profits of any kind; and

- any relief obtained by carry back of the loss to previous accounting periods; and

- any part of the loss surrendered to group or consortium members in the accounting period concerned.

For expenditure incurred on or before 1 April 2012, a further restriction applied, as a cap was set by the PAYE/NIC liabilities due under PAYE Regulations for the relevant accounting period of claim (*s 1059*).

Unlike the large scheme R&D expenditure credit, the tax credit payment is not regarded as income of the company for tax purposes. The repayment is also subject to the satisfactory payment of unpaid corporation tax whether on a provisional basis or not.

Example 4.11 – RDTC

Big Invention Co (BIC) has carried out valid in-house R&D project work during the accounting period. It reported a loss of £80,000 to December 2013. It subcontracts out some of the activity, but most of its expenditure is upon activity carried out in-house.

There is little to adjust in its tax computation which shows losses in 2013 of £80,000; its R&D spend in the year was £100,000. There are no group relief surrenders or losses carried back. It has just signed a sales contract for its mobile satellite tracking system and will be profitable from 2015.

Analysis

BIC can claim relief under *Ch 2* and is therefore entitled to the repayable tax credit for 2013.

The repayable tax credit is based upon the company's surrenderable loss.

The surrenderable loss is the lower of:

- the company's trading loss for the accounting period, £80,000; or

- the company's R&D expenditure as enhanced = £225,000 (225% × 100,000).

The company may claim a repayable tax credit of 11% × £80,000 = £8,800.

In doing so the company will reduce its loss carry forward by £80,000.

Once surrendered, it will not be able to relieve losses of £80,000 in the future, the corporation tax loss 'lost' is a minimum of 20% × £80,000 = £16,000.

Chapter 5

Research and development tax relief – large companies

Contents

SIGNPOSTS

- **Backgound** – R&D tax relief for large companies went largely unchanged since the relief was first introduced in 2002. But the new RDEC was introduced by *FA 2013* which significantly added to the incentives available (see **5.1**, **5.5**).

- **Alignment with other R&D incentives** – The RDEC aligns the UK to other EEA R&D incentives. It also assists loss bound companies previously without R&D incentivisation, making a repayable tax credit available for the first time to large company claimants.

- **Legislation** – The legislation for large companies is therefore found in both *CTA 2009, Pt 13* and the new *Ch 6A*, following the *FA 2013* changes. Transitional rules apply to large companies switching from the legacy large company scheme before it becomes mandatory from 1 April 2016 (see **5.13**).

- **Three eligible areas** – The definition of R&D and eligible cost headings remains unaltered. Relief for large companies is split into three eligible areas of R&D expenditure (see **5.12**).

- **Adverse effect** – Group dynamics are relevant to the organisation of R&D and this can have a potentially adverse impact upon the large company reliefs available. Special legislation has been present since the scheme was first introduced to counteract any adversity (see **5.17**).

- **Restricted activity** – The large company can only engage in subcontracted R&D activity in a narrow range of circumstances (see **5.6**). Similarly, large companies are only able to obtain R&D tax relief for activity contracted out to third parties in a narrow set of circumstances (see **5.7**). These rules apply equally to SME companies claiming R&D tax reliefs at the lower large company rate of relief (see **4.6**).

- **Prior to RDEC** – Until the RDEC, the benefit from RDTR was available either as a straightforward reduction of corporation tax liabilities or the surrender of losses as group relief in a tax-efficient manner on a group-wide basis. No repayable tax credit was available (see **5.5.1**).

- **Aligning corporation tax liabilities** – The mechanics of the new credit and the detailed rules applying to the set-off process act to align the company's real time corporation tax liabilities and PAYE payments on a group-wide basis (see **5.5.3**).

- **The Patent Box** – This is a significant consideration for many large companies performing R&D with UK or EEA patent rights. Special rules preserve the benefit of RDTR against the fall in corporation tax rates of relief for R&D expenditure (see **5.20**).

> • **Examples** – A number of examples show that the relief available under the legacy super deduction scheme are almost equivalent to the value of the relief in the RDEC scenario. The amounts will depend inter alia upon whether the company is a profit, or loss maker (see **5.12**).

OVERVIEW – LARGE COMPANY SCHEMES

5.1   RDTR for large companies was introduced by *FA 2002*, which provided a super deduction of 25% (now 30%) for eligible R&D expenditure. The relief mirrors many of the features of the SME scheme. The main rules were at *CTA 2009, Pt 13, Ch 5* but have been supplemented by *CTA 2009, Pt 3, Ch 6A* until 1 April 2016, when the 'old' legislation will be abolished.

The large scheme went unchanged for almost ten years until the introduction of the RD expenditure credit (RDEC), which was announced in the 2011 Autumn Statement. The new credit-based relief switches the relief away from a 'super deduction' to a credit which acts to reduce the company's R&D costs. For the next two years, the new credit scheme will run in tandem to the legacy 'super deduction' large scheme until it becomes mandatory in 2016.

The large company scheme provided relief of £770 million, for around £9.7 billion of R&D expenditure in 2011/12. The scheme accounts for approximately 81% of the value of claims filed to HMRC R&D Units. The advent of the RDEC and the Patent Box opportunity into the UK tax environment may enhance the use of the scheme yet further.

The key feature of the new large company credit scheme is a pre-tax credit of 10%, which is administered and settled through the corporation tax self-assessment (CTSA) system. The credit is set off against the company's corporation tax liability of the current period. Unlike the SME scheme, the credit is not 'below the line' but acts to reduce the cost of R&D and attract investors. It is 'payable' net of corporation tax and is aligned to the group's corporation tax and PAYE payment account. It is safeguarded from abuse by a PAYE/NIC cap. A higher rate of credit is payable to companies within the oil and gas ring-fence.

The introduction of the credit followed industry consultation which ended with the publication of the legislation on 11 December 2012. The 'legacy' super-deduction scheme had, until the changes in 2012, changed only once, increasing from 25% to 30% from 1 April 2008. The enhancement scheme did little to promote the 'visibility' of R&D activity for large innovators. It provided no access to cash as a repayable tax credit, which made many a large company with locked in corporation tax losses unable to access 'real' R&D relief.

5.2   *Research and development tax relief – large companies*

R&D reliefs available to large companies and SMEs with capped or subsidised project costs are therefore twofold from April 2013 to April 2016. There is no change to the definition of what activity is regarded as 'R&D' for companies under either scheme. The key eligible project costs are similarly unchanged. The Government have stated the future of the SME credit is also unaltered.

LEGISLATION

5.2   The large company scheme was introduced on 1 April 2002 (see **4.1**) and provided a super deduction of 25% of the eligible R&D costs as additional tax relief. A minimum project limit was set at £25,000 but this was reduced to £10,000 for accounting periods beginning on or after 1 April 2003, aligning the limit to the SME threshold. This was eventually abolished by *FA 2012*.

Most of the legislation affecting the large company scheme was consolidated within *CTA 2009*. Like the SME scheme this had been regularly updated through successive *Finance Acts*.

FA 2012 was particularly relevant for large companies, introducing the RDEC which has been outlined at **1.1**, the 'line credit' in the consultations preceding its introduction. This will become mandatory for large company R&D reliefs from 1 April 2016.

The definition of R&D for tax purposes applies as equally to large companies as to SMEs. The impact of EC Regulations is less pronounced in the large company scheme as the relief is not regarded as a State Aid. However, the fundamental definition of 'What is a large company' derives from EC Recommendation 361/EC/2003 (see **4.2**).

Large companies are also affected by the introduction of the Patent Box legislation and may need to consider aspects of that legislation in tandem with the R&D relief calculation (see **5.20**).

The large company scheme is subject to the revenue capital cost distinction and that the R&D activity begins with the same accounting principles discussed in **Chapter 2**.

WHAT IS A LARGE COMPANY?

5.3   A large company is defined in negative terms, and the definition is taken from EC Recommendation 361/2003. This says a large company is:

> 'A company which does not qualify a small or medium-sized enterprise…'

(FA 2002, Sch 12, para 2)

When the large company scheme was first introduced, the 1996 Recommendation applied for accounting periods ending before 31 March 2005 (see **4.3**).

A condition of the EC Directive is that the company must be large through the entirety of the accounting period concerned. This means that companies 'becoming' large remain eligible for SME relief for the final period in which they are regarded as SMEs (see **4.13**).

Transition from or to SME status can take place under a variety of circumstances and these are explored at **4.6**.

LARGE COMPANY RELIEF – ELIGIBLE R&D ACTIVITY

5.4   The legislation recognises expenditure arising within three distinct R&D activities. Like the SME schemes it is feasible that a company may combine any of these relief heads into one claim.

The expenditure qualifying for relief under the large company scheme(s) is based upon the company's total R&D costs incurred in respect of the following:

SME rates of relief

Activity	*CTA 2009*	**Reliefs available FY 2013**
In-house direct expenditure upon R&D s 1077	130% enhanced deduction/RDEC	
Contracted-out R&D activity	*s 1078*	130% enhanced deduction/RDEC
Contributions to independent R&D	*s 1079*	130% enhanced deduction/RDEC

The first two categories are parallel to the SME scheme, although the contracting out of R&D activity in the large scheme contains detailed rules. Contributions to independent R&D activity are not a category of expenditure that is within the SME scheme.

In-house R&D activity

5.5   Where R&D activity is carried out 'in-house', a number of conditions and features apply:

● The R& D must be relevant to the company, which should be carrying on a trade.

- The company must meet the minimum threshold for accounting periods ending before 1 April 2012.

- The company must be regarded as 'large' throughout the accounting period of claim.

Section 1077 confirms that the costs eligible for relief are:

- staffing costs (see **4.30**) – *CTA 2009, ss 1123, 1124*;

- costs incurred upon software or consumable items – *s 1125*;

- expenditure on externally provided workers – *s 1127*;

- expenditure on capital equipment where research development allowances (RDAs) may be claimed.

Like the SME scheme, the expenditure must be 'relevant' to the claimant company.

Limited relief is given for subcontractor costs where third parties are engaged upon the large company's R&D project work (see **5.7**). It is not possible for third parties to subcontract this work further as it must be 'directly performed'.

Large company as a subcontractor

5.6   Where the claimant is contracting in R&D, relief is limited to work carried out on behalf of a large company or 'any person otherwise than in the course of carrying on a chargeable UK trade'.

The large company can obtain relief where the project work is performed 'in-house', upon the costs at **5.7**. If the large company in turn contracts out the activity, relief is limited to the very specific bodies at *s 1078* (see **5.7**), and no further subcontracting is permitted.

Qualifying expenditure on contracted out R&D activity – s 1078

5.7   Large companies are able to claim relief upon the costs of work contracted out by them to third parties only in very limited circumstances.

Section 1078 prescribes four special conditions for the relief to be available. The foremost condition is that the expenditure is incurred in making payments to either:

- a qualifying body,

- an individual, or

- a firm comprising individuals.

Additionally, the body, individual or firm must directly perform the R&D and cannot subcontract the work further.

Should the work contracted out be subcontracted in by the claimant, it should be from a large company or entity outside the scope of UK corporation tax or income tax.

In practice, many large companies perform R&D on behalf of other large companies and bodies outside the scope of UK corporation tax or government agencies, and the relief is a useful one.

Example 5.1 – Subcontracted-in R&D activity – large companies

This example from HMRC *Tax Bulletin* 2002 has stood the test of time. It represents the position of the large R&D performer asked to undertake R&D activity on behalf of others.

GE plc is a large company. It is contracted by the Government of Freedonia to undertake R&D for it. GE spends £2.4 million upon research and can claim a super deduction of 130% × £2.4 million when it calculates its profits chargeable to corporation tax for the year ended 30 April 2012.

Analysis

GE plc would also be able to claim RDTR if the work was contracted to it by another large company, a charity or a UK government agency.

It is possible for GE to subcontract this activity further, but only to:

- qualifying research bodies; and/or
- individuals or partnerships of individuals.

These bodies must perform the contracted-out activity directly and no further subcontracting can take place.

Group situations

5.8   As can be seen, contractor companies carrying on R&D activity are restricted to a limited species of subcontractor costs. This is unhelpful in group situations because it is very common for high-tech industries to subdivide R&D activity on a group-wide basis.

The legislation recognises this difficulty and relaxes the subcontracting rules to permit bona fide R&D group subcontracting activity. This is discussed at **5.17** below. *Section 1082* updates the original group activity/group relief provisions introduced within the original scheme at *FA 2002, Sch 12, para 14.*

Reliefs available: expenditure upon contributions to independent R&D

5.9   *Section 1079* recognises contributions to independent R&D activity carried out by

- a qualifying body;
- an individual not connected with the contributor;
- a firm, each member of which is an individual.

'Funded' R&D has many indirect benefits for the large company, enabling it to be associated with leading research or development projects as a marketing tool or enabling the company to become a long-term stakeholder in specialist areas and have first sight of the intellectual property or expertise generated by the developer's work.

The expenditure is not argued by HMRC to be capital in so far as it may represent an investment in the company's longevity or status, or represent a duality of purpose.

Conditions D and E of *s 1079* require that the parties to the funded work are unconnected individuals or corporates, preventing one company effectively subsidising the other's R&D activity.

Contributions to independent R&D have been recognised as a fundamental part of the pattern of large company research work and have been eligible for relief since the scheme was first introduced in 2000.

Qualifying body

5.10   Qualifying bodies (QBs) are recognised as institutions dedicated to research or development activity, such as scientific research organisations, health services, charities, higher education institutions (*FA 2002, Sch 12, para 18(1)*), or any other body prescribed by Treasury Order (*Research and Development (Qualifying Bodies) (Tax) Order (SI 2012/286)*).

The list of qualifying bodies recognised for these purposes is updated at CIRD82250, which provides further guidance for cases of difficulty. *IRC v Gull* [1937] 4 All ER 290 suggests that charities must be UK resident, in order for them to be regarded as eligible QBs.

Subsidies

5.11   Unlike the SME scheme, no restrictions on the relief due to the large claimant apply where expenditure is subsidised. The scheme is not regarded as 'State Aid' for the purposes of RDTR. As with the SME scheme, the relief available is prescribed by the nature of the R&D activity itself.

SME companies – reliefs available at the large company scheme rate

Three of the SME schemes of R&D tax relief carry relief *at the large company rate of 130%:*

- expenditure incurred upon R&D where the SME acts as a subcontractor (*CTA 2007, Pt 13, Ch 3*) (see **4.4**);

- expenditure that is subsidised (*CTA 2007, Pt 13, Ch 4*) (see **4.5**);

- expenditure incurred on projects exceeding the project cap (*CTA 2007, Pt 13, Ch 5*) (see **4.6**).

Because of the way the legislation is written, the schemes of relief do not place the SME company 'within' the large scheme but restrict the amount of the relief to the large company rate and attach further conditions upon the subcontractor costs that are eligible for relief.

This is an important distinction and it is not correct to state that SMEs 'enter' the large company scheme as a result of the above activities. They will retain SME status for the accounting period concerned.

Because of the express legislation enabling such SMEs to obtain access to the RDEC, a repayable R&D tax credit is available in any or all of the above circumstances from 1 April 2012 for the first time.

Eligible costs: SME acting as a subcontractor

The detailed conditions of SME subcontractor activity is discussed at **Chapter 4** above. The SME must be engaged, similarly to a large company, to perform R&D on behalf of:

- a large company; or

- 'any person otherwise than in the course of carrying on a chargeable UK trade' (*CTA 2009, Pt 13, Ch 3, s 1065(2)(b)*).

The SME will be able to claim the costs of staff and externally provided workers, and software and consumable items but relief for subcontractor costs will be limited to payments to:

- individuals or firms of individuals; and

- qualifying bodies.

No further subcontracting costs are eligible.

Where the SME engages in project work that has been subsidised or exceeds the project cap, limited relief is available at the large company rate, which is discussed at **Chapter 4**.

LARGE SCHEME RELIEF BENEFITS

The legacy scheme: enhanced corporation tax deduction

5.12 The large scheme super deduction was introduced in its original state by *FA 2002, Sch 12, para 11* providing a 25% enhancement for eligible R&D costs. But the mainstream rate of UK corporation tax has fallen dramatically, and the rate was raised to 30% by *FA 2008*.

Financial year (FY) 2014 provides that a company carrying on eligible R&D activity as above can claim an additional 30% of the qualifying expenditure as a 'super deduction' in the computation of its profit or loss. The relief benefit can be taken as a reduction in corporation tax liabilities becoming due or can act to enhance or create a trading loss. The trading loss has no special definition for corporation tax purposes and can be carried forward to the previous accounting period or carried back. Any excess relief in the current accounting period can be surrendered as group relief subject to the usual restrictions.

Unlike the SME scheme, the large company scheme has never made a repayable R&D tax credit available to large companies or SMEs claiming at the large company rate. The new RDEC will correct this deficiency for expenditure incurred on or after 1 April 2013, subject to complicated set-off rules.

The enhanced deduction relief is useful for groups/companies paying their corporation tax liabilities in quarterly instalments, and the enhanced deduction could be used predictively to ease cash flow.

But the 'enhanced deduction' basis of R&D tax relief is drawing to a close for large companies and restricted SMEs and will only now be available for expenditure incurred before 1 April 2016.

If the company chooses to elect into the new expenditure credit, this will apply on an irrevocable basis to future claims. The company would not then have the option to claim the enhanced deduction relief in the future.

There has been little change to the mechanics of the super-deduction scheme since its introduction which can be shown by way of a simple example.

Example 5.2 – Large R&D company: relief through enhanced 130% deduction (legacy scheme)

Legacy Co (LC) performs R&D on a recurrent basis, its annual spend is £2 million, its accounts to 30 September 2012 show profits of £10 million.

Analysis

LC can claim a deduction of £2 million × 30% against its taxable profits for the year to September 2012.

The deduction is 'below the line' in the company's tax computation and not 'visible' as a relief.

It has until 30 September 2014 to file its claim to relief.

The problems with the super deduction scheme are shown in **Example 5.3** below and went unchanged for almost ten years from when the relief was first introduced.

Example 5.3 – Large R&D company with substantial corporate losses – problems with the legacy enhanced deduction scheme

Legacy Loss Co (LLC) spends around £500,000 on R&D each year. It has substantial losses brought forward of £5 million and its operations are continuing to struggle. It is not part of a group.

Analysis

LLC can claim a super deduction of £500,000 × 130% and supplement the losses carried forward by £150,000. Given the amount of losses locked in, LLC has no surplus capacity to ever absorb any benefit from RDTR.

It is aware of the scheme but does not claim RDTR – there is no UK R&D incentive. The position was unlikely to change until the expenditure credit was introduced for expenditure from 1 April 2013.

LLC can now claim a repayable pre-tax credit based on 10% of its eligible R&D spend.

R&D expenditure credit

Structure and location of legislation

Transitional period 1 April 2013 to 1 April 2016

5.13   Partly in response to the above problem, the 2011 Budget Speech announced an 'expenditure credit' for large companies, which became known as an 'above the line tax credit' and then was introduced as an R&D expenditure credit (RDEC). The credit was legislated for by *FA 2012* into what will become *CTA 2009, Pt 3, Ch 6A*. The new Chapter will include the provisions of *CTA 2009, Pt 13, Chs 3, 4 and 5*. These provisions which concern the application of large company scheme reliefs to SME companies will then be repealed in 2016.

The legislation therefore permits the credit to apply on a voluntary basis to expenditure incurred on or after 1 April 2013, but before 1 April 2016. This applies equally to large companies and SME companies claiming within the large company scheme for subcontracted or subsidised R&D project work, or where the overall project cap has been exceeded.

During the transitional period between 1 April 2013 and 1 April 2016, companies may choose whether to elect, on an irrevocable basis, into the scheme, or stay within the enhanced deduction scheme. This will give rise to a number of accounting considerations, which are discussed below.

The scheme mirrors the SME repayable credit for losses surrendered in exchange for a refund. The RDEC differs because it is taxable and heavily dependent upon the company/group being up to date with all tax liabilities, including PAYE/NIC duties. The credit applies a direct discount to the eligible R&D expenditure instead of providing a tax-based refund. In this way, and as the discount is visible in the company's accounts, rather than detailed in the tax computation, the claimant gains visibility for the extent of its R&D work.

There is no alteration to the fundamental definition of R&D for tax purposes or its framework.

RDEC – relief mechanics

5.14 The RDEC works by providing a taxable credit of 10% upon eligible expenditure (*CTA 2009, s. 104M*). The 10% rate of relief was calculated to equate with the existing 130% rate; based upon a 23% corporation tax rate, the net value is 7.7%.

The following table shows how the RDEC applies in practice.

Large company 31.03.2014	£m	Legacy scheme	RDEC
Turnover	5,000		5,000
R&D expenditure	(1,000)		(1,000)
Expenditure credit	10%	–	100
Other expenditure	(1,000)		(1,000)
Profit	3,000		3,100
R&D relief @30%	(300)	–	
Taxable profit		2,700	3,100
Tax charge @23%	621	713	
RDEC utilised		–	(100)
CT payable	621	613	

The credit is utilised to reduce the corporation tax (CT) payable by the company on 1 January 2015. If PAYE duties were outstanding, the credit would be partially absorbed there first.

The credit is entirely reliant upon the company having no outstanding corporation tax liability. A detailed seven-step set-off in respect of outstanding corporation tax liabilities must be followed and a PAYE/NIC cap exists, limiting the effectiveness of the relief for some companies.

As an alternative, a group surrender is available. These steps are contained at *s 104N* and discussed below. The current drafting of the legislation does not include a discount facility for quarterly instalment payers likely to benefit from the credit.

The credit is also dependent upon the company being a 'going concern' at the time of claim.

The differing benefits of the credit can be seen by way of an example.

Example 5.4 – Large company with substantial losses

Effectiveness of the RDEC

Large Credit Co (LCC) has carried on eligible R&D activity for the past six years. It has substantial losses brought forward and has never really bothered with RDTR as it had little UK CT capacity to benefit from further enhancements to the company's losses. From 2013 it has chosen to claim RDEC and obtain a repayment credit based upon expenditure of £100,000. It still has losses brought forward of £500,000.

Analysis

LCC has little UK CT capacity and did not claim RDTR. Opting into the RDEC scheme locks LCC into this scheme as its use is mandatory once the company opts in prior to April 2016. This is unlikely to cause any problems.

Based upon its £100,000 of eligible expenditure, LCC may claim a credit of 10%.

The repayment will not be paid before the end of the subsequent (2014) accounting period.

RDEC: Set off process (CTA 2009, s 104M)

5.15   In its current state, the RDEC legislation provides seven stages funnelling the relief only to companies completely up to date with corporation tax and other taxes and duties.

Steps for RDEC repayment

Claims must follow each of the steps below, prior to the credit being repaid by HMRC:

Step 1

Set off credit against CT liability for the accounting period of claim. Apply surplus to Step 2.

Step 2

Apply PAYE/NIC cap – if credit exceeds PAYE/NIC of R&D project staff costs of claimant in year of claim, excess is carried forward to next accounting period.

Step 3

Set off any remainder from Steps 1 and 2 against any CT accounting period deficits.

Step 4

Optional set off for surplus from end of Steps 1 to 3 against group companies' relevant CT liabilities.

Step 5

Calculate full rate of CT from residue after Steps 1 to 4 have been calculated.

Step 6

Test for set-off against other outstanding tax liability of claimant (PAYE etc).

Step 7

Any remainder is payable as cash if company is a going concern.

RDEC: Accountancy issues

5.16   The credit entails an 'above the line' reporting requirement. This raises the question, 'When and how should the credit be recognised?'. There are a number of valid arguments to support *IAS 12* treatment, including the ability for the credit to be offset against the corporation tax liability of group entities. Similarly, profitable entities have no additional criteria or conditions applying to the eligibility of the company to receive the credit. The possibility of a restriction to the credit in the event of an open corporation tax enquiry means the credit reflecting its dependency upon both the real time and potential tax position.

The fact that the credit meets the basic definition of a government grant and is not structured as an additional tax deduction would support *IAS 20* treatment.

Consideration of accountancy issues will be necessary when adopting the RDEC and during the transitional period prior to April 2016.

LARGE COMPANY RELIEF: GROUP SITUATIONS

Relevant activity

5.17   *Section 1042* of *CTA 2009* tells us that RDTR is only available where the performer's activity is 'relevant' to its trade. In group situations, it is not uncommon for one member to be assigned R&D activity to perform on behalf of another. This may put the performer in a position of carrying out prima facie ineligible activity and is best illustrated by a simple example.

Example 5.5 – Relevant Group Activity Co

BAE1 carries on an R&D project for a number of years developing a new eco engine for the aerospace industry. It needs its prototype to be tested. The industry requires stringent testing to take place and it assigns this to its sister company BAE2, a specialist engine testing company.

Analysis

Testing is not usually regarded as an R&D activity and BAE2 is not carrying on R&D in its own right or a separate R&D activity relevant to its own trade. BAE1 needs the testing to be carried out on its prototype and this is relevant to both BAE1's project work and its trade.

Because of the relaxation in the rules of relevant R&D in group situations, a view of the activity of the parties as a whole can be taken to consider the overall relevance of the R&D.

BAE1 can claim the costs of the work carried out by BAE2 even though, in isolation, the work is not relevant to BAE2 or valid R&D for that company.

Large company issues – consortium relief

5.18   There are restrictions on the amount of consortium relief which can be surrendered by an SME where a large company is a consortium member.

The amount of the loss created by the R&D relief cannot be surrendered by way of consortium relief to a large company – the relief is restricted purely to members of the consortium who are SME companies.

This corrects the position where large companies may otherwise access SME rates of R&D relief through the surrender of losses enhanced at the 225% rate.

Large company scheme – insurance companies

5.19   Insurance companies carrying on life assurance business can claim under the large or SME company schemes for R&D activity carried on as part of the company's trading business.

Funding

The large company may claim relief for pre-trading R&D expenditure in the same way as the SME. This enables valuable cash flow benefits during start up. As the large company scheme is not regarded as State Aid for the purposes of the relief, there is no 'tax relief' barrier to seeking funding for project work.

PATENT BOX INTERACTION

5.20   Many large companies will consider the usefulness of the Patent Box as part of their R&D strategy and wider approach to intellectual property (IP) and other intangible assets.

As the introduction of the Patent Box into the UK reflects the Government's published 'Plan for Growth' document published in March 2011 and the 'Taxation of Innovation' document in 2010, it is not surprising to see that special rules apply to prevent the erosion of the benefit of claiming RDTR for R&D expenses associated to patent streams.

Patent Box

Preserving the benefit of RDTR

5.21   Without special rules, the value of RDTR would diminish, reflecting the lower taxation rate of relevant patented income.

The issue is addressed through the 'streaming rules', which are available through an election by the R&D claimant, or which become mandatory in certain circumstances. The legislation is at *CTA 2010, s 357D(1)* and provides the R&D claimant with relevant patented income, an opportunity to allocate R&D costs in a tax-efficient manner whilst at the same time benefiting from the reduced corporation tax rates within the Patent Box. The streaming election is complex and will require consideration of income streams that are within patent and those which are 'off patent' to determine a just and reasonable apportionment of R&D costs between the various activities comprising the company's trade.

Group R&D arrangements

5.22   Cost sharing arrangements are common where group companies carry on simultaneous R&D work. Helpfully, HMRC have published an interpretation reflecting a practical approach to the integration of this type of income and group cost sharing into the Patent Box. The example at CIRD260130 demonstrates the approach.

Example 5.6 – Patent Box: joint venture/collaborative R&D

Three companies have R&D facilities which allow them to carry on complementary R&D in different fields of research with a view to combining the results into one specific product. There is no guarantee that the costs of each specialist area of research will be equal, so the participators may agree that the income arising from any resultant IP (including, but not exclusive to, patents) will be split according to the relative costs incurred by each participator. Alternatively they may agree that the costs incurred by each participator should be recorded and that the greatest contributor will be reimbursed a proportion of their costs by the other participators. The income arising from the resultant IP would then be split equally between the participators.

Accordingly, each of the participators will have contributed to the development of the IP and will be entitled to a share of the income from that IP as a result. To the extent that this income includes income from a qualifying patent it should qualify for the Patent Box.

CHAPTER SUMMARY

5.23   The large company super deduction scheme will be repealed and replaced by a new R&D expenditure credit from 1 April 2016 (*CTA 2009, Pt 3, Ch 6A*). This will also repeal the large company rules affecting SME claimants. For expenditure incurred on or after 1 April 2013, the legacy deduction scheme runs in tandem to the new taxable credit scheme which enables large loss makers to receive a cash-based relief. Moving into the scheme will involve a review of appropriate accounting reporting policies and good management of group-wide corporation tax payments.

The RDEC follows a detailed repayment process and aligns itself to the 'real time' corporation tax and PAYE liabilities of the claimant. As the 10% credit is taxable at the company's prevalent rate of corporation tax, the net value is worth around 7.7% of the R&D spend. The credit scheme harmonises the UK with the EEA position which has made R&D credits available to large companies for many years.

The definition of RDTR, and the detailed rules applying to the calculation of eligible costs are completely unchanged. The move to the credit system for large companies will not disturb the identification of eligible project work and the R&D documentation requirements.

The large schemes provide relief for in-house activity and R&D undertaken in other circumstances. Limited reliefs are available to large companies contracting in R&D activity. The effect of these detailed rules, is to exclude the possibility of other companies duplicating relief for the same expenditure. Similarly, limited relief is available for the large company contracting out R&D work to third parties.

The Government has clearly listened to companies using the large company scheme and, following the 2012 consultations, introduced a valid extension to the large company relief. It has also provided an assurance that there is no intention to change the SME R&D tax credit scheme. The interaction of the Patent Box opportunity with the large company scheme reliefs will require careful evaluation over the long term, particularly as opting out of the Patent Box currently carries a further five-year exclusion period.

PRACTICAL EXAMPLES

Example 5.7 – RDEC profit maker

Large Profit Co (LPC) presents the following results and claims the repayable RDEC to the full extent possible. It has no group companies and is up to date with its corporation and other tax liabilities.

	RDEC
	(£000m)
Turnover	10,000
Expenses	(1,000)
R&D costs	(2,000)
2000 × 10%	
ATL credit	200
Profit/loss	7,200
Tax 23%	1,656
ATL credit	(200)
Tax payable	1,456

Example 5.8 – RDEC loss maker

The following year LPC made a substantial loss. It can claim a repayable credit of £371 as follows:

	RDEC (£000m)
Turnover	3,000
Expenses	(2,000)
R&D costs	(2,000)
2000 × 10%	
RDEC	200
Profit/loss	(800)
Tax 23%	–
Loss carry forward	N/A
Group relief	N/A
Tax payable	–
Tax repayable	200
Less tax withheld 23%	46
Payable RDEC net of tax	154
Cash benefit of R&D relief	154

Example 5.9 – Profit maker: comparison of legacy scheme and RDEC claimant

£000	No claim	Super deduction	RDEC
Turnover	10,000	10,000	10,000
Expenses	(1,000)	(1,000)	(1,000)
R&D costs	(2,000)	2,000	2,000
ATL credit 10%			200
Super deduction 130%		600	
Profit/loss	7,000	6,400	7,200
Tax 23%	1,610	1,472	1,656

145

£000	No claim	Super deduction	RDEC
ATL credit			200
Tax payable	1,610	1,472	1,456

Example 5.10 – Loss maker: comparison of legacy scheme and RDEC claimant

£m	No claim	Super deduction	RDEC
Turnover	3,000	3,000	3,000
Expenses	(2,000)	(2,000)	(2,000)
R&D costs	(2,000)	(2,000)	(2,000)
ATL credit 10 %			200
Super deduction 130%		(600)	
Profit/loss	(1,000)	(1,600)	(800)
Tax 23%	–	–	–
CT loss	(1,000)	(1,600)	(800)
Tax payable	–	–	–
RDEC	–	–	200
Less: tax withheld 23%	RDEC net of tax	–	46
			154*

*£154 million is then subject to Steps 1 to 7 to determine the amount of credit repayable.

Chapter 6

Claim administration

Contents

SIGNPOSTS

- **Who can claim?** – RDTR may only be claimed by companies within the scope of UK corporation tax. This can include companies in foreign ownership and non-corporate entities liable to UK corporation tax. Joint ventures are common in R&D projects, corporate members of hybrid partnerships may claim RDTR, but will need to identify any 'subsidy' received from the partnership or other related parties (see **6.2–6.5**).

- **Late claims** – Claims for R&D tax relief are made through the corporation tax self-assessment (CTSA) system. Late claims for relief are not accepted unless a bona fide 'reasonable excuse' prevailed in the accounting period (see **6.6, 6.9**). Interest and penalties can apply to overstated claims for relief. These can in theory be based upon 100% of the tax involved (see **6.14**).

- **Repayable R&D tax credits** – Claims for repayable R&D tax credits are similarly filed through the company's tax return but are subject to the 'going concern' condition (see **6.10**).

- **Who should claim and where?** – A company may find it preferable to claim R&D reliefs elsewhere. Relief of up to 400% is available in a few territories such as Singapore. This decision would need to consider any intellectual property right requirements and other conditions imposed by overseas tax codes (see **6.6**).

- **Administration of claims** – HMRC have responsibility for administering R&D tax reliefs and therefore review claims carefully and with precision. Any claim should be based upon good documentation and the underlying records form part of the company's tax return for the period. This Chapter provides a checklist for suitable R&D records (see **6.12**). Substantial anti-avoidance legislation is available to HMRC to counteract synthetic claims to relief, particularly in group situations or contrived tax credit claims (see **6.10**).

- **R&D case law** – Case law upon R&D legislation has been infrequent. Two cases have been useful in identifying the principles of R&D in practice, and how a claim should be quantified and documented. If no evidence of the project work is provided, a claim will fail (see **6.15**).

INTRODUCTION

6.1   RDTR is administered by HMRC. The SME scheme also requires compliance with EC regulations as the relief for small and medium-sized enterprises is regarded as 'State Aid'. An overall cap of €7.5 million applies to State Aid provided to SMEs on a per project basis.

Latest statistics show that approximately 12,000 claims were filed to HMRC in 2012, providing relief of around £1,174 million. Large companies accounted for over £750 million of the reliefs claimed, although SME companies filed the largest volume of claims at 9,875. It is estimated that 75% of companies eligible to claim RDTR fail to do so. This reflects both a lack of awareness and the complexity of the legislation.

The most common way for SMEs to claim R&D tax relief was by deduction from their corporation tax (CT) liability (5,390) as opposed to a cash tax credit repayment (790) and combination claims (2,000). Although relatively few claims were made by large companies (1,930) and SME subcontractors (520), the amounts claimed by large companies were generally much higher than before.

The UK system compares well with R&D tax incentives in other EEA countries. Further, the UK tax system is not territorial, enabling R&D activity to be carried on anywhere in the world. The UK corporation tax system provides an indefinite loss carry forward facility if the company carries on the same trade and ownership. The UK rates of tax relief, and headline corporation tax rates therefore compare well with many OECD countries. Additionally, the UK provides substantial grant-based assistance for R&D projects and a range of practical incentives such as procurement programmes and research centres.

HMRC are tasked with administering the relief and review claims with care and precision. An insight into the HMRC approach to the legislation generally can be gained from the cases of *Gripple Ltd v HMRC* [2010] EWHC 1609 (Ch) and *BE Studios Ltd v Smith & Williamson Ltd* [2005] EWHC 1506 (Ch). Both cases provide useful commentary upon the 'micro' requirements of the relief rules (at *CTA 2009, Pt 13*) and the 'qualitative' nature of R&D activity itself if a claim is to be competent.

The early part of this book has discussed the matrix of the R&D framework. This Chapter discusses the relief administration including:

- who may claim RDTR?

- time limits for claiming or amending claims for R&D tax relief?

- mandatory filing and record-keeping requirements;

- interest and penalty charges for incorrect returns or tax credit repayment claims;

- common errors found in R&D tax relief claims.

WHO CAN CLAIM RDTR?

6.2   RDTR can only be claimed by companies within the scope of corporation tax. This extends to a body corporate or unincorporated association, but would not include a partnership, local authority or local authority association (*CTA 2009, s 1121*).

Overseas ownership

6.3   An overseas permanent establishment of a UK company which is within the charge to UK corporation tax can claim RDTR. This principle also applies to UK permanent establishments of foreign companies.

In practice, R&D is often 'performed' in the UK on behalf of an overseas parent or associated company. For example, in the pharmaceutical industry, over 40% of the industry's funding comes from overseas investment. Group dynamics and funding arrangements for R&D work can trigger both the subsidy and contracting rules, and draws no distinction between UK/UK or UK/non-UK funding arrangements. Some exceptions apply provided the R&D is performed within a trading 'group' (see **5.10**). This applies whether the subcontractor is based in the UK or overseas.

Group dynamics

6.4   Any of the companies within a group may claim RDTR provided they are within the scope of UK corporation tax. If a trading group is not established for tax purposes, it will be important to establish the facts of what the UK company has been asked to do and the extent of its economic risk and control over the R&D project work. The case of *Gripple Ltd v HMRC* establishes the importance of documentation establishing the boundaries of the R&D project and its purpose, no matter how high-tech the company's environment may be.

Joint ventures

6.5   Where companies carry out R&D in a joint venture, the venture is regarded as 'transparent'. Provided that the company bears its own expenditure and risk, the treatment is the same as any other claimant. The influence of the joint venture may have an impact on the rate of relief available. Certain exceptions are made for institutional investors and business angels, but if these are not met, the company may not meet the requirements for relief at the SME rate. This may be because either it needs to amalgamate its accounting data with linked or partner enterprises, or because the joint venture provides an effective or 'subcontracting' relationship for the R&D project (see **4.6**).

Partnerships, hybrid structures and joint ventures will therefore need to consider carefully the influence and extent of 'linked' and 'partner' enterprises to establish entitlement to SME rates of relief.

ADMINISTRATION

6.6 The R&D claim is filed through the corporation tax self-assessment (CTSA) system and administered by HMRC. The company must include the amount of qualifying expenditure upon its corporation tax return 'CT 600' for the period, and the amount of any tax credit repayment claimed. The company must specify the amount of relief claimed in the corporation tax computation. A claim can only be amended or withdrawn through the self-assessment system.

Who should claim?

6.7 The RDTR rules are not prescriptive as to which industry sectors are eligible for the relief. The case of *Gripple Ltd v HMRC* [2010] EWHC 1609 (Ch) highlights that, in practice, there is no retrospective relief to be had by adjustments to inter-company accounts. The relief will simply follow the accounting treatment of the expenditure as detailed in the claimant company's accounts. This can be disappointing as it is often assumed that there is some 'choice' available where companies hold R&D costs on an intercompany account.

This problem is highlighted by a simple example:

Example 6.1 – Group Claim Co – who incurs the R&D costs?

Sub Co is part of a large group. It carries on R&D activities on behalf of Sister Co, charging £1 million through the intercompany account at the end of each year. Sister Co is part of an EEA group and receives funding from Parent Co SA of around £2 million per annum reflecting this in its short-term creditors.

Sister Co reflects the expenditure in its profit and loss computation and intends claiming RDTR upon £1 million in its accounts to December 2012.

Analysis

Sister Co is able to act as a subcontractor within the group as a whole because of the relaxation of the subcontractor requirements (see **4.18**).

There are a number of considerations. Sister Co does not appear to actually 'perform' the R&D activity but allocates the work to Sub Co who then performs the R&D work in its capacity as a subcontractor. These costs are eligible for SME relief and there is no requirement that Sub Co performs the work directly.

It is harder to see if the costs paid by Sister Co are 'incurred' and reflected in the profit and loss account as there is only an intercompany account entry via Sub Co. But Parent Co is also linked to the intercompany account transactions. The merits of the claim would need to be reviewed in conjunction with establishing the extent of any 'subsidy' provided by Parent Co. Subject to a review of what the contracts between the group members state, it is possible that either Parent Co or Sister Co may have a tenable claim to relief.

The rules concerning the 'relevance' of the R&D project itself to the individual companies are relaxed in a group situation like this, but it is still necessary to look at the mechanics of the 'payments' between the companies.

Who should claim and where?

6.8   In a group situation such as the above, the location of the R&D performer may be decided not only on the cost of labour hire and skillsets but the availability of relief in other territories and the detail of other tax codes. The UK schemes are not territorial and allow R&D activity to be carried on anywhere in the world. This is not the position in many other countries. The UK schemes are also supported by grant facilities as discussed below.

This issue is discussed in detail at Chapter 7 below. A simple summary of the principal EEA reliefs highlights the issue:

Summary of 2013 RDTR regimes

Territory	CT rate (full)	Tax credit	RDTR rate SME	Territorial limit	IP requirements
UK	22% (FY 2014)	Yes	225%/130%/ grant funding Patent Box SME cap at €7.5 million	None	None
Eire	11%	Yes	25% offsetable credit	Eire, EEA only	None
Canada	11–31%	Yes	SRED credit plus provincial credit	Some exceptions but mainly required to be performed in Canada	No

Territory	CT rate (full)	Tax credit	RDTR rate SME	Territorial limit	IP requirements
US	15–35%	Yes	20%/14% credit	US activity only, incurred by US resident person. No IP requirement	No
France	34.3%	Yes	30% first €100 million, 5% thereafter. Innovation tax credit for small projects	Must be performed in EU.	No
Germany	15% plus surcharges and levies	No	Grant based incentives up to 50% eligible costs	Must be performed in Germany. IP to be retained and exploited in Germany.	Yes
China	25%	Yes	150% or 15% reduced CT rate	Maximum of 40% external activity. IP must reside in China.	Yes

International comparisons

The UK is one of 14 territories providing a 'super deduction'-based tax incentive. The UK SME rates places the current regime at an 'average' level (19th), by international comparison. The top end of the ranges exceeding 200% are available in just a handful of territories such as Singapore, topping 400%, Lithuania and Croatia.

Although the UK large scheme rate features at the lower end of the scale, the relaxation of rules applying to IP ownership and the absence of a 'clearance' type mechanism to obtain relief are helpful.

The UK is one of only 11 territories offering relief for subcontracted R&D activity. The 65% SME rate for payments to unconnected subcontractors mirrors the US relief, but unlike the US, there is no requirement that the subcontractor be located in the host country.

Only two territories are entirely grant-based in their provision of incentives – Mexico and Germany.

TIME LIMITS

6.9   Ordinarily, the company has up to two years from the end of the accounting period to claim relief for R&D activity. This is not always the case, where for example, HMRC have served notice for a company tax return to be prepared for a different period of account.

The filing of a company tax return, or an amendment to it, opens an 'enquiry window' during which HMRC may raise queries by way of a written notice to the company. In practice, many HMRC officers will raise queries informally by way of a telephone call, or short letter. Although there is no legal basis for a response to be provided, the approach is helpful in settling potential difficulties at an early stage.

The corporation tax enquiry windows are summarised in the table below and have applied since April 2008.

CTSA enquiry windows

The enquiry notice is to be made by HMRC within the following time limits.

Returns filed within time limit:

Filing by a company that is part of a small group	12 months of receipt of return by HMRC.
Filing by a company that is part of a medium/large group	12 months from mandatory due date for return
Returns filed late (all companies)	12 months plus quarter date in which late return delivered
Amendment to an original return	12 months plus quarter date in which amended return is delivered

HMRC are able to make 'discovery' assessments where the possibility of fraud or negligent conduct is established. This covers all claims to corporation tax reliefs and RDTR claims fall within this power. Similarly, HMRC are able to levy penalties under the 'incorrect corporation tax return' legislation. HMRC have won a number of discovery issues recently and the issue is particularly relevant to R&D relief where full details of borderline project work are able to be disclosed.

R&D claimants are advised by HMRC to approach the R&D Unit upon contentious issues; for a short while an 'advance assurance' pilot was available to smaller companies claiming the relief for the first time.

Late claims

HMRC take a stringent approach to late claims. A 'reasonable excuse' would require the serious illness or death of a key director or adviser. Although tax cases have shown that even in these extreme circumstances, the application will not necessarily be accepted without reference to the lower tax tribunals (SP 5/01).

REPAYABLE SME TAX CREDITS

6.10   There are no special administrative procedures to claim repayable tax credits in respect of R&D activity. A claim is filed through the company's tax return and detailed in the relevant tax computation. The credit is entirely dependent upon the company having a 'surrenderable loss' in the accounting period or during a period of pre-trading activity. From August 2008, the credit is also subject to the proviso that the claim is made at a time when the company is a 'going concern', based upon its published accounts for that period. Subsequent failure will not affect previous claims to the credit. The SME tax credit excludes activity where the company has performed work subcontracted from a large company.

For expenditure incurred on or after 1 April 2013, both SME and large companies may now claim a tax credit under the 'RDEC' provisions which are discussed at **Chapter 5**. A detailed order of set-off applies to the claimant's corporation tax liabilities, including PAYE and NIC duties. The claim is similarly subject to the company being a 'going concern' based upon its published accounts for the period.

Interest may be due to the company in respect of delayed repayments of R&D tax credit under the provisions for interest on tax overpaid that applies generally to corporation tax. The interest is payable from the material date until the payment is issued. The material date is defined as the later of the company's:

(a)   filing date for the accounting period for which the credit is claimed; and

(b)   date on which the return (or amended return) containing the claim is delivered to HMRC.

Recovering overpaid R&D tax credits and tax relief

FA 2013 updated the provisions which enabled HMRC to recover overpaid R&D tax credits. The effect of *Sch 15* is to extend the right of recovery to credits paid under the RDEC large company scheme. Over-repayments of tax credits are subject to interest. In cases of negligence, penalties are exigible as if the company had made an incorrect corporation tax return.

Anti-avoidance

In common with claims to tax relief for R&D activity, both tax credit schemes are subject to anti-avoidance legislation counteracting artificially inflated claims to relief/tax credit repayments. These apply equally to the SME and RDEC schemes, and are based upon the concept of preconceived corporate 'transactions' manipulating a position where a company obtains relief to which it would not otherwise be entitled. CIRD97100 provides examples of the HMRC approach to artificial ownership arrangements to contrive 'enterprises' or towards arrangements with little commercial justification, devised to obtain the credit/relief.

HMRC – R&D UNITS

6.11 The RDTR scheme is administered by HMRC with the express policy objective to administer the relief in a positive way. This fits with the Government's published strategy to promote investment by UK companies in R&D.

As awareness of the benefits of the relief grew, HMRC formed specialist units to process claims and provide HMRC's opinion on technical issues. Seven specialist R&D Units were set up in November 2006. This has been reduced to six to accommodate the setting up of a Patent Box Unit in October 2013. The Units process claims to relief on the basis of the company's postcode (see **Appendix 8**).

The Units process around 12,000 claims each year. The following guidance, urging expediency in handling claims, is found in the HMRC Corporate Intangibles Research & Development Manual at CIRD80520. It is provided to tax inspectors, and the whole process is subject to independent 'audits' from time to time.

> 'The R&D tax relief schemes are intended to encourage expenditure on R&D. Payable credit claims should be dealt with quickly ... For some companies, particularly small start up companies, the cash flow that can result from a payable credit can make the difference between success and failure. Where an enquiry has been opened without making payment of a credit that has been claimed HMRC officers should keep under review whether it is possible to make at least a partial payment.
>
> ...
>
> An open-minded approach should be adopted as to whether a project, or part of a project, is relevant R&D. It is important to gather all of the facts, and listen to the company's representations before making a decision.'

Unlike some EEA territories, UK claims to RDTR do not require any type of 'pre-transaction clearance'. A pilot voluntary assurance scheme was offered by HMRC offering feedback on the viability of project work where required. This was relatively short lived, but in practice the units are able to offer informed feedback in cases of doubt or difficulty.

RECORDS AND DOCUMENTS

6.12 The RDTR claim forms part of the company's statutory accounts and tax returns. Information and records relevant to the claim are part of the company's tax return. HMRC are permitted to charge a penalty of £3,000 if a company does not maintain or retain these records. The required period of retention is six years from the end of the relevant accounting period.

The types of documents that will be necessary to formulate the claim to RDTR are discretionary. Usually these will break down into three aspects:

(i) Records of expenditure incurred upon projects – accounting documents, PAYE records and expense records.

(ii) Records of the nature of payments to and from third parties – contractual records:

- engaging and paying third parties;

- the terms upon which the company itself is engaged to perform R&D involving third parties.

(iii) Project related records:

- setting out the substance of the R&D project work – its objectives and outcome.

Contractual records will be particularly useful when establishing entitlement for SME relief for subcontracted R&D activity. Similarly, the terms upon which the services of staff providers and controllers are engaged will be relevant to calculate the amount of payments to 'externally provided workers'. Where the 'tripartite' arrangements are relevant to a claim, these documents will be particularly useful.

Qualitative records supporting the company's R& D strategy are often collated in hindsight where the SME is unaware of the benefit of RDTR and the underlying record requirements. HMRC appreciate the reality of this situation and that not all project activity is undertaken by established claimants.

Despite any unfamiliarity with the tax relief schemes, the company will still need to demonstrate the systematic nature of its activity and the technical boundaries of the project work if R&D activity is to be demonstrated and relief found.

The technical rationale of the company's approach to project work underlines the tax definition of R&D. A key requirement is that the company has sought an advance, and embedded within that objective is activity seeking to resolve scientific or technological uncertainty. The nature of the technical advance will require clear explanation, as will the fact that this was not readily deducible to a 'competent professional'.

The records underlying the R&D activity go far beyond the company's statutory documents and will support the basic proposition that the company has not simply 'used' science or technology, or found a 'Eureka' moment. As HMRC state at CIRD 80560:

> 'There is a difference between making an unexpected discovery and the carrying out of R&D.'

The qualitative records will establish:

- what the R&D aim of the project is, ie what advance in science or technology is being sought;
- a link between the outcome of the R&D project and its effect on the commercial prospects for the company;
- a review of the current state of technical knowledge;
- what uncertainties were foreseen for the project;
- a structure and methodology for the project;
- notes on the technical knowledge base of the industry and project area;
- a summary of the expertise of the team and the competent professional.

COMMON ERRORS

6.13   The most common error made in R&D claims, particularly for SME relief, is the absence of key documents establishing the qualitative R&D and its objectives.

RDTR is a complex area of corporation tax and, without full adherence to the rules set out in *CTA 2009, Pt 13* and the associated legislation, errors are easy to make (see **2.1**).

Without a full appraisal of the commercial environment in which the company undertakes R&D, or has raised venture capital, it is also easy to overlook the possibility of subcontracted activity, subsidised expenditure and the R&D boundaries.

HMRC publish lists from time to time of the most common errors made in claiming the relief. It is common practice that, once established, HMRC will open an enquiry into previous years' claims and consider the application of interest and penalties.

The most recent list of errors for SME claims includes:

- the inclusion of project activities outside the scope of R&D for tax purposes within the claim to relief;

- expenditure outside the scope of *Pt 13*;

- staffing costs claimed in respect of people who are not employees of the claimant;

- claims in respect of overheads that do not qualify as consumable items;

- special rules for connected parties not having been applied;

- Companies not recognising that they are not SMEs/SMEs failing to make claims under the large company scheme.

INTEREST AND PENALTIES

6.14   As the RDTR claim is submitted through the company's self-assessment, errors in the claim may place the whole return within the penalty regime applying to incorrect company tax returns. The rules were changed from April 2008 and are based on the concept of 'potential lost revenue'. Clearly RDTR can substantially understate a company or group's liability to corporation tax and incorrect claims can carry a heavy cost.

The penalty regime extends to underpayments of corporation tax arising from overclaimed group relief, or repayable tax credits.

Separate rules apply to incorrect estimates of quarterly instalment payments. The current legislation on RDEC seems to prevent anticipated RDEC relief from reducing quarterly instalments on account. Penalty proceedings under the *Corporation Tax (Instalment Payments) Regulations 1998 (SI 1998/3175), reg 13* are usually taken only where reckless or deliberate failure is demonstrable.

Late payment interest applies to all delayed payments of corporation tax, and RDTR may have a significant impact upon the corporation tax liability. Where errors are made, the company will have an exposure to late payment interest. On the upside, HMRC credit repayment interest (supplement) for overpayments of the tax. This background highlights one of the practical difficulties with the relief. The length of the enquiry window is an unwelcome source of uncertainty. This is emphasised by the interest and significant penalties available to HMRC in the case of both errors in the return, or deficiencies in the accounting records. The absence of any type of agreement or clearance for the claimant's R&D activity can cause real difficulties for company's cash flow where some kind of 'certainty' is needed. HMRC are aware of this feedback, but will not be drawn into a shortened enquiry window for one particular business sector, even where substantial repayments are received whilst the window is open. Careful collation of the claim is essential. The cases below are useful preliminary guidance.

CLAIM GUIDANCE: CASE LAW

6.15 HMRC have published their 'approach' to deficient claims by way of commentary upon the two prominent R&D cases.

The earlier case of *BE Studios Ltd v Smith & Williamson* demonstrates the 'qualitative' substance of the legislation providing RDTR relief. This case reviewed the technical content of the work undertaken by BE Studios Ltd, a software company that, interestingly, had tried to sue its tax adviser for not providing an awareness of the relief or filing claims to relief on the company's behalf.

BE Studios Ltd (BES) claimed £113,500 of R&D tax relief on its corporation tax returns for the three years to June 2002. It ceased trading shortly afterwards due to the cash flow problems for which it placed at least some of the blame upon its tax adviser.

HMRC raised an enquiry into the claims and served a notice of rejection. The company made an appeal to the High Court. During the hearing, a critical weakness of the claim was the absence of evidence that the company had formulated its claim from the project work carried on in the accounting period to June 2002. In fact, it was shown that the approach of the company in making its claim was to amalgamate all expenditure on technical work in the accounting period and deduct obvious costs such as marketing and administrative costs, claiming relief upon the global balance. Reviewing the nature of the employees' work, it was found that two key employees referred to as project managers had no technical background. In tandem no evidence was provided for the work upon project objectives by any of the employees within the claim.

As a result of either a project based approach, or any documents supporting the construction of the claims, each was rejected in the High Court.

HMRC now base their qualitative guidance upon claims for relief almost entirely on the principles aired by Mr Justice Evans highlighting the following relevant comments:

● The high tech nature of the company's setting is almost irrelevant.

● The enhanced functionality attained by activities perceived to be R&D is not an indication that eligible activity takes place.

● High tech activity is not in itself sufficient to demonstrate that R&D has taken place.

● The absence of project methodology, as outlined within the BIS Guidelines, will rule out the possibility of a claim to relief.

● The claim must demonstrate a scientific or technological advance by reference to the work carried out as well as the broader objectives sought.

- The claim must also show the technical uncertainties targeted by the project.

- The technical contribution of project employees must be demonstrable.

The precision of the case of BES contrasts sharply with the examination of detail that was aired in *Gripple Ltd v HMRC*. The issues in *Gripple* were highly specific and concentrated upon the dissection of the accounting entries behind the company's claim and their compliance with the rules at *Pt 13*.

The case of *Gripple* went to the High Court in 2010. Interestingly, the case was the result of one of the last commissioners' hearings to provide an 'expression of dissatisfaction' and to reach the High Court. The arrival of the tax tribunals took over the jurisdiction of the general and special commissioners on 1 April 2009.

Gripple Ltd (GL) was an engineering company and had made three years' claims to RDTR SME relief upon eligible activity from 2004 to 2006. The mainstay of the claim was payments 'made' by way of a recharge of the director's salary, to an associated company, Loadhog Ltd (LHL), for the services of GL's director, Mr Facey. Mr Facey was a director of both LHL and GL at the time of the claim. At around the time of the claim, the parent company had made a tax clearance application for share buy-back from the subsidiary which highlighted the collaborative nature and economic dependence of the companies' R&D activity.

It became accepted ground that GL was able to claim RDTR only if the payments constituted 'staffing costs' within *CTA 2009, Pt 13*, or alternatively (but not validly in this case), payments for the services of 'externally provided workers'. Just to recap, staffing costs are defined in the legislation at *Pt 13* as:

'(a)   the emoluments paid by the company to directors or employees of the company, including all salaries, wages, perquisites and profits whatsoever other than benefits in kind;

(b)   the secondary Class 1 national insurance contributions paid by the company; and

(c)   the contributions paid by the company to any pension fund ... operated for the benefit of directors or employees of the company.'

(Then *FA 2000, Sch 20, para 5(1)*)

The substance of the recharge from LHL to GL was consistent with the entries made upon Mr Facey's tax return for the period of claim. However, the possibility of the charge representing the cost of an 'externally provided worker' was not consistent with the entries made.

In GL's defence of the R&D claim, the court was asked to consider the company's collaboration in the project work. A number of cases where the 'corporate veil' could be lifted were highlighted. It was argued that where two associated companies collaborated upon R&D, cross-charging expenses from one to the other, relief was tenable. Although the representations were as realistic as they were erudite, the HC found that the strict language of what is now *Pt 13* prevented any relief being due.

Taken as a whole, the 'code of the relief at *Part 13*' was extensive and written 'meticulously' allowing no possibility of purposive construction. The RDTR claim must be demonstrable from an 'audit trail' of the expenditure concerned and then tested against the strict definitions of the relief.

With regret, the company's appeal was dismissed by Mr Justice Henderson, highlighting the conclusion that R&D relief turns purely upon the facts rather than any purposive construction of the legislation.

> '27. The commissioners reached their conclusion with avowed reluctance. I can understand their feelings, because the group could easily have arranged matters in such a way as to attract relief for the full amounts paid to Mr Facey. Gripple was not attempting any form of tax avoidance, but inadvertently failed to obtain the maximum relief to which it might otherwise have been entitled. However, as the Commissioners rightly appreciated, their duty was to apply the law to the transactions which the parties had actually entered into, and not to some alternative transactions which they might have entered into with the benefit of better advice. The mere fact that the same economic result could have been achieved in a different, and more fiscally attractive, manner cannot avail the taxpayer where the clear words of the relevant legislation preclude the grant of relief for the transaction which the taxpayer has actually undertaken.'
>
> 28. For these reasons Gripple's appeal will be dismissed.

(Justice Henderson, *Gripple Ltd v HMRC*)

The full text of *Gripple Ltd v HMRC* is to be found at **Appendix 12**.

Taken together, *both* cases underline the fact that the anchors of R&D tax relief are both quantitative and qualitative. *Gripple* highlights the fact that the specific rules of Pt 13 must be followed 'meticulously' and do not permit purposive construction of 'payments' or contra accounts as representing R&D costs. Book entries will not attract R&D tax relief, no matter how strong the justification may be.

Although the rules upon EPW have been softened, the changes in FA 2012 would not prevent a similar scenario. Group cost recharges are common within the R&D scenario, but collaborative costs have no special footing in the R&D legislation and *Gripple* shows that there is no legal basis for looking at the 'wider picture'.

Chapter 7

'The Innovation Gap' – grants and State Aid for research and development

Contents

SIGNPOSTS

- **Grant funding** – Grant funding provides a viable alternative to tax incentives for R&D. Both UK and EU funding agencies can support generic R&D project work as well as projects aimed at specific technologies and sciences (see **7.2**).

- **Technology Strategy Board** – The UK's Technology Strategy Board (TSB) has provided the equivalent of 60% of the R&D tax relief programme, funding around £1 billion per annum for indirect R&D (see **7.2**).

- **Other funding** – Regional Growth Funds supplement programmes such as SMART funding and can aid R&D in specific areas such as Northern Ireland and Scotland. SMART schemes run in annual rounds of funding programmes and can offer up to £250,000 towards R&D projects developing 'first of class technologies' (see **7.3–7.8**).

- **Practical support programmes** – Procurement and partnership schemes can provide the vital first link towards the commercialisation of R&D project work. A number of practical support programmes are coordinated through the TSB such as the Small Business Research Initiative Scheme (see **7.6**).

- **EU funding programmes** – EU funding programmes have very significant budgets for R&D support. The new programme 'Horizon 2020 Projects' will run from 2014 to 2020 and focus upon a range of emerging technologies. Successful programmes have included both the Eureka/Eurostars programmes and FP 7 Framework programmes (see **7.14, 7.15**).

- **Impact on tax relief** – Grants and subsidies can have a significant impact upon tax relief for SME companies. This is highlighted through a number of case study examples (see **7.19**). Both strategies should therefore be considered in tandem, over the length of the R&D project(s) (see **7.18**).

OVERVIEW

7.1   Innovative companies will not always find tax relief an appropriate incentive for R&D activities. This 'Innovation Gap' is common in start-up enterprises, and for work preceding the R&D company's first valuable contracts. There are a number of alternatives to tax relief, but some may have an adverse impact on later claims to tax relief, whilst others carry caps and conditions, which will require consideration. As with tax relief, the effectiveness of grant support depends significantly upon the commercial environment in which the R&D takes place. Many schemes are aimed at bridging the practical gap between product concept and development and the commercialisation of innovative ideas. These offer resource-based expertise, assistance and collaboration in getting new innovations into market.

The UK agencies offering grant support target both generic R&D project work as well as the promotion of specific technologies and industries. UK companies may also access EU funding opportunities, of course, as well as regional assistance schemes which include a variety of R&D incentives within specific UK locations.

The lead UK grant agency is the Technology Strategy Board, which states it has provided funding for innovation of £2.5 billion in the past five years. The agency has a long history in R&D incentivisation, almost predating the UK R&D tax relief schemes. It is funded by the Department for Business & Innovation Skills (BIS). More recently, the agency has set up 'excellence/ catapult centres' which are focused upon technically ambitious R&D activities which may lead to large global market potential for UK firms.

A number of other government agencies and departments offer support for R&D work. Current programmes include the following:

Department of Energy & Climate Change

The Entrepreneurs' Fund

Opportunity: R&D work involving the area of low carbon technologies – various projects running to 2015.

Bioenergy funding schemes

Opportunity: R&D work involving bioenergy – various funding schemes launched January 2013.

Research-based programmes

Research Councils UK

Funding of £3 billion per annum aimed at multi-disciplinary research in high-end sciences.

The wide availability of grant funding makes for some complexity. There are currently in excess of 7,000 schemes in the UK alone. Additionally, as can be seen from the partnership initiatives offered by the TSB, procurement contracts, such as the SBRI schemes, can be a vital commercial pathway for emerging technology.

Several tax cases such as *Smart v Lincolnshire Sugar Co Ltd* (1937) 20 TC 643 and *Burman v Thorn Domestic Appliances (Electrical) Ltd* (1981) 55 TC

493 establish that grants and subsidies for revenue costs are often regarded as taxable receipts, but this is an area of difficulty as other tax cases have established that such grants are not treated as trading receipts in certain circumstances, particularly where capital expenditure is involved. Although no R&D relief is available for capital expenditure, to ease the confusion, the starting point is that GAAP requires grant funding and subsidies to be recognised as part of the company's income for the relevant accounting period, and that subsidised expenditure is also brought in as a deduction, and therefore eligible for RDTR. The large company scheme does not prevent subsidised expenditure from qualifying for RDTR, but the SME scheme applies a barrier to relief at the SME rate where any type of funding has been obtained. This stands even if the funding is repaid.

UK-BASED GRANT FUNDING

The Technology Strategy Board (TSB)

7.2   The agency's primary objective is to promote high-tech economic growth. The TSB coordinates both financial and practical assistance for UK R&D companies. This fits with the UK's wider growth policy objective to become a 'magnet for technology-intensive companies'. The TSB was established in 2004 to assist both SMEs and large companies carrying out 'ground breaking' R&D project work. The way in which this works has changed significantly over this period. The growth of commercial sponsorship for innovation and the isolation of specific technologies for support have grown as key features of TSB R&D support.

Recent measures announced increased funding for the board. The limits for 2013/14 have increased from £40 million to £100 million, with a further £200 million being available in 2014/15. Funds are targeted particularly at these industries and technologies:

- Advanced materials
- Biosciences
- Built environment
- Digital economy/ICT
- Electronics
- Energy
- Food supply
- Health care
- High value manufacturing
- Space
- Transport

The Board is currently operating 25 diverse funding schemes providing assistance through a range of both practical and financial means. The most popular schemes currently on offer are:

- SMART funding – investment in R&D projects;

- competition 'rounds' for funding in specific industries;

- specialist facilities;

- catapult centres – technical expertise and advice;

- SBRI schemes – government procurement opportunities;

- international programmes;

- networking and partnership opportunities.

SMART funding scheme

7.3 UK SMEs meeting the EC definition of a small or medium-sized enterprise may apply for SMART funding.

The TSB's SMART scheme provides assistance to start-up companies engaging in early stage technology, engineering and science-based R&D projects that may lead to successful new products. SMART funding is aimed at strengthening the innovation concept the business has and providing the R&D activity with commercial traction.

The grants are split into three functionality-based categories, each subject to absolute limits and a competitive application process. The SMART scheme runs on an annual basis. In 2013 there were six funding rounds, the last of which closed on 27 March 2014. Applications are assessed by independent review boards. The amounts on offer are similar in absolute value to the support provided for many SMEs through the R&D tax relief schemes.

Summary of SMART funding schemes 2013/14

Type of SMART grant	Purpose	Maximum £
Proof of market	Assistance with assessing potential markets	25,000
Proof of concept	Assistance with technical feasibility	100,000
Prototype development	Assistance with first of class	250,000

Advantages

- Eligible costs are less restrictive than RDTR.

- Confidentiality – funding assistance is not disclosed.

167

- Possibility of making further applications if unsuccessful.

- There is no impact on 'Seed EIS' investors.

Disadvantages

- Match funding is required which may not be available.

- Appointment of an auditor is obligatory.

- The work must be carried out only in the UK or wider EEA for a specified period after funding is obtained.

- Impact upon UK R&D tax relief for project costs – claim reduced to large company rate only.

Funding competitions

7.4   The TSB runs around 20 funding competitions at any one time, spanning a wide range of technologies in a number of industries. Assistance involves a lengthy, quality-intensive application process where the applicant will set out at high level the aims of the development/research work and its excellence. The application will also need to match up with the current aims of the TSB's innovation investment strategy.

Catapult centres

7.5   In late 2011 TSB published its aim to create seven resource/'catapult' centres aimed at maturing R&D project work with a relevance to international markets. The catapult centres concentrate on the 'very best' scientists and engineers within seven target industries with strategic importance for the UK economy, including:

- high value manufacturing R&D;

- renewable offshore energy;

- cell therapy;

- connected digital economy;

- satellite applications;

- future cities;

- transport systems.

The centres assist with the commercialisation of research projects and builds upon ideas published in the Hauser report upon the future of UK innovation centres which were further developed in the Dyson 'Ingenious Britain' review of 2010.

Small Business Research Initiative

7.6   The Small Business Research Initiative (SBRI) provides companies with the opportunity to develop R&D activity by entering into government contracts. The procurement-based incentive is popular and replaces grant funding with real sales contracts over a medium- to long-term basis.

The TSB publishes a number of 'success stories' from a variety of technologies, emphasising the usefulness of the scheme as a pathway from concept to market place for the R&D company.

A range of statistics is published about the assistance provided by this scheme, which is highly promoted by the BIS. The 2014/15 budget has been set at £200 million, representing a £100 million increase on the 2013/14 provision.

Innovation vouchers

7.7   Coordinated by the TSB, the innovation vouchers scheme works by providing resources for technical work. The 'Buy an Expert' incentive is aimed at providing practical assistance to target technologies and industries.

Companies with fewer than 250 employees can 'purchase' expertise from universities and research centres to progress R&D activity. The scheme is linked to a number of leading academic institutions in the UK and operated on a regional basis.

REGIONAL GROWTH FUNDS

7.8   Regional Growth Funds (RGFs) have provided around 2,700 SMEs with economic assistance of some kind or other. The funds are run by the Government's BIS department. The funds are not specifically focused at encouraging R&D activity alone, promoting a range of broader economic objectives driving specific local employment and investment opportunities.

The application process is open to UK-based SMEs wishing to 'bid' for investment funds through spending rounds but who may have been unable to obtain funds elsewhere. The funds are usually regarded as a 'State Aid' for RDTR purposes. A further 'Exceptional Regional Growth' programme runs in tandem to the main BIS scheme for monies to be allocated outside of the RGF bidding processes.

A bewildering array of government statistics surround the private capital stated to be leveraged by the fund and the employment opportunities generated by the RGF. The published statistic from BIS (January 2013) states that the fund is running at £2.6 billion from 2012 to the mid-2020s. This provides good assurance about its longevity, if not its effectiveness.

NORTHERN IRELAND

7.9 The TSB also works closely with two agencies within Northern Ireland – 'Invest Northern Ireland' and 'The Department of Enterprise & Trade Northern Ireland'. The initiatives provide wide ranging economic assistance to local businesses. The work focuses on a number of economic objectives, but also focuses upon significant technology lead industries such as:

- telecommunications,
- ICT/digital,
- life/health sciences,
- agrifood,
- engineering and advanced materials.

Taken together the above sectors represent 77% of business-led R&D performed in Northern Ireland.

'Invest Northern Ireland' – grants for R&D work

7.10 'Invest Northern Ireland' (INI) is Northern Ireland's economic development agency. It provides a range of grant-based financial assistance for R&D projects undertaken by businesses operating in that region. In addition, it provides an umbrella of R&D assistance tools such as that available through the UK TSB such as:

- centres of excellence/Northern Ireland 'spinouts';
- innovation advice, advice upon intellectual property and patents;
- innovation vouchers, grants and venture capital funding;
- collaborative R&D support service;
- SBRI government procurement schemes;
- proof of concept funding.

Support is offered in two stages:

- project definition maximum funding 40–75% of eligible costs up to £50,000;
- direct grant for R&D: maximum funding 25–70% of eligible costs depending upon business size.

New businesses can receive a one-off R&D grant for first projects of up to 75% of costs capped at £50,000. The grant is not regarded as State Aid.

The Government are so keen to encourage R&D tax relief claims in the region that it has produced a special promotional brochure upon the benefits of the scheme and a 'guide' upon eligible project work. HMRC also have a specialist corporation tax office in the area, the Northern Ireland Corporate Tax Office, which leads the R&D initiatives for local companies.

SMART SCOTLAND

7.11   Focusing upon SME R&D, the agency provides two streams of R&D grant support depending upon the stage of the R&D work for businesses and university spin-outs based in Scotland:

Early stage R&D/feasibility studies

Early stage R&D/feasibility studies attract funding of up to 75% of project costs with a maximum ceiling of £100,000. Funding is usually provided quarterly in arrears, around a quarter of grants are provided 'up front'.

Product/prototype development

Product/prototype development attracts funding of up to 35% of eligible costs, maximum grant £600,000, minimum £75,000. This is paid quarterly in arrears.

Assistance provided by the Board is strengthened if the business can demonstrate ownership of the resultant intellectual property. Registration of a patent is not essential.

EU GRANT FUNDING

7.12   A vast array of funding and assistance schemes is run from the EU with significant budgets for the promotion of innovation and investment in research and development both in particular industry sectors and specific technologies and research disciplines. The definition of R&D is very broad, much wider than that adopted for tax purposes. This enables a wider range of costs to be included in the funding circle.

The key schemes currently available include:

- Horizon 2020 projects (from 2014);
- Eureka/Eurostars programmes;
- FP7 Framework programmes;
- Innovation and Competitiveness programmes.

Information and resources for many of the schemes and their spin-offs are coordinated as a portal by the Community R&D Information Service

(CORDIS) on behalf of the European Commission (EC).Collectively, the schemes operate as part of the reinforced EC '2020' Economic Strategy, incentivising economic growth through investment in R&D. The CORDIS service was established in 1990 and is a useful first point of access for EU-wide grants and assistance. Many of the programmes and sub-programmes referred to in the CORDIS hub have recently been simplified into the 'Horizon 2020' project opportunity which is due to commence next year.

Horizon 2020 project

7.13   Set to begin in 2014, the Horizon 2020 project is a brand new EC R&D programme with the stated aim of enhancing the EC's ability to compete in R&D with the US.

The Horizon 2020 budget is estimated at €72 billion, the greater proportion of which will be aimed at research excellence. The 2020 project pulls together the diverse Framework programmes explained below, with a stronger focus upon innovation.

One of the 2020 key objectives is excellence in science, funding the best science through funding competitions, with an emphasis upon future and emerging technologies.

Eureka/'Eurostars' programmes

7.14   The scheme is aimed at SMEs bringing innovation to the market place. It provides maximum project funding of £300,000/50% of eligible costs. Entry into the scheme is made difficult by the preconditions that:

● projects must be collaborative and involve at least two European member entities;

● the project must have a maximum duration of three years; and

● the product must be brought to market within two years of the project.

If the above are surmountable, the funding limits are generous, and the scope of the scheme covers almost all mainstream R&D activities performed by SMEs.

Seventh Framework programme (FP7)

7.15   The most remarkable aspect of the FP7 Framework programme is its significant €50 billion budget published from 2007 to 2013.

The framework is divided into four programmes and is accessible to 27 main EEA countries as well as a number of dependent states. The programmes are similar in structure to the SMART funding opportunity, focusing upon specific aspects of R&D commercialisation such as marketing opportunities and networking as well as research and technology infrastructures.

The schemes are wider in nature than the Eureka/Eurostars programmes and are open to individuals and non-corporate enterprises, including public organisations.

A scorecard evaluation is used to award funds to applicants. The quality of the application is essential and high, and fewer than 20% of applicants receive any type of funding at all.

Competitiveness and Innovation Framework Programme (CIP)

7.16   The CIP is aimed at SMEs and had a budget of €3,621 million for its first period of activity from 2007 to 2013.

The CIP is split into three specific areas aimed at promoting innovation across the 27 EU member states. The central themes are eco-efficiency and biodiversity. The specific headline programmes are:

Intelligent Energy Europe

A fund aimed at new and renewable energy sources and peripheral activity. The programme is aimed at promoting the technical knowledge base, focusing upon:

- information exchange;
- education/training; and
- spreading of know-how.

The fund provides an average grant of €1 million and is aimed at universities and research institutions in addition to the business owner.

ECO Innovation

As the name suggests, the fund develops the EC's environmental technology action plan. The objective of the fund is to narrow the gap between R&D and the commercialisation of 'eco-friendly' products. Eco-innovative techniques, products, processes or practices come within the umbrella of the scheme, which recently included the following priority projects:

- eco-innovation in the supply and waste chains;
- sustainable construction materials for building projects;
- materials recycling/reclamation/new markets for recycled products.

Average grants are around €750,000 with a maximum of 50% of a project's eligible cost over a further maximum of three years.

The fund publicises its preference for SME applications, but is open to large companies.

Entrepreneurship and Innovation Programme

The programme is particularly aimed at SMEs. The priority is to provide access to finance and markets for growth firms. The programme strategy emphasises the promotion of eco-innovation. This drives particularly at stimulus for environmental technologies.

UK R&D TAX RELIEF V EU FUNDING SOURCES

7.17 EU funding programmes have significantly helped many UK-based companies to invest in R&D. The longevity of these schemes is secured beyond 2020 as the area focuses on keeping apace with emerging technologies in the US and Tiger Economies/East.

The illustration below shows the historic pattern of funding for UK R&D has been heavily dominated by support from the EU. In particular the Sixth and Seventh Framework Programmes have provided around €5.5 billion in support from 2002 through to 2013. Over the same period UK direct tax relief has provided around £1 billion of support per annum.

Indirect sources of R&D funding

£0.09 billion per annum	....................The cost to government of providing R&D tax relief increased by 1,111% between the 2000-01 and 2010-11 financial years	£1.09 billion per annum
EU funding	6th Framework Programme: £1.58 billion provided to the UK between 2002 and 2006	7th Framework Programme: £4.02 billion provided to the UK between 2007 and 2013

Source: NAO Report 'Research and Development Funding for science and technology in the UK'.

GRANT ASSISTANCE: IMPACT ON RDTR

7.18 The treatment of R&D grants and subsidies depends upon their EC notification status and can be unfavourable for an SME if funding of any amount is obtained for a project, even where it is later repaid.

The examples at **7.19** show it is possible to claim both R&D relief and an R&D grant assistance for the same project depending upon the status of the grant funding concerned.

SME scheme relief

If the grant is a 'notified State Aid'

As the SME Scheme is itself a notified State Aid, none of the R&D costs will qualify under the SME scheme. However, the company may still be able to claim relief for the project under the large company scheme at 130% of the gross allowable expenditure. From April 2013 the RDEC is available in these circumstances.

If the grant is not a 'notified State Aid'

The grant should be deducted from the SME qualifying expenditure and relief is due on the net costs under the SME scheme at 225%. The costs excluded by the grant may also qualify for relief under the large company scheme at 130% and obtain the RDEC.

The general rule ensures EC rules against the accumulation of State Aid are not breached. 'Notified State Aid' is a State Aid (other than R&D tax reliefs or R&D tax credit) notified to and approved by the EC.

Any grant towards an R&D project out of government or public funds or from the Commission itself would normally fall into this category (subject to certain exemptions). As an example, most SMART awards (see **7.3** above) constitute notified State Aid. This rule covers any funding whatsoever and not just funding received to cover wages or consumable stores. Should the company wish to repay the grant to secure RDTR, HMRC publicise their viewpoint that simply 'obtaining' funds in the first place will negate the possibility of tax relief for the project concerned.

CASE STUDIES

Impact of grant funding upon RDTR

7.19

Example 7.1 – SME company obtaining grant which is a notified State Aid

R&D costs	£100,000
Less: grant or subsidy	(£40,000)
Net cost of project	£60,000

No claim under SME scheme but can claim under large company scheme

Large scheme R&D relief	£100,000 @ 30% £30,000
Tax saved (using 24% tax rate)	
Enhanced expenditure	£30,000 @ 24% £7,200
Plus already claimed in accounts	£100,000 @ 24% £24,000
Total tax relief	£31,200
Grant assistance obtained	£40,000
Total project R&D support	71.2%

Example 7.2 – SME company – grant is NOT a notified State Aid

R&D costs	£100,000
Less: grant or subsidy	(£40,000)
Net cost of project	£60,000
Claim under both SME and large company schemes possible:	
SME scheme R&D relief	£60,000 @ 125% £75,000
Plus	
Large scheme R&D relief	£40,000 @ 30% £12,000
Total R&D relief	£87,000
Tax saved (using 24% tax rate)	
Enhanced expenditure benefit:	£87,000 @ 24% £20,880
Plus already claimed in accounts	
£100,000 @ 24% £24,000	
Total tax relief £44,880	
Grant assistance obtained	£40,000
Total project R&D support	60.88%

Example 7.3 – Large company grant applicant

In the large company scheme, grants are not deducted from the qualifying expenditure and the R&D claim can be made on the gross allowable expenditure.

| R&D costs | £100,000 |
| *Less:* grant or subsidy | (£40,000) |

Net cost of project	£60,000
Large scheme R&D tax relief	£100,000 @ 30% £30,000
Tax saved (using 24% tax rate)	
Enhanced expenditure	£30,000 @ 24% £7,200
Plus already claimed in accounts	£100,000 @ 24% £24,000
Total tax relief	£31,200
Grant assistance obtained	£40,000
Total project R&D support	47.20%

SUMMARY

7.20   As the following 'directory' shows, a broad range of R&D incentives is available from both within the UK and the wider EU. Additionally, regional financial and practical assistance is available for R&D activity in specific UK locations and a range of similar, broader employment-focused resources are also on offer.

Provided the grant company can attain match funding, many of the schemes may not have an adverse impact upon R&D tax relief in the long run. This is helped by the division of the reliefs into 'project' funding. For the R&D entity running parallel or a number of long-term projects, there is no reason why both fiscal and grant-based assistance should not be considered.

Grant directory

UK grant assistance schemes

Agency/scheme	Key features	Aim	Funding
Technology Strategy Board		Various schemes Target technologies and tech industries	£440 million 2013/14
SBRI	Government contracts for R&D. Not grant-based	Develop R&D in the private sector through government procurement	Scheme limits high: £100 million 2013/14 £200 million 2014/15

SMART (Formerly 'Grants for R&D')		Match funding for R&D: Three schemes: • Proof of concept • Proof of market • Prototype development	Maximum grant assistance £25,000– £250,000
Funding competitions	Competition rounds run throughout the year		
UK Innovation Investment Fund	Run by BIS	Funding for venture capital to invest in tech companies	£300 million budget
Technical resources			
Catapult/ Innovation Centres	Technology Strategy Board	Provide resource centre	Set up in 2010
Innovation vouchers	Technology Strategy Board	SME assistance	Micro R&D companies
Research Councils	Some R&D industries	Bioscience/ biotech and Engineering, Physical Sciences Research Council	Set up in 2002 Central government funding

Chapter 8

Worldwide trends in research and development

Contents

SIGNPOSTS

- **Influence of worldwide trends** – R&D activity is interdependent in its character. UK companies carrying on R & D are likely to be heavily influenced by worldwide trends. This Chapter looks at these trends and the elasticity of corporate development expenditure (see **8.1, 8.2**).

- **Sectorial excellence** – Good tax breaks for R&D do not necessarily stimulate external investment in R&D and vice versa (see **8.3**). Sectorial 'excellence' is a key factor in attracting R & D investment and has led to the dominance of sectors such as automotive production and pharmaceuticals over a sustained period of time (see **8.6, 8.9**).

- **Features of R&D** – An interesting feature of R&D investment is that activity 'follows' patent registrations and particularly impacts upon 'copy cat' SME activity (see **8.10**).

INTRODUCTION

8.1   Investment in research and development (R&D) activity is rarely driven by tax incentives. Neither is this a UK phenomenon; no obvious correlation between the major EU and US R&D investors and their respective tax codes is apparent from patterns observed over a lengthy period from 2002 through to 2013. The gap between incentivisation and investment in R&D is also apparent in industry specialisations. For example UK construction and engineering companies engage upon very significant R&D project work, but fewer than 140 R&D claims companies in that sector were processed by HMRC in 2012.

This begs the question, 'What is the wider pattern of worldwide R&D investment?' The top 2000 R&D investors account for around 90% of the €22.6 billion expenditure upon R&D by businesses worldwide. The EU places around 500 companies in the top 2000 and attracted 22% of the inflow of foreign direct investment in R&D in 2012/13. The expenditure of the top ten largest global R&D investors exceeds the combined total of the expenditure claimed by UK companies as R&D tax relief by 5:1.

Studies of R&D business investment show an obvious focus upon both technological and industry specialisations. For example, the pattern of R&D investment in the EU differs to industries leading US and Asian R&D activity. The top five most numerous R&D industries in the EU are led by industrial engineering and biotechnologies. The US R&D activity is traditionally dominated by ICT and healthcare companies, with nine out of ten of the world's leading healthcare companies being based in the US.

But emerging technologies have performed well in sustaining R&D investment over the last ten years. For example, US R&D investment in emerging sub-technologies of healthcare is very progressive. It is estimated that investment in therapeutic biotechnology in the US will develop over 50% of new drugs by 2018 compared to 12% in 2003.

The EC Study of the 'Worldwide Business Expenditure upon R&D in 2012/13' shows R&D expenditure patterns are resilient despite significant economic uncertainty. The average growth in R&D spending over the period from 2008 to 2013 shows growth of 6.3% in R&D (EU) and 8.3% (US). The UK compares equally favourably, despite relatively weak GDP performance. Indeed, within the EU, the UK became the second most dominant R&D investor nation on the 2013 worldwide R&D Scoreboard, behind Germany. But both countries fare relatively poorly on the ratings for global tax incentivisation, being placed 18th and 38th (last) in the table of countries with established R&D tax relief frameworks.

Worldwide trends in corporate R&D

8.2   The most recent R&D Scoreboard is contained in a study of worldwide corporate R&D investment which was published by the EU in late 2013. The '2013 EU R&D Scoreboard' shows trends in R&D expenditure made by the world's top 2000 investing companies.

The main R&D trends are long-term patterns. These establish that R&D expenditure is traditionally focused upon a handful of industries, reaching across a diverse range of entrenched and emerging technologies and sciences. These industries are concentrated geographically, with the US leading pharmaceutical and biotechnical R&D activity and the EU leading R&D in industrial engineering.

Regional EU R&D patterns

8.3   EU R&D investment is dominated by Germany. This is largely accounted for by the activity of a singular company (Volkswagen) and the cascade effect upon the automotive industry there.

Worldwide R&D Scoreboard 2012

EU R&D investor companies by country

8.4   The following list shows the number of companies per EU country in the top 2000:

- Germany 130;
- UK 107;
- France 75;

- Sweden 40;

- Netherlands 35;

- Italy 30;

- Denmark 25;

- Finland 20;

- Spain 16;

- Belgium 13;

- Austria 12;

- Ireland 11;

- Luxembourg 4;

- Portugal 4;

- Czech Republic 1;

- Greece 1;

- Hungary 1;

- Malta 1;

- Slovakia 1.

Which industries invest in R&D?

Sectorial R&D trends

8.5   A handful of industries account for the €22.6 million invested by the world's 2000 leading R&D investors during 2012. The US has dominated global R&D expenditure upon ICT hardware and software development and this has been sustained over the last ten years.

This trend has had a knock on effect on EU pharmaceutical R&D investment as well as investment in EU software and hardware R&D projects. This shows that R&D activity within emerging and successful technologies cascades globally. This is very evident in the UK's new tech 'hub' cities as R&D activity trickles down to micro SME level.

2013 Global R&D Investment Scoreboard

EU: Top ten most numerous R&D sectors

8.6   Sector/(number of companies with significant R&D investment)

- Industrial Engineering 62;

182

- Pharmaceuticals and Biotechnology 58;

- Electronic and Electrical Equipment 38;

- Software and Computer Services 37;

- Automobiles and Parts 36;

- Technology Hardware and Equipment 29;

- Chemicals 24;

- Banks 23;

- Health Care Equipment and Services 20;

- Aerospace and Defence 18.

These top five sectors account for 43.8% of the 527.

Non-EU: Top ten most numerous R&D sectors

- Technology Hardware and Equipment 264;

- Pharmaceuticals and Biotechnology156;

- Software and Computer Services 151;

- Electronic and Electrical Equipment139;

- Industrial Engineering 116;

- Chemicals 94;

- Automobiles and Parts 90;

- Health Care Equipment and Services 63;

- General Industrials 54;

- Construction and Materials 39.

The top five sectors account for 56.1% of the 1,473.

Source: EC 2013 Worldwide R&D Report

The longevity and tenacious nature of R&D investment may have a number of economic causes. But the investment patterns also tend to follow the complexity involved in the technology itself, as well as the sheer scale and commercial significance of the uncertainties involved in the R&D.

For example, the domination of US R&D investment by healthcare and ICT sectors has remained unchanged since 2004. The EU R&D investment in industrial engineering and automotive R&D has been similarly sustained.

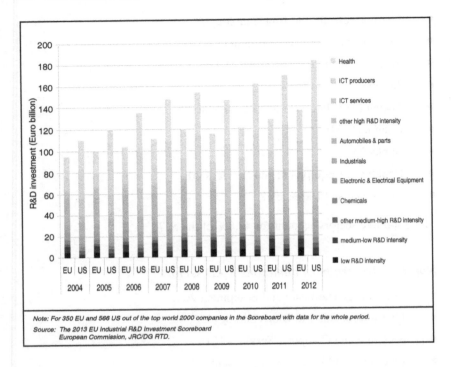

Note: For 350 EU and 566 US out of the top world 2000 companies in the Scoreboard with data for the whole period.
Source: The 2013 EU Industrial R&D Investment Scoreboard
          European Commission, JRC/DG RTD.

R&D – economic sensitivity

8.7   The above is given support by the fact that during the three years following the financial crisis in 2008/09, Scoreboard companies increased their R&D investments by an average 6.2% per year (from 2010 to 2012).

The diagram below shows the longer-term R&D trends for a subset of Scoreboard companies with available data for the past nine years.

The impact of the recession shows the resilience of commercial R&D investment during a period of economic uncertainty reflecting the strategic importance that companies attach to such investment and the fact that the resolution and exploitation of technological complexities are so commercially lucrative.

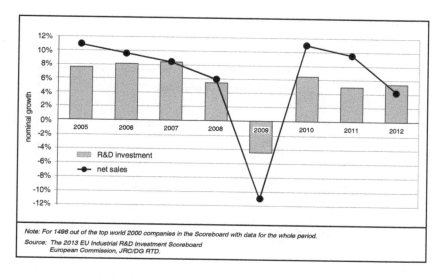

Note: For 1496 out of the top world 2000 companies in the Scoreboard with data for the whole period.
Source: The 2013 EU Industrial R&D Investment Scoreboard
European Commission, JRC/DG RTD.

Emerging trends – collaborative R&D

8.8   The scale of complexities has added to the frequency with which industries and companies within industries collaborate in joint venture R&D projects across more than one technology. For example, centres of research excellence in the US 'Silicon Valley' are becoming common ways of developing new R&D partnerships such as that between IBM and Continental – a software/ automotive component partnership for the 'self-drive car' technology.

Whereas global patent registrations for low emission engine technologies have doubled in the past three years, interestingly, the pattern of R&D investment in the automotive industry shows a demographic shift from the US to EU and Asian companies. However, despite the shrinkage in the US of R&D volume in established technologies, there is a refocus there into collaborative R&D directed at new combinations of technologies.

R&D investment patterns

8.9   The EU, together with the US, plays a major role in the international R&D investment scenario, both as a source and destination of knowledge-intensive foreign direct investments (FDIs). From 2003 to 2012, the EU attracted 22% of FDI projects on R&D from the set of non-EU companies while the US received only a share of 8 % (see Figure S7). Six out of the ten countries with the highest number of international projects are European.

FDIs in R&D are concentrated mainly in three sectors:

●   IT hardware

8.10   *Worldwide trends in research and development*

- Automobiles and parts; and
- Pharmaceuticals and biotechnology.

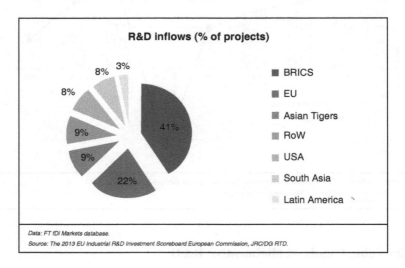

R&D inflows (% of projects)

- BRICS
- EU
- Asian Tigers
- RoW
- USA
- South Asia
- Latin America

Data: FT fDi Markets database.
Source: The 2013 EU Industrial R&D Investment Scoreboard European Commission, JRC/DG RTD.

R&D specialisation – patent trends

8.10   The Thompson Reuters index of global R&D activity is based on a narrower sample of worldwide R&D companies. The index comprises the top 100 innovators but is interesting as its methodology reflects the propensity for patent application within the R&D sector. It is led by the semi-conductor and electronic components industry, followed by computer hardware, chemicals; transportation; telecommunications and consumer manufacturing.

The composition of the index is based upon the propensity for patent registration and the ratios of published applications to granted patents; global presence and subsequent technological citation by other companies.

The fact that global R&D 'follows' patenting trends is very evident. This is given further support as the expiration of 'blockbuster' patents in the US coincides with a relative slowdown in US biotechnology expenditure in 2012.

UK TRENDS

8.11   The National Audit Office estimates UK expenditure on R&D reached £27 billion in 2011. UK businesses make the largest contribution, accounting for £17.4 billion (64%) of R&D investment. R&D in the UK is concentrated in a small number of large companies; fewer than 50 UK companies account for 68% of the above total R&D activity, of which ten companies account for 44% or £7.7 billion of the above total.

However, it is very evident that this cascades into SME R&D activity, although fewer than 5% of R&D activity is carried out by smaller enterprises, the industries in which SME innovation is performed mirror large company activity.

Pharmaceuticals are now the largest performer of UK R&D, although this was not the case ten years ago when the sector was responsible for only 25% of R&D in the UK. BIS data shows that just two organisations accounted for more than 70% of expenditure on R&D in the sector in 2009, spending a combined total of £6.4 billion. Interestingly overseas investors funded £1.5 billion of expenditure in the pharmaceutical industry, accounting for 40% of funding in that sector. The next most prominent industries are computer-related businesses, automotive industry, aerospace and telecommunications.

The largest growth in UK R&D is led by computer-related technologies, automotive industry and technical testing and analysis services.

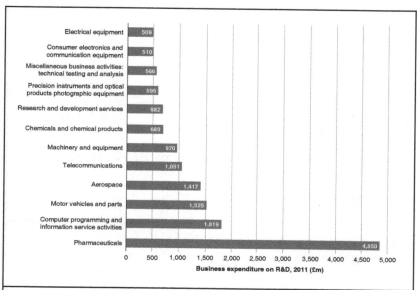

NOTES:

1. The Figure shows the largest 12 sectors of the UK, in terms of business spending on R&D undertaken in the UK in 2011.

2. The Figure excludes business sectors which spent less than £500 million each on R&D in 2011. These sectors collectively spent £2.2 billion on carrying our R&D in 2011.

Source: Office for National Statistics data. Data are available at: www.ons.gov.uk/ons/publications/re-reference-tables.html?edition-tcm%3A77-283184, UK Business Enterprise Research and Development, 2011– Datasets, table 8

8.12   *Worldwide trends in research and development*

By way of international comparison, UK spending on R&D is ranked as in the 'middle' of OECD R&D levels at 1.9% of GDP. This is some way behind the 3% target set for 2020. A study by the National Audit Office found the investment in R&D activity by UK companies has stagnated since 2001. Besides the GDP statistics, no UK companies featured in the 2012 Thomson's Reuters 'Top 100 Global Innovators' Index, although this index favours fast-paced, high-tech industries, with short product lifecycles, rather than the pharmaceutical and biotechnology companies that dominate R&D within the UK.

Some UK larger company R&D activity is very substantial. This has placed the UK reasonably well in the survey of top 2000 worldwide companies as a significant EU R&D investor. But the UK R&D investment in industrial engineering, for example, is a long way behind the European average, with three-quarters of the UK's R&D investors performing below the EU average for R&D investment.

Over the long term, the UK R&D expenditure as a proportion of GDP lacks the pace of the US, German and OECD averages, and shows a decline despite the absolute increases discussed above.

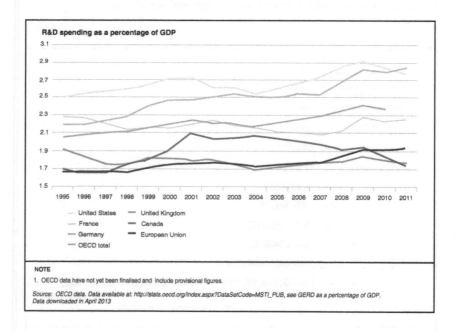

UK SME R&D

8.12   The growth of independent SMEs performing R&D is very evident. SMEs spent £4 billion undertaking R&D in 2011 (23% of total UK business spending on R&D performance). However, spending by independent SMEs, which are not part of a larger group, was significantly lower at £627 million (4% of total UK business spending).

Since 2000, the amount spent by SMEs on conducting R&D has increased by 48% for all SMEs and 40% for independent SMEs. Spending as a proportion of total UK business spending has increased for SMEs from 18% in 2000 to 23% in 2001.

In terms of volume, SMEs dominate claims for tax relief filed to HMRC. However, just a fraction of the UK's SME expenditure is relieved under the R&D tax relief schemes, with SME claims accounting for just £420 million of relief in 2011/12.

Global R&D trends are therefore influential on industry R&D investment patterns and will continue to influence which technologies are exploited by SMEs. The 'cascade' effect of large company R&D has dominated the economics of technology for a sustained period. But the study of R&D in UK industry at a micro level shows the universal way in which complexity can apply.

These micro trends are discussed in **Chapter 9** and can have a significant impact on the tax relief available for R&D in industry.

Chapter 9

Research and development in industry – case studies

Contents

SIGNPOSTS

- Case studies on R & D intensive industries are published on a regular basis, both by BIS and government agencies (see **9.1**).

- The case studies in this Chapter highlight just a few of the important practical opportunities and pitfalls that are relevant to the tax relief claim. These are drawn from practical examples drawn from a range of industries (see **9.2–9.12**).

- Emerging technologies, new cities and traditional UK industries are earmarked as significant R&D investors in the future (see **9.13–9.15**).

INTRODUCTION

9.1   As **Chapter 8** shows, R&D covers a completely diverse range of innovation and will follow international patterns of investment.

The earlier part of the book discusses how the BIS Guidelines and legislation in general shows that the tax definition of R&D applies universally to all industries. Yet some industries are more prominent upon HMRC R&D Scoreboards and can claim tax relief more effectively than others. There are many barriers that prevent efficient claims to R&D tax relief but the discussion shows that the many pitfalls are equally matched by opportunity.

The empirical data in **Chapter 8** shows that many UK SMEs shadow 'giant' technologies supplementing and diversifying baseline products and processes through significant R&D investment. But the definition of R&D for tax purposes is much narrower than the OECD meaning and from which much of the above empirical data is drawn. Case studies are a useful tool for putting many of the opportunities and pitfalls in applying the definition of R&D for tax purposes into practice.

Many of the issues highlighted in large company R&D have wider application to other industries and smaller companies. This overlap highlights the fact that the BIS Guidelines apply equally to all branches of science and technology and are not industry-specific. Although HMRC have published guidance upon software and pharmaceutical R&D, at no point does the legislation upon R&D apply industry-specific rules, outside the gas and oil and insurance sectors.

The case studies represent industries in which SMEs are involved significantly in R&D activity. The conclusions can, of course, apply equally to any type of company in any industry.

ENGINEERING AND CONSTRUCTION

9.2   Work carried out by engineering and construction companies upon advanced materials and design work can quickly become very technical and complex. Around 18% of SME companies in the sector believe they carry out significant R&D activity. Yet the level and volume of R&D relief claims filed to HMRC by engineering and construction companies is historically weak.

Almost no construction or engineering contracts are undertaken without significant input from specialist engineers. Technological uncertainty is such a common feature of many engineering and construction projects that almost no contract will be completed without extensive indemnity and retention clauses. These are often useful pointers for R&D activity in construction and engineering projects, showing new technologies that have been developed and areas of technical uncertainty. Stage payment contracts will also point to the resolution or continuation of technical milestones.

For companies investing in the development of alternative or advanced materials, prototype technologies will be common place. This is usually regarded as an R&D activity in its own right, provided there is sufficient technical uncertainty present at the prototype stage. Construction and construction materials can often engage in R&D unaware, as worldwide markets demand increasing cost efficiencies and high specification in materials, that building designs have accelerated the R&D hallmarks in the sector.

Gaps in the theoretical study of many new materials and their physical properties can mean construction and engineering companies have an almost constant approach to R&D. The extent to which this is identified will dictate how successfully the company can claim relevant R&D tax incentives.

Despite the predominance of a number of technical issues, the construction and its support industries accounted for just 140 of the 8,700 R&D claims filed to HMRC in 2012. HMRC are so concerned about the low take-up by companies in the civil engineering sector that the industry was recently chosen to feature in HMRC's promotional R&D case studies material.

Activity likely to be regarded as R&D

9.3

- Development of new cheaper, or greener structures and materials;

- Development of fire retardant and combustive materials and structures;

- Development of 'green timber' materials and structures, responding to worldwide regulations upon newer and sustainable resources;

- New tooling and machinery processes for eventual sale or commercial use;

- Prototype development;

- Packing solid materials and structures for export markets;

- Adapting technology for off-site fabrication;

- Modifying coating methods, technologies or coating products;

- Trialling new steel and heavy metal materials for sale or production.

R&D Issues in the engineering and construction industries

9.4   The use of subcontractors is a common feature in the engineering and construction sectors. HMRC will often take the stance that the 'contractor/subcontractor' relationship will be mirrored in R&D activities. This can be a risk for SME 'subcontractors' as it may be argued that the reduced, large company rate of relief outlined in *CTA 2009, Pt 13, Ch 3* may be appropriate where the R&D is performed under the direction of a large company.

Example 9.1 – Establishing subcontracted R & D Activity: Tower Co

Tower Co has engaged Crane Co to build a safety platform during the construction of a pioneering glass and steel building in the City. The contract between the companies complies with RICS (Building Control) Regulations and gives details of stage payments to be made to Crane Co as the safety platform is designed and constructed. Crane Co has had to incur significant research activity into the behaviour and performance of some of the platform components and their interaction at levels above 500m. It has developed a cradle to access the platform which will be safe in the event of high winds. The R&D costs are £1 million and Crane Co wishes to claim R&D relief at the SME rate of 225%. It does not have an obligation to assign the intellectual property rights back to the contractor, Tower Co.

Analysis

Crane Co and Tower Co have a contractual arrangement governing the construction of the final platform. This is probably distinct from a contract to 'perform R&D' as envisaged at CIRD84250. If the facts support the economic risk and the initiative and responsibility for the R&D activities lie with the SME, relief is due within *Ch 2* at the higher SME rate. Stage payments are not an indication of a subcontractor relationship, but a common feature of contracts in the construction industry.

In practice, it is likely that Crane Co may delegate the installation, design or construction of the platform to further third parties. Crane Co has engaged in R&D that it can exploit subsequently. This has been carried out for its own economic risk and benefit. No subcontracting of R&D has taken place.

Example 9.2 – Tower Co continued

Continuing with Crane Co's project, a number of third parties are engaged by Tower Co to design and install the safety platform. Costs of £800,000 are incurred by Tower Co and relief is claimed at the SME rate.

Analysis

As an SME entitled to claim within *Ch 2*, Tower Co will be able to claim relief for relevant costs incurred upon both subcontractors and externally provided workers. Whilst the subcontractors need not be based in the UK, the restrictions and requirements relating to the subcontractor costs permissible in the claim will need to be met.

Had Tower Co been a large company or been performing subcontracted R&D on behalf of Crane Co no relief for subcontracting costs would be available unless these were individuals or partnerships of individuals who performed the work directly.

SOFTWARE AND COMPUTER SERVICES

9.5   ICT and telecommunications industries are so fast moving that there is an almost perpetual flow of worldwide R&D. Technological uncertainty is so fundamental to the business services sector, and failure so widely publicised, that there is a constantly unpredictable environment for both hardware and software companies.

This partly derives from the concentration of expertise and skilled excellence centres in the US and Asia, leaving the copycat technologists in a state of perpetual darkness and catch-up.

However, there are an equal number of ICT companies using completely routine methodologies for copycat solutions to simply add functionality to established technologies with little or no advancement or even uncertainty that would not be deducible by peer-to-peer discussions.

These types of companies often highlight the uniqueness or added functionality of their innovative product but there is little, if any, substance to regard such commercial innovation as activity within the tax definition of R&D. As an active example of this issue, HMRC material refers to website development as an example of copycat R&D with little evidence of technical advance. The company is simply 'using' science or technology, rather than furthering the understanding of technological complexities within it. This is not an activity that can be regarded as R&D for tax purposes (see **3.2**).

Example 9.3 – BE Studios Ltd v Smith & Williamson Ltd

Establishing the R&D project

> 'Management believe that the evolution in the technologies of interactive platforms heralds the beginning of another dramatic (IT) revolution.'

(*BE Studios Ltd v Smith & Williamson Ltd* [2005] EWHC 1506 (Ch))

When the directors of BE Studios Ltd explained the background of their industry and its highly innovative nature, only very informed advisers would discount the possibility of an R&D claim. Indeed the company was so convinced that this implied a competent R&D relief, that they sued their tax advisers for the absence of claims and specific R&D advice.

Even where a company is on the 'ground floor' of a technological revolution, an R&D claim may fail if project documentation is insufficient. When providing evidence of the carrying on of R&D activity, the case of *BE Studios Ltd v Smith & Williamson Ltd* is a salutary one, showing the onus upon the company to demonstrate the existence of a project and its relevant boundaries.

The case highlights the common 'misconception' that presence, even at its very inception, within a high-tech environment is not sufficient to justify a claim to tax relief. It is rarely useful to highlight the complexities and high-tech environment in which the company operates. Neither is it sufficient to be 'one of the first companies to' without a defined project aimed at the resolution of specific technical uncertainties.

For a claim to tax relief to be valid, the project and its technical uncertainties must be understood and apparent as a first step to establishing qualifying R&D costs.

Many R&D software claims are similarly rejected by HMRC on the basis that the work simply adds functionality or enhances user experience in already defined technology. But, and almost by contradiction, strong R&D activity can exist within established technologies, particularly where legacy systems are involved.

For example, many activities involving bona fide system certainty engineering in established technical fields are within the BIS definitions of an 'advance in technological capability' despite the established nature of the environment. This can be shown in the following example.

Example 9.4 – Larger tech company (LTC): system certainty projects

LTC is responsible for the integrity, security and accuracy of Big Bank's (BB's) IT data. BB runs many powerful computers on mainly legacy systems and LTC has an annual cost of £1.5 million on IT personnel deployed on the project.

BB has its own software packages which have been adapted over a number of years and it is responsible for its own hardware equipment.

LTC wishes to make a claim for R&D relief upon the annual costs of £1.5 million so far as they relate to this technical work.

Analysis

The nature of the R&D activity is unclear. Whilst LTC is not engaged upon either software or hardware development, it has responsibility for the resolution of a significant amount of technological uncertainty relevant to BB's legacy IT system. This activity is 'relevant' to its trade as an IT services provider.

The areas of uncertainty probably focus upon platform and architecture or 'system' certainty under the key headings in the contract it has with BB.

Provided economic risk and responsibility can be established by LTC, it may be able to demonstrate a valid R&D project if supported by the facts. If both companies are 'large', it may still be feasible for LTC to act as a subcontractor to BB, as it is a large company: the scheme recognises the costs of large company to large company activity as eligible for relief. The relief available to LTC would then be limited to the costs eligible within the large scheme, ie primarily the costs of staffing and externally provided workers, rather than subcontractors.

R&D funding – Software and hardware development

9.6 Statistics published by the National Audit Office show the growth in R&D business funding for tech firms. There is a good awareness of the Enterprise Investment Scheme (EIS) incentives in the sector. 'Crowd funding' is common within the industry and a number of grant-based initiatives are taken up from the Technology Strategy Board.

But start-up technology companies will often have a significant 'no income' lead into commercialisation of R&D activity. Pre-income R&D tax credit relief can be particularly useful here.

197

Example 9.5 – Start-up expenditure – deemed trading loss – R&D tax credits

New App Co (NAC) is investing significantly in the development of pioneering algorithms and application programming interfaces (APIs) breaking new grounds in an emerging branch of computer science. Whilst many elements of application (App) design are generic and involve little deducible technical uncertainty, this company's work has extended technological knowledge and is not readily deducible to the competent professional.

NAC has raised two tranches of VCT and EIS capital since 2010 and is pre-income. It has developer salary costs of £400,000 and is preparing its first accounts to 31 December 2012.

Analysis

NAC is a typical SME tech start-up company and may take advantage of the pre-trading tax credit by surrendering its losses in its first accounting period in exchange for a repayable tax credit.

NAC is probably aware of the SMART grant funding schemes but has been fortunate enough to attract first-tier funding, which will not be regarded as a 'subsidy'. In the future NAC may be able to consider commercialisation of the App through e-sector marketing agencies but it is unlikely to access hardware contracts with key players until its technology is well established.

NAC is a going concern and will be able to claim a tax credit in its first accounting period on £400,000 without the PAYE cap that existed for accounting periods prior to April 2012 being an issue.

The potential tax credit will be based upon 11% of the lower of the R&D expenditure as enhanced or the adjusted tax loss shown in the first accounts.

If NAC's first accounting period shows an adjusted loss of £900,000, it might obtain a tax credit repayment of 11% of that amount upon a claim being filed.

Investments from institutional investors, business angels or EIS stakeholders are not regarded as 'subsidies' for the purposes of the relief.

Software and telecom industries: employee incentivisation

9.7   Start-up tech companies frequently find it difficult to recruit and incentivise key technical employees. As a bare minimum, an experienced developer with sufficient skills to lead an R&D programme will require a substantial base salary in addition to share-based incentives.

Traditional EMI incentives are routine in the industry and have no impact on the availability of R&D tax relief. But non-emolument-based remuneration does not attract R&D relief.

The position is unlikely to change but there has been a useful development in the tax breaks for key tech employees. From 1 September 2013, new 'employee status' exemptions from capital gains tax now mean that the first £50,000 of employee share ownership is exempt from charge. The £50,000 is valued at the time of the initial award and although subject to a 'material interest' test and other conditions is very likely to provide further traction for share incentivisation. The rules avoid the cumbersome applications and HMRC liaison attached to EMI awards.

Tech Co: grant funding or tax relief?

Continuing the discussion in **Example 9.5** above, NAC may have been made aware of UK or EU grant funding for the technology it is developing. Had it claimed a grant that would be regarded as 'State Aid'; this may deny any tax relief upon the project costs. The HMRC viewpoint is well set out at **Chapter 7** above, and obtaining any State Aid funding will be fatal to a future tax relief claim.

Industry summary

ICT/software/hardware – activity likely to be regarded as R&D

- Developing the first version of a software product or hardware prototype
- Developing inferior, less complex or cheaper versions of new software or hardware products
- Development of new search engine methodologies
- Development/exploitation of new semantic programming languages
- Development of new hardware technologies or operating systems
- Development of system integration methodology/architecture beyond routine solution fixing
- Developing new malware and security encryption techniques
- Developing interaction of software and/or hardware methodologies beyond knowledge deducible in the industry at large
- Exploitation and development of new algorithms or APIs beyond knowledge deducible in the field at large
- New and pioneering visual/data exchange or integration

Activity unlikely to be regarded as R&D

- Capital expenditure*
- App development by way of routine methodology
- Added user functionality, visual displays
- Extending routine data retrieval or display
- System maintenance or routine protection
- Routine bug fixing or routine system integration patches/fixes
- Website creation and enhancement

*Where in-house ICT-based projects are undertaken HMRC frequently explore the possibility of the expenditure being regarded as capital. The viewpoint is well set out at CIRD81700 and will need to be considered for tax relief purposes.

PHARMACEUTICALS, CHEMICALS AND BIOTECHNOLOGY

9.8   The sheer scale of pharmaceutical and chemical manufacturing R&D project work, together with gaps in the theoretical knowledge relating to each science, can make the boundaries of the company's R&D work hard to define.

For example, in the pharmaceutical sector, significant pre-clinical research activity will be a key phase of project work. The subsequent lead into commercialisation may then cross over several parallel R&D projects. For example, very stringent guidelines are produced by the World Health Organisation upon the transfer of pharmaceutical research and technology into commercial production. The performance and behaviour of starting materials and excipients will be unknown. Similarly the active pharmaceutical ingredients may be unpredictable until well into the productive and packaging processes, and across many of the supply chain logistics. Finished pharmaceutical product information will need to have rigorously tested the integrity of each stage through 'assays' and replication tests. In turn, these phases will be denoted against acceptable testing and performance criteria.

Clinical trials are common in the pharmaceutical industries. Two practical issues can arise in this situation, which are shown in the following examples.

Example 9.6 – Testing as 'relevant' R&D: group companies

New Drug Co (NDC) develops a cheaper version of a coagulant drug after significant pre-clinical research into alternative synthetic ingredients. It asks its sister company (Sister Co) to undertake clinical trials up to 2016.

Analysis

(1)   The start and end point of the R&D activity frequently reappears as an issue for pharmaceutical and similar companies. R&D might take place at any of the key discovery/research, pre-clinical or clinical stages in bringing new products into commercial production. NDC will need to document the timeline for technical uncertainty during the course of the clinical trial and its response to the findings, to establish whether an 'end' point was reached and when, or if an extension to the project's uncertainties is evident.

(2)   After commercial production is well established, it is possible that advancing into new commercial markets with different health regulations, or alterations to existing regulations, may lead to fresh technical uncertainty, restarting R&D activity.

(3)   HMRC's published viewpoint upon coincidental progress in R&D projects is that 'Eureka' activity is not eligible for relief. R&D must be conducted within an exploratory environment.

(4)   HMRC relax the 'relevant' R&D test in group situations. Whilst the testing undertaken by Sister Co is not R&D by reference to the trade of that company alone, because of the relaxation in the rules of relevant R&D in group situations, a view of the activity of the parties as a whole can be taken to consider the overall relevance of the R&D.

Continuing the example, suppose the testing company were unconnected to NDC. It is clear from the analysis that Sister Co, whilst operating in a highly technical field, faces few technical uncertainties that could be regarded as R&D in its own work. No R&D claim would be possible for costs incurred in testing and analysis of the new drug.

AUTOMOTIVE INDUSTRY AND AUTOMOTIVE PARTS

9.9   The automotive industry is an established 'leader' on the R&D Scoreboard – VW tops the EU leading R&D companies with an R&D spend of around €9.5 billion in 2012.

Many of the technical issues involved in R&D activity in manufacturing and engineering companies are played out in the automotive industry. For example, industry safety regulations around the design of new components and technologies are so demanding in the automotive industry that safety testing may represent up to 20% of the entire R&D project and may be conducted over a very significant time period.

Amounts spent upon middle and end product testing are so significant in the automotive industry that very significant amounts of tax relief may be denied where HMRC argue that testing costs relate to commercial and safety objectives rather than the resolution of technical uncertainties.

Example 9.7 – Industry regulation standards

Car Co has had a carbon replacement technology project ongoing for the past four years. It has reached an acceptable level of prototype. Industry regulations require the company to produce 1,000 trial cars before commercial production may begin. Car Co incurs labour costs of £2.5 million per annum on the trial runs which it anticipates will be completed in 2016. It wishes to claim R&D relief on the basis that technical uncertainties re-emerged during the trial.

Analysis

Big Car Co would need to establish when the technical uncertainties emerged and their substantive nature. Similarly, the availability of a 'readily deducible' solution would make a claim difficult unless fundamental uncertainty is apparent.

If Big Car Co can establish that uncertainties requiring advances in technology or scientific knowledge correlated to the trial run, it may be able to identify the boundaries of a further R&D project or continuation of the carbon technology project.

The re-emergence of uncertainty is a common feature within prototype development in the automotive industry and many manufacturing and engineering activities. The extent to which this can be documented and recorded will clearly be helpful when R&D costs are considered.

MANUFACTURING COMPANIES

9.10   The regional government incentives for industrial manufacturing are well publicised. The UK R&D tax relief incentives were introduced in the first place, largely as a result of the UK's aim to account for a technology led growth in UK GDP.

Less well publicised has been the growth in technical product development and technological advances in consumer led manufacturing. For example, UK food and drinks manufacturers now account for an increasing number of claims to R&D tax relief in 2012.

Case study: food and drinks industry

The BIS Guidelines apply equally to all branches of science and technology. Uncertainty about the behaviour of many chemical ingredients and processes in food and drinks production is just as relevant as R&D into 'pure' chemical and agrichemical manufacturing processes.

Similarly, the BIS Guidelines apply equally to all branches of science and technology irrespective of the scale of activity involved.

Example 9.8 – Food/drink manufacturer – product development R&D

Small Gourmet Co (SGC) has invested £300,000 in bringing a gluten-free beer to market. It has used a food chemist and its production managers over an 18-month period and used up around £50,000 in consumables used in trial pre-production.

SGC wishes to claim R&D relief on £300,000 for the past two years.

Analysis

The production methods for gluten-free products are well known to the industry at large. But the knowledge has been gained by large scale food and drinks manufacturers rather than in a 'micro' climate. Not only are these likely to be highly secretive but chemical processes within bacterial and allergen complexes will be completely different in small batches of raw ingredients to large ones.

To surmount the requirements of para 6, the BIS Guidelines require the advance in capability to go beyond simply extending the company's own knowledge. Paragraph 21 suggests the company must be able to demonstrate the inadequacy of knowledge on the processes:

- '• several companies are working at the cutting edge in the same field, and are doing similar work independently; or

- • work has already been done but this is not known in general because it is a trade secret, and another company repeats the work; or

- • it is known that a particular advance in science or technology has been achieved, but the details of how are not readily available.'

(BIS Guidelines, para 21)

Provided SGC can demonstrate the technical need for the project work, an R&D claim should be considered. The cost of salaries and particularly the materials used during the course of establishing technical 'certainty' would be relievable as 'consumables' (*CTA 2009, ss 1125, 1126*).

Precision manufacturing

R&D in precision industries: research development allowances

9.11 Precision manufacturing often requires significant investment in new capital equipment. This forms a critical part of new product development and technological processes. Research development allowances (RDAs) provide 100% relief for plant and equipment purchased for use in R&D projects.

The definition of R&D follows those for corporation tax reliefs (*Income Tax Act 2007,s 1006*). Detailed legislation can be found at *Capital Allowances Act 2001, ss 439–440*. RDA is useful in R&D scenarios where the annual investment allowance is already used up, although no double allowance as revenue expenditure is possible. Clearly the allowance is not intended for plant and equipment used for ordinary production. Case law in *Gaspet Ltd v Elliss* (1987) 60 TC 91 has also established that only where the research or development activity relates directly to the company's trade is an allowance possible. The subsequent rental of equipment to third parties would compromise this.

Case study: UK printing industry

9.12 R&D activity within the printing industry can be costly and complex. As with most 'practical' R&D in industry, significant amounts may be spent upon prototype and pre-production processes to ensure high levels of product quality and precision.

The industry highlights the importance of RDAs as a useful supplement to conventional capital allowances in manufacturing and process-based companies.

Example 9.9 – Precision manufacturing company claiming RDA

Practical Printing Co is a major printing company. It has invested in many improvements in production processes for a number of years. Lately, the printing industry at large has become technology led, partly in response to the growing interaction of IT and hardware equipment.

Being a significant 'leader' in the market, the company has invested in new machinery costing £1.8 million, which is so 'high-tech' it is one of only two companies in the UK to have done so. Significant technical uncertainty exists as to how the machinery will be used for currently unexplored but emerging technology such as 3D printing and the plant is an integral part of the company's R&D project into those uncertainties.

Analysis

The plant is not part of the company's ordinary production equipment. It has purchased the equipment to move into new products and technologies and to revolutionise a number of the production processes currently in use in its factories.

The equipment is clearly being purchased for use in the printing company's trade and to further development/research activity being undertaken by that company which is relevant to the business activity. Although the development work will enable the company to extend its trade and move into new commercial markets, it should be possible to regard the whole cost of the equipment as relevant to the original rather than a new trade.

The extent to which the machinery is used in ordinary non-R&D work will need to be established. Once this is done, the company will be able to claim 100% capital allowances upon the cost of the equipment as RDAs.

Complex rules may apply to any subsequent disposal, dealt with in the HMRC Capital Allowances manual at CA64000. Ceasing to use machinery in R&D activity is not regarded as a disposal event. If relevant, the company can also disregard RDAs, and indeed any other patent allowances under *CAA 2001, Pts 6* and *8* when calculating routine deductions for the purposes of the Patent Box.

EMERGING UK TECHNOLOGIES

9.13   As established R&D sectors such as IT and pharmaceuticals gain in technical momentum and diversity, so too a number of emerging technologies have significant direct R&D funding incentivisation earmarked by both EU bodies such as Horizon 2020 and the UK's Technology Strategy Board. This trend is also a response for the EU/UK to keep up with Asian/US technological advances.

Future cities

9.14   The planning, design and management of future cities is an important area of EU sustainable development, with significant funding for projects earmarked to 2020. For example, technical developments within carbon technologies, engineering and construction will fall under the umbrella of incentives targeted towards sustainable urban growth. Smart cities and the built environment may emerge as a key R&D sector as the OECD anticipate an urban population of 75% by 2050.

Traditional industries

9.15   Finally, a number of traditional UK industries have begun to feature on the R&D Scoreboard. This includes sectors as steeped in crafting tradition as fishing, agriculture, high quality consumer goods and food production.

As demand for British-made quality goods accelerates, particularly in the East, these traditional industries have had to rise to the demand for much larger scale production methods and much more enhanced quality assurances and may become more significant R&D investors in the future.

Chapter 10

Creative industry tax reliefs

Contents

SIGNPOSTS

- **Investment in the creative sectors** – A range of tax incentives were introduced by the 2012 Budget to encourage investment in the creative sectors. Many companies in the creative sectors already claim R&D tax relief (RDTR) and will welcome the simpler definitions the creative reliefs offer (see **10.1**).

- **Delay in legislation** – A lengthy delay followed the announcements for Video Games Tax Relief (VGTR) as relief was blocked by the European Commission's review which was announced in April 2013. The review focused upon the cultural equivalence of games to film and was successfully completed on 27 March 2014. During the course of the EC review, detailed legislation was drafted. This subsequently became law (*FA 2013, s 36*) for expenditure incurred by eligible companies upon eligible games on or after 1 April 2014 (see **10.1, 10.2**).

- **Scope of creative sector reliefs** – The creative sector reliefs do not replace RDTR for this sector but it is not possible to claim both reliefs upon the same expenditure. The reliefs are based upon an enhanced deduction and can provide a tax credit repayment to loss making companies (see **10.2–10.16**).

- **Rates of relief** – Production companies in high-end television or animation and in the future, video games development can claim the 'super deduction'. This has been introduced as 80% of eligible expenditure. The rate of enhancement has been set at 100% for expenditure incurred on or after 1 April 2013. A repayable credit is available for loss making companies. The rate has been set at 25% for FY 2013 (see **10.17**).

- **British cultural test** – A 'British cultural test' underlines each of the reliefs. The company will need to obtain certification that the production reaches a minimum number of qualitative cultural aspects in its work. The certificate accompanies all claims to tax relief (see **10.21**).

- **Creative Sector Unit** – HMRC have established a 'Creative Sector Unit' to administer the reliefs. This is supported by the successful Film Tax Relief Unit and works alongside the mainstream R&D specialists (see **10.27**).

- **Legislation** – Detailed legislation applies to both the activity and eligible expenditure within the scope of the reliefs. This is set out at *CTA 2009, Pt 15A* (see **10.7**).

- **Basis of the schemes** – Each of the schemes is based upon the successful film tax relief model, bringing the UK corporation tax reliefs for the creative sector to four and aligning the UK's creative industries with the tax incentives on offer in the US and EEA (see **10.5**).

INTRODUCTION

10.1   The 2012 Budget announced the introduction of a series of 'creative sector tax reliefs'. Three new reliefs were announced, intended to help support technological innovation in these specific industries. The reliefs are aligned to the objective to the UK's economic growth models.

The schemes are modelled on the successful film tax relief. They relate to expenditure incurred on or after 1 April 2013 by eligible UK companies. With the exception of video games development relief (VGR) which is subject to EC State Aid approval. Creative companies can apply for industry specific corporation tax relief:

- high-end television tax relief;

- animation production tax relief;

- video games development tax relief (VGR);

- film tax relief (FTR).

The reliefs do not replace R&D tax relief but act as an alternative. Many of the conditions of the creative relief will assist the narrow band of production companies currently within the R&D framework to obtain relief more quickly. The reliefs are not dependent upon an annual accounting period and provide much clearer and simpler guidelines on eligible expenditure and production costs.

As with R&D tax reliefs, the schemes are only available to UK companies falling within the charge to corporation tax. The relief provides a 'super deduction' based upon 'core expenditure' production costs provided that at least 25% of these costs relate to UK expenditure. As with the SME R&D scheme, the resultant loss can be surrendered for a 25% repayable tax credit or relieved against profits of the same trade.

The reliefs contain a number of key definitions established by the film tax relief, which production companies will meet for the first time. For example, television tax relief is based upon the company having 'eligible' programmes, defined in term by average 'core expenditure' per hour of slot length. Specific productions such as advertisements, news, current affairs and discussion programmes etc. are not be included in the relief.

The Chapter is split into four parts outlining the key opportunities in each of the reliefs. Some of the conditions for TV and animation reliefs overlap. In particular, 'television production relief' (TVPR) is aimed at both companies engaged in the production of qualifying 'high end' television programmes as well as companies engaged in animation productions. All the creative reliefs require certification as having 'culturally British' content. The rules for the TVPR and animation reliefs have been written into *CTA 2009, Pt 15A*. The certification rules for VGR will be set by Statutory Instrument once State Aid is approved.

10.2 *Creative industry tax reliefs*

The choice of relief is potentially complex. It is feasible that the activities of video games developers, in particular, may continue to qualify under one of the R&D schemes. One of the benefits of retaining R&D relief is the significant capital allowances scheme attached to R&D.

The absence of territorial limits for R&D relief is also relevant. The creative industry reliefs are based on minimum UK cost requirements and are territorially driven. The certification process is similarly driven by UK considerations.

BACKGROUND – WHAT IS THE CREATIVE SECTOR?

10.2   In his Budget speech of 2012, George Osborne announced the Government's commitment to the creative sector and the intention to make the tax reliefs available 'the best in the world'. This followed lengthy lobbying and consultation with representatives from the entertainment and media industries.

The reliefs now available target three key activities and provide enhanced corporation tax deductions for UK companies engaged upon:

● television production;

● animation production; and

● video games development.

The tax breaks were outlined in a Ministerial Statement published in February 2013, by Maria Miller, Minister for the Department of Culture, Media and Sport. She explained that the UK's creative industries are worth around £36 billion per year, employ at least 1.5 million people in the UK and account for 10% of the UK's export trade. She also highlighted the ability of the UK's media industry to symbolise an open and free society. Fearing the migration of the creative sector to favourable tax regimes such as Canada and Japan, the UK announced its own reliefs.

The video games industry has long been a proponent of a creative industry relief: unsurprising as it is estimated that at least 30 million people in the UK now watch some type of game-related media.

10.3   There are around 27 different 'cultural tax credit' schemes in OECD countries. Several EEA states, the US and Canada subsidise television and animation productions by as much as 40% of the production budget. Reform to the UK tax regime was long overdue. The animation production industry in particular, contains a large proportion of loss making companies unable to access any type of relief. A study of the UK animation industry, conducted in 2009, found up to 40% of the 620 or so UK companies in the sector were loss making. Without an equal international playing field for tax credit relief, the industry faced a very difficult future in the UK.

10.4 At the same time, the Government has been part of an economic strategy dedicated towards assisting the 'digital economy'. The *Digital Economy Act 2010* set the scene for a number of stimuli, with further benchmark publications such as Professor Ian Hargreaves' 'Digital Opportunity – a review of intellectual property and growth', which was published in May 2011. This provided ten key recommendations aimed at assisting innovators and investors in new technologies choosing to register patents and protect intellectual property. The creative industries were seen as being important contributors into the digital innovation drive.

10.5 The legislation for the creative sector largely mirrors the existing FTR model. This has been a successful relief with a high success rate for claim processing and a high filing rate by companies eligible to claim the relief, unlike the R&D schemes. HMRC have estimated that FTR has supported £5.5 billion of investment into 825 British films since its introduction in January 2007.

ELIGIBLE COMPANIES

10.6 Only companies liable to UK corporation tax can claim creative industry tax reliefs, which will include corporate members of LLPs but not partnerships or unincorporated enterprises.

Joint ventures: TVPR recognises the importance of joint ventures engaged in TV production. The high cost nature of the industry means that joint ventures are often involved in creative sector activities. An election is possible where one company is not as 'directly involved' as another in this situation to switch the relief favourably (*CTA 2009, s 1216AE*).

The legislation also permits group management and intercompany charges to fall within the definitions of qualifying core and/or UK expenditure. This is in contrast to the approach established by *Gripple Ltd v HMRC* [2010] EWHC 1609 (Ch) for R&D purposes where no purposive reliefs are available for expenditure based upon management or intercompany charges.

Subject to the joint venture exceptions, the relief then depends upon the extent to which the company is *directly* involved in the development of specific film or animation productions or video games material. The company does not necessarily need to own the production but the responsibility for costs is a pre-requirement. These conditions are set out in detail at *CTA 2009, Pts 15A* and *15B*.

The entity will then need to follow the special computational rules in *CTA 2009, Pts 15A, 15B* and *16* which require that a 'separate trade' is established.

Finally, the company will need to comply with the specific rules upon eligible expenditure and certify that this meets the 'culturally British' certification requirement.

10.7 *Creative industry tax reliefs*

Companies operating within the new creative industry reliefs will therefore face three preconditions. The claimant will be:

● an eligible entity liable to UK corporation tax;

● preparing accounts and tax computations according to the specific tax rules of the scheme;

● complying with the specific rules of the relief claimed concerning eligible expenditure, eligible production costs and the British Cultural test.

LEGISLATION

Television and animation production companies – legislation finder

10.7   The reliefs take effect for accounting periods ending on or after 1 April 2013. *Finance Act 2013, Sch. 16* introduced *Pt 15A* into *CTA 2009* which details the conditions of the relief and the special tax computational rules the company must follow.

The legislation at *CTA 2009, Pt 15A* can be summarised as follows:

Chapter 1

An overview and introduction to the legislation, definition of key terms and eligible company requirement.

Chapter 2

● Taxation of the activities of a television/animation production company; concept of separate trade.

● Explanation of profit/loss calculations.

Chapter 3

Detailed tax relief provisions, and further definitions.

Chapter 4

Loss provisions, interim repayment calculations.

Chapter 5

● Provisional relief claims and repayments, interim accounting periods.

- Certification process.
- Avoidance provisions.

Video games development tax relief: legislation finder

10.8 The framework for VGR tax relief was subject to delay. The proposed scheme was introduced by *FA 2013, Schs 17* and *18* and is contained in *ICTA 2009, Pt 15B.*The conditions of the relief and the special tax computational rules for the separate trade apply in a similar way to TVPTR.

The core requirements of the legislation at *CTA 2009, Pt 15B* can be found at:

Chapter 1

Introduction and overview of the relief, interpretation and definitions.

Chapter 2

Identification of a separate trade; calculation of profits and losses of the video game trade.

Chapter 3

Outline and availability of video games tax relief.

Core expenditure at least 25% UK expenditure.

Certification as British video game through Statutory Instrument.

Video game tax credit – loss making companies.

Chapter 4

Further provisions for loss making companies.

Chapter 5

Provisional relief claims; avoidance provision.

TV PRODUCTION TAX RELIEF

10.9 The relief has a number of other titles, including 'high-end TV tax credits' and 'Television tax credits'. Animation production companies are included in the relief, almost as if they were television companies.

10.10 *Creative industry tax reliefs*

TV production tax relief (TPTR) works by providing an enhanced deduction of 80% to qualifying expenditure. This can be used to reduce corporation tax or where a surrenderable loss arises, the company can claim a repayable tax credit subject to various conditions.

Some of the special terms in the relief framework will be new to media companies approaching the relief for the first time. Although the relief works in a similar way to the FTR, there are key differences. The company will need to consider the following steps:

A   Establishing the company is a qualifying one.

B   Identifying the 'relevant programme'.

C   Identifying eligible 'core' expenditure arising in the UK.

D   Preparing a 'separate trade' computation for each production.

E   Compliance with the British Cultural Certification process.

Within this framework, a number of detailed conditions apply, and are outlined as follows:

A.   What is a qualifying company?

Responsibility for core activity and intention to broadcast (CTA 2009, s 1216AE)

10.10   The company must be able to demonstrate key management and risk engagement for the production including:

- being responsible for pre-production, principal photography, post-production and delivery of the relevant programme;

- directly negotiating pay for rights, contracts and goods and services in relation to the relevant programme; and

- being actively engaged in the production, planning and decision-making during the pre-production, principal photography and post-production.

B.   What is a qualifying programme?

'The relevant programme'

10.11   A 'relevant' programme must meet four key conditions, which are set out at *CTA 2009, Pt 15A, ss 1216A–1216D*. These define the TV programme's type, length and core expenditure. A series is regarded as one programme.

Condition A and B: Programme type – the programme must be either a drama, documentary or animation production. This will include comedy but exclude programmes within Condition B, such as advertisements, live productions and quiz shows, training programmes, current affairs and news broadcasts.

Condition C: Programme length – the relevant programme must be commissioned to last at least 30 minutes. This permits series of programmes to be 'averaged' as one programme.

Condition D: Core expenditure – this covers expenditure on pre-production and post-production costs and principal photography. The average core expenditure per hour of programme time must be a minimum of £1 million. It is anticipated that these costs will include group recharges and relevant overheads. This limit does not apply to animation productions.

The availability of tax relief depends upon the relevant programme being:

- intended for broadcast to the general public, which includes the internet;

- certified as a British programme* under the Cultural test which is implemented by the BFI; and

- at least 25% of the relevant programme 'core' expenditure** must be UK expenditure.

The criteria are evaluated at the time that production is planned ('intended'), rather than upon the 'end' result.

*As an alternative to the certification as a British programme, the programme can be a qualifying co-production. This covers programmes which are co-produced under a relevant co-production treaty. Currently, the UK has treaties for TV programmes with Australia, Canada, France, Israel, New Zealand, and the occupied Palestinian Territories.

**'Core expenditure' is expenditure on pre-production, principal photography and post-production of the programme. Certain development costs such as distribution and finance, are not core expenditure and will not attract the tax relief.

C. Which costs qualify?

10.12   The programme must identify two separate cost heads – 'total' production expenditure and 'core' production expenditure (*CTA 2009, s 1216AG*):

- *Production expenditure:* meaning all production costs relevant to the programme in its widest sense.

- *Core expenditure:* meaning pre-production, principal photography and post production costs of the programme. Certain development, distribution and finance costs will not attract tax relief. The Government conceded at the final stages of the Bill that production fees will qualify towards the £1 million threshold provided they are less than 10% of the pre-production budget to avoid abuse.

For animation companies, post-release costs such as de-bugging and relevant quality assurance work will qualify, but not service maintenance costs.

Tax relief is only available for 'core' expenditure, at least 25% of which must be UK core expenditure. Pre-production costs are eligible for relief, once the end product is defined and the programme 'intended' for broadcast and the certification process is passed.

The concept of having goods and services 'consumed in the UK' is fraught with difficulties and can be best understood by an example:

Example 10.1 – Core UK expenditure

Beckham Boy is a relevant 'British' programme documentary following the thrills and spills of a boys' football team on their way to the top of the league from Hackney marshes. A number of brave Californians are recruited by BBTV Co to carry out the principal photography, and spend ten months on location invoicing the company $30,000 per month.

Analysis

BBTV is an eligible company and is engaged upon the production of a relevant programme. The expenditure is core UK expenditure because it is 'consumed' in the UK. The fact that non-UK personnel are located in the UK for the photography is irrelevant as the photography takes place and is paid for here. The expenditure will count towards the UK expenditure pot.

Co-productions

To establish the 25% test in a co-production, all of the entities' costs attributable to the UK will be *pooled*, although not all of the parties will qualify for relief.

D.   Computation of the relief – separate trade

10.13   The company's activities in relation to a programme are treated as if they are a separate trade *(CTA 2009, s 1216A)*.The trade is deemed to commence when pre-production commences, or if earlier, when any income is received by the company *(s 1216B)*.

The profits or losses of the trade are calculated by deducing costs incurred to date from the proportion of estimated production income. This is treated as 'earned' at the end of the relevant period and costs are offset to the extent that they have not previously been brought into account and relieved. Expenditure unpaid within four months of the accounting period is ignored. Accounting periods do not need to be annual, which provides the ability for credits to be repaid at more frequent intervals.

All expenditure relates to costs incurred on or after 1 April 2013.

Aggregating income

10.14   The tax computation differs from 'ordinary' tax computations and is based upon a formula, C/T × I, where C represents total costs incurred to date, T represents the total programme costs and I represents the estimated total income from the programme including royalties, payments for rights and merchandise etc. (*CTA 2009, ss 1216BA, 1216BB*).

The benefit of this approach is that it greatly simplifies the extraction of costs for the relevant programme and provides a clear formula for cost collection in comparison to the R&D relief scheme which is based upon the subjective opinion of 'when' technical work begins and ends.

Income recognition/expense recognition

10.15   The calculation of the profits or losses of the 'separate programme trade' are described at *s 1216BB*. It is important to note that there is a concept of 'estimated total income' for the relevant production. Relief focuses upon expenditure incurred and previously accounted for in previous accounting periods. From this it is clear to see that the structure of the relief is to provide an interim tax credit facility based upon cumulative anticipated total income and expenditure. This is formulated at *s 1216BA*.

What is income?

10.16   Income from the relevant programme includes all receipts by the company which are relevant to the 'making or exploitation' of the programme or its rights and merchandise and so on. Capital receipts are expressly regarded as being revenue in nature (*CTA 2009, s 1216BB*).

Costs are taken to be incurred when they are capable of being regarded in a state of completion and transferred to work in progress. Creditor expenditure must document an unconditional payment obligation to be included as relevant costs. Payments in advance are ignored until the work is carried out.

Pre-trading expenditure is recognised in the familiar way. To recap, this will be included as expenditure for the production company as if it was incurred on the first day that trading begins. Where alternative tax reliefs have been claimed the company is required to amend its corporation tax return accordingly (*s 1216BE*).

Relief benefit – calculation of the relief

10.17 Assuming eligibility, TVPR enables the company to claim an additional corporation tax deduction for qualifying expenditure incurred upon the relevant programme (*s 1216CF*).

The amount of the deduction is the lesser of:

• UK expenditure; or

• 80% of total qualifying expenditure.

This means that the additional deduction and payable credit are to be calculated on the UK core expenditure up to a maximum of 80% of the total core expenditure by the TV production company. The additional deduction is 100% of qualifying core expenditure and the payable tax credit is 25% of losses surrendered.

This means that the maximum tax credit can be 25% of UK core expenditure but restricted to 80% of total core expenditure. So if 80% or more of the total core expenditure is incurred in the UK, the payable tax credit will be 20% (25% of 80%) of the total core expenditure. This is in line with the current rules for the film tax credit.

Loss making companies

10.18 The television tax credit may be surrendered for a repayable credit. The legislation permits repayments to be made for a provisional amount if there are queries on the overall amount of relief claimed. This mirrors the R&D schemes where HMRC raise technical enquiries on part of the relief claim. The company is still entitled to an amount of repayment that is 'just and reasonable' (*s 1216CJ(3)*).

The repayable credit is net of any outstanding arrears of the company for HMRC duties such as outstanding corporation tax, PAYE, National Insurance or 'visiting performer' levies under *ITA 2007, s 966 (CTA 2009, s 1216CJ(4))*.

Besides the usual carry forward provision, there is the ability to utilise losses in two further ways (*CTA 2009, Pt 15A, Ch 4*):

• group relief surrender; and/or

• terminal loss relief – a television production will cease once the production is suitable for public viewing.

E. Certification – the cultural test

10.19 Certification as a British programme involves either passing the appropriate 'cultural test', or qualifying under a co-production treaty where production is carried on partially abroad. The certification process is dealt with by the British Film Institute (BFI) on behalf of the Department for Culture, Media and Sport. The BFI is a charitable body which acts to assist and process certification applications from potential claimants of the television and animation reliefs.

The certification process is discussed further at **10.22** below.

ANIMATION PRODUCTION RELIEF

10.20   As with TVPR, a company engaged in the production of qualifying animated productions can claim an additional deduction in computing their taxable profits. A 20% tax credit surrender relief is similarly available for loss making companies.

An animation programme is defined in one of two ways as:

- a programme that is 'animation' (in the ordinary meaning of the word);

- a programme that is a drama or documentary but contains at least 51% animation.

The animation production must meet the eligible programme and core expenditure requirements outlined in the TVPR legislation, ie:

- the conditions relating to programme content and broadcast;

- the cultural test;

- the computation of costs and tax computations.

'Animation' has its ordinary meaning. Mixed content production is permissible; the test is that 51% of the programme's production costs must represent animation activity. Animation produced for advertisements, training material, news and documentaries is excluded.

There is no budget minimum for the animation production budget core expenditure test. 'Core expenditure' follows the rules for TVPR above and the established FTR rules.

The relief applies for accounting periods ending on or after 1 April 2013.

THE CULTURAL TEST

The 'culturally British' production test

10.21   A TV or animation programme must be certified as a 'British programme' by the Secretary of State. The BFI administers this administrative process on behalf of the Department for Culture, Media and Sport at the end of 2012. This is known as the 'cultural test' and mirrors the FTR certification process. An interim or final certificate is available. The contact details for the BFI are: http://www.bfi.org.uk/

Certification points

10.22   The test is based upon a points scoring system requiring a minimum of 16 points from a range of characteristics. These characteristics include the presence in the production of:

- British cultural content and contribution;

- British cultural hubs and the use of UK facilities;

- UK personnel across the range of production, casting and crew activities.

There are separate cultural tests for: (a) drama and documentaries; and (b) animation programmes, but both are substantially the same as the existing cultural test for films. Sixteen points will be required out of a possible 31 points in order to qualify as British. It is possible to score more than 16 points on these tests alone. To score under other parts of the test, an accountant's report may be required. No extra relief is possible for additional points scored.

Expansion of cultural content section to include EEA

10.23   The main difference to the film cultural test is the expansion of the 'cultural content' section to include the EEA, not just the UK. So points will be awarded for programmes:

(i)   set in the UK or another EEA state;

(ii)   with lead characters from the UK or another EEA state; and

(iii) depicting a British story or a story which relates to an EEA state.

There is no modification to the so-called 'cultural practitioners' test, which remains the same as the cultural test for films, so there is no additional flexibility to hire non-EEA key talent.

For animation productions, additional cultural points are available for 'British' voice-overs during production. The relevant cultural tests are set out at by way of Statutory Instrument – the *Cultural Test (Television Programmes) Regulations 2013 (SI 2013/1831)*.

VIDEO GAMES DEVELOPMENT TAX RELIEF

Relief for video games production

10.24   The industry successfully lobbied for a specific relief in 2010, only for the proposals to be dropped in the June 2010 Coalition Budget. The benefit of the relief is stated by its proponents to stimulate around 4,600 jobs in the UK and to encourage around £188 million of expenditure upon technical development.

The industry rightly found R&D tax relief obscure and, in practice, difficult to claim. Significant pressure from the gaming industry body, 'TIGA' and other industry representatives upheld the relief and the UK as a focus point for the industry's R&D. In their present form, the reliefs require both the company and the game to meet specific qualifying conditions. Once these conditions are met, the relief applies as an enhanced deduction or repayable tax credit for expenditure incurred on or after 1 April 2014.

Qualifying conditions

To qualify for relief, the video game must be intended for supply to the general public when the video game development activities begin. There is no specific definition of a 'video game', which takes on its ordinary meaning for tax purposes. However, a video game does not include:

- material produced for advertising or promotional purposes; or

- material produced for the purposes of gambling;

- games with extreme or pornographic content.

The Government has decided not to introduce a minimum spending threshold.

Qualifying companies – video game development

10.25   The relief applies in the same way that R&D tax reliefs do to companies within the scope of UK corporation tax. It does not apply to LLPs. In contrast to the TV reliefs, there is no 'co-production' recognition of the activity of companies resident elsewhere.

To claim VGR the company must show it has responsibility for:

- designing, producing and testing the video game;

- active engagement in planning and decision-making during the design, production and testing of the video game; and

- direct negotiation of contracts and payments for rights, goods and services in relation to the video game.

221

Legislation – key definitions

10.26 The draft legislation introducing VGR was contained in *FA 2013, Schs 17* and *18* and *CTA 2009, Pt 15B*. A number of requirements apply.

Core expenditure

Core expenditure is the starting point for the calculation. This is defined as meaning 'expenditure on designing, producing and testing the video game' (*ss 1217AC, 1217AD*). At least 25% of the total 'core expenditure' must be 'UK expenditure', ie 'expenditure on goods or services used or consumed in the UK'.

The following costs are excluded from being core expenditure:

- any expenditure incurred in designing the initial concept for the game;

- any expenditure incurred in debugging a completed game or carrying out any maintenance in connection with such a video game.

The relief recognises that games often do not have a single production run and release date, and that development continues after release – this will be allowable expenditure but pure maintenance will not.

There is currently no relief for speculative or abortive costs.

Minimum UK expenditure

The same minimum 25% of total core expenditure must be UK expenditure (*CTA 2009, s 1217*). This has the same 'goods or services used or consumed in the UK' meaning as the television/animation reliefs.

Singular trade

The video game development company is deemed to carry on a singular trade relating to the relevant video game.

Cultural test

To qualify for the reliefs, the game must pass a 'cultural test', similar in principle to the television and film tax credit schemes. The test focuses on four key questions:

- Is the video game made in the UK or another EEA state?

- Does the game feature the UK or another EEA state?

- Does the game promote the UK or another EEA state?

- Are the production personnel ordinarily resident in the UK or another EEA state?

As with the sister reliefs, at least 16 out of a possible 31 points must be obtained for accreditation.

Income and expense recognition

As with the television tax credit, a separate trade is established for each eligible production.

The income and expense recognition of the relevant game follows the television tax credit reliefs. Income includes all receipts, royalties, rights payments and profit sharing arrangements relevant to the game. Expenditure is recognised using the 'unconditional contract' principle discussed above, and must be represented by work in progress.

Capital expenditure and receipts are expressly regarded as being of a revenue nature, in similarity to the television and animation schemes (*CTA 2009, s 1217BC(3)*).

Video Game Cultural Test

VGR depends upon certification of the material as 'culturally British' (*CTA 2009, ss 1217CB–1217CD*). Applications lie to the Secretary of State and the qualifying conditions mirror, to some extent, those in the film and television certification progress.

Detailed steps have yet to be announced.

Regulations are to be made separately by Statutory Instrument.

Relief value

VGR is calculated as a super deduction for eligible expenditure. It can be given by either:

- a reduction in the company's corporation tax liability; or
- surrendered for a repayable tax credit at 25%.

The deduction or payable credit is calculated against UK core expenditure, up to a maximum of 80% of the total core expenditure.

Therefore a company will be able to claim a tax credit equal to 25% of the core expenditure that was spent in the UK (up to the cap of 80% of total core expenditure).

Once approved, the relief will be very useful for the video games industry. Previously companies had to struggle with the complexities of the R&D scheme and were often vulnerable to 'subcontracting' arguments from HMRC, restricting any tax relief to a maximum of 130% of the development budget.

Example 10.2 – VGR tax credit

V Co is a video games production company. It produces a video game which is commissioned. Income received from the commissioning publisher totals £200,000. The total expenditure incurred is £300,000 of which £200,000 is core expenditure on the commissioned game.

Total income	£200,000
Total expenditure	£300,000
Pre-relief loss	(£100,000)
Enhanceable expenditure	
80% × 200,000	£160,000
Additional deduction: 80% × 160,000	(126,000)
Post-tax relief profit/loss	(226,000)

Surrenderable loss:

● The post-tax relief trading loss of £226,000, and

● The enhanceable expenditure of £160,000.

Repayable tax credit: 25% × £160,000	£40,000
Loss c/f	(66,000)

HMRC CREATIVE INDUSTRIES UNIT

Claims procedure

10.27   Creative sector reliefs form part of the company's self-assessment and are subject to the same time limits (see **Chapter 6**).

The HMRC Unit responsible for the creative sector reliefs has been nominated as Manchester. The contact details are:

E-mail: randd.manchester@hmrc.gsi.gov.uk

Tel: 03000 510 795.

The Unit is responsible for processing claims and providing advice on the reliefs to companies and their representatives within these industries. The turnaround rate is targeted at processing or repaying 98% of claims within 28 days. The Unit is based alongside the FTR unit and the Manchester R&D Unit.

COMPARISON TO R&D RELIEF

10.28   The promising feature of the creative industry reliefs is that there seems to be more clarity about the eligible costs upon which relief may be claimed. In contrast to the tax definition of R&D reliefs, core expenditure is clearly defined and matches up to how costs are incurred in the industry.

For companies formerly within the R&D relief regime, the creative sector reliefs remove a number of difficulties such as:

- identifying the precise advances sought in technical work and matching these up to the relevant BIS Guideline;

- identifying baseline knowledge or meeting the 'hypothetical knowledge'/'readily deducible' test. This aligns the relief to what companies actually do, rather than a theoretical benchmark for what they could do;

- dissecting project activities into multiple categories of directly, indirectly or non-contributing activity;

- letting a company use shorter accounting periods for the relief credits;

- being able to account for the tax 'cost' of a production on a fair and reasonable basis, without the uncertainty of quarrels with HMRC as to the extent of tax relief made available.

The recognition of income and expenses for both television and video games production specifies when income should be recognised and when expenses are to be regarded as incurred. Capital expenditure and receipts are within the scope of the relief.

SSAP 13 – Accounting for research and development

(Issued December 1977; revised January 1989)

The provisions of this statement of standard accounting practice should be read in conjunction with the (Explanatory) Foreword to accounting standards and need not be applied to immaterial items.

PART 1 – EXPLANATORY NOTE

Basic concepts

1 The accounting policies to be followed in respect of research and development expenditure must have regard to the fundamental accounting concepts including the "accruals" concept by which revenue and costs are accrued, matched and dealt with in the period to which they relate and the "prudence" concept by which revenue and profits are not anticipated but are recognised only when realised in the form either of cash or of other assets the ultimate cash realisation of which can be established with reasonable certainty. It is a corollary of the prudence concept that expenditure should be written off in the period in which it arises unless its relationship to the revenue of a future period can be established with reasonable certainty.

The different types of research and development expenditure

2 The term "research and development" is currently used to cover a wide range of activities, including those in the services sector. The definitions of the different types of research and development used in this statement are based on those used by the Organisation for Economic Co-operation and Development for the purposes of collecting data world-wide.

3 Classification of expenditure is often dependent on the type of business and its organisation. However, it is generally possible to recognise three broad categories of activity, namely pure research, applied research and development. The definitions of the individual categories are set out in Part 2.

4 The dividing line between these categories of expenditure is often indistinct and particular expenditure may have characteristics of more than one category. This is especially so when new products or services are developed through research and development to production, when the activities may have characteristics of both development and production.

5 Research and development activity is distinguished from non-research activity by the presence or absence of an appreciable element of innovation. If the activity departs from routine and breaks new ground it should normally be included; if it follows an established pattern it should normally be excluded.

6 Examples of activities that would normally be included in research and development are:

(a) experimental, theoretical or other work aimed at the discovery of new knowledge, or the advancement of existing knowledge;

(b) searching for applications of that knowledge;

(c) formulation and design of possible applications for such work;

(d) testing in search for, or evaluation of, product, service or process alternatives;

(e) design, construction and testing of pre-production prototypes and models and development batches;

(f) design of products, services, processes or systems involving new technology or substantially improving those already produced or installed;

(g) construction and operation of pilot plants.

7 Examples of activities that would normally be excluded from research and development would include:

(a) testing analysis either of equipment or product for purposes of quality or quantity control;

(b) periodic alterations to existing products, services or processes even though these may represent some improvement;

(c) operational research not tied to a specific research and development activity;

(d) cost of corrective action in connection with break-downs during commercial production;

(e) legal and administrative work in connection with patent applications, records and litigation and the sale or licensing of patents;

(f)   activity, including design and construction engineering, relating to the construction, relocation, rearrangement or start-up of facilities or equipment other than facilities or equipment whose sole use is for a particular research and development project;

(g)   market research.

The accounting treatment of research and development

8   Expenditure incurred on pure and applied research can be regarded as part of a continuing operation required to maintain a company's business and its competitive position. In general, no one particular period rather than any other will be expected to benefit and therefore it is appropriate that these costs should be written off as they are incurred. Expenditure on pure or applied research may not be treated as an asset (Companies Act 1985, Schedule 4, paragraph 3(2)(c)).

9   The development of new products or services is, however, distinguishable from pure and applied research. Expenditure on such development is normally undertaken with a reasonable expectation of specific commercial success and of future benefits arising from the work, either from increased revenue and related profits or from reduced costs. On these grounds it may be argued that such expenditure, to the extent that it is recoverable, should be deferred to be matched against the future revenue.

10 It will only be practicable to evaluate the potential future benefits of development expenditure if:

(a)   there is a clearly defined project; and

(b)   the related expenditure is separately identifiable.

11 The outcome of such a project would then need to be examined for:

(a)   its technical feasibility; and

(b)   its ultimate commercial viability considered in the light of factors such as:

    (i)   likely market conditions (including competing products or services);

    (ii)   public opinion;

    (iii)   consumer and environmental legislation.

12 Furthermore a project will be of value:

(a)   only if further development costs to be incurred on the same project, together with related production, selling and administrative costs, will be more than covered by related revenues; and

(b)   adequate resources exist, or are reasonably expected to be available, to enable the project to be completed and to provide any consequential increases in working capital.

13   The elements of uncertainty inherent in the considerations set out in paragraphs 11 and 12 are considerable. There will be a need for different persons with different types of judgement to be involved in assessing the technical, commercial and financial viability of the project. Combinations of the possible differing assessments which they might validly make can produce different assessments of the existence and amounts of future benefits.

14   If these uncertainties are viewed in the context of the concept of prudence, the future benefits of most development projects would be too uncertain to justify carrying the expenditure forward. Nevertheless, in certain industries it is considered that there are a number of major development projects that satisfy the stringent criteria set out in paragraphs 10 to 12. Accordingly, when the expenditure on development projects is judged on a prudent view of available evidence to satisfy these criteria, it may be carried forward and amortised over the period expected to benefit.

15   At each accounting date the unamortised balance of development expenditure should be examined project by project to ensure that it still fulfils the criteria in paragraphs 10 to 12. Where any doubt exists as to the continuation of those circumstances the balance should be written off.

16   Fixed assets may be acquired or constructed in order to provide facilities for research and/or development activities. The use of such fixed assets usually extends over a number of accounting periods and accordingly they should be capitalised and written off over their useful life. The depreciation so written off should be included as part of the expenditure on research and development and disclosed in accordance with SSAP 12.

Exceptions

17   Where companies enter into a firm contract:

(a)   to carry out development work on behalf of third parties on such terms that the related expenditure is to be fully reimbursed, or

(b)   to develop and manufacture at an agreed price calculated to reimburse expenditure on development as well as on manufacture,

any such expenditure which has not been reimbursed at the balance sheet date should be dealt with as contract work-in-progress.

18   Expenditure incurred in locating and exploiting oil, gas and mineral deposits in the extractive industries does not fall within the definition of research and development used in this accounting standard. Development of new surveying methods and techniques as an integral part of research on geological phenomena should, however, be included in research and development.

Disclosure

19 While there are uncertainties inherent in research and development projects, such activities are important in forming a view of a company's future prospects. Detailed disclosure raises considerable problems of definition and the disclosure requirements of this standard are therefore limited to:

(a)   accounting policy as required by FRS 18 *Accounting Policies*;

(b)   disclosure of the total amount of research and development expenditure charged in the profit and loss account, distinguishing between the current year's expenditure and amounts amortised from deferred expenditure;

(c)   the movements on deferred development expenditure during the year.

20 Having regard to the problems of definition and disclosure referred to above, the scope of disclosure required under paragraph 19(b) is (except in the case of Republic of Ireland companies) restricted in effect to companies which are public limited companies, or special category companies, or subsidiaries of such companies, or which exceed by a multiple of 10 the criteria for defining a medium-sized company under the Companies Act 1985.

PART 2 – DEFINITION OF TERMS

The following definition is used for the purpose of this statement:

21 *Research and development expenditure* means expenditure falling into one or more of the following broad categories (except to the extent that it relates to locating or exploiting oil, gas or mineral deposits or is reimbursable by third parties either directly or under the terms of a firm contract to develop and manufacture at an agreed price calculated to reimburse both elements of expenditure):

(a)   *pure (or basic) research:* Experimental or theoretical work undertaken primarily to acquire new scientific or technical knowledge for its own sake rather than directed towards any specific aim or application;

(b)   *applied research:* Original or critical investigation undertaken in order to gain new scientific or technical knowledge and directed towards a specific practical aim or objective;

(c)   *development:* Use of scientific or technical knowledge in order to produce new or substantially improved materials, devices, products or services, to install new processes or systems prior to the commencement of commercial production or commercial applications, or to improving substantially those already produced or installed.

PART 3 – STANDARD ACCOUNTING PRACTICE

Scope

22 This standard applies to all financial statements intended to give a true and fair view of the financial position of profit or loss, but, except in the case of Republic of Ireland companies (see paragraphs 45 and 46), the provisions set out in paragraph 31 regarding the disclosure of the total amounts of research and development charged in the profit and loss account need not be applied by an entity that:

(a)　is not a public limited company or a special category company (as defined by Section 257 of the Companies Act 1985) or a holding company that has a public limited company or a special category company as a subsidiary; and

(b)　satisfies the criteria, multiplied in each case by 10, for defining a medium-sized company under Section 248 of the Companies Act 1985, as amended from time to time by statutory instrument and applied in accordance with the provisions of Section 249 of the Act.

Application to smaller entities

22A　Reporting entities applying the Financial Reporting Standard for Smaller Entities currently applicable are exempt from this accounting standard.

Accounting treatment

23　The cost of fixed assets acquired or constructed in order to provide facilities for research and development activities over a number of accounting periods should be capitalised and written off over their useful lives through the profit and loss account.

24　Expenditure on pure and applied research (other than that referred to in paragraph 23) should be written off in the year of expenditure through the profit and loss account.

25　Development expenditure should be written off in the year of expenditure except in the following circumstances when it may be deferred to future periods:

(a)　there is a clearly defined project, and

(b)　the related expenditure is separately identifiable, and

(c) the outcome of such a project has been assessed with reasonable certainty as to:

   (i) its technical feasibility, and

   (ii) its ultimate commercial viability considered in the light of factors such as likely market conditions (including competing products), public opinion, consumer and environmental legislation, and

(d) the aggregate of the deferred development costs, any further development costs, and related production, selling and administration costs is reasonably expected to be exceeded by related future sales or other revenues, and

(e) adequate resources exist, or are reasonably expected to be available, to enable the project to be completed and to provide any consequential increases in working capital.

26 In the foregoing circumstances development expenditure may be deferred to the extent that its recovery can reasonably regarded as assured.

27 If an accounting policy of deferral of development expenditure is adopted, it should be applied to all developmental projects that meet the criteria in paragraph 25.

28 If development costs are deferred to future periods, they should be amortised. The amortisation should commence with the commercial production or application of the product, service, process or system and should be allocated on a systematic basis to each accounting period, by reference to either the sale or use of the product, service, process or system or the period over which these are expected to be sold or used.

29 Deferred development expenditure for each project should be reviewed at the end of each accounting period and where the circumstances which have justified the deferral of the expenditure (paragraph 25) no longer apply, or are considered doubtful, the expenditure, to the extent to which it is considered to be irrecoverable, should be written off immediately project by project.

Disclosure

30 The accounting policy on research and development expenditure should be stated and explained.

31 The total amount of research and development expenditure charged in the profit and loss account should be disclosed, analysed between the current year's expenditure and amounts amortised from deferred expenditure.

32 Movements on deferred development expenditure and the amount carried forward at the beginning and the end of the period should be disclosed under intangible fixed assets in the balance sheet.

Date from which effective

33 The accounting and disclosure requirements set out in this statement should be adopted as soon as possible and regarded as standard in respect of financial statements relating to accounting periods beginning on or after 1 January 1989.

PART 4 – NOTE ON LEGAL REQUIREMENTS IN GREAT BRITAIN AND NORTHERN IRELAND

All paragraph references unless otherwise indicated are to the Companies Act 1985 and the Companies (Northern Ireland) Order 1986.

34 Paragraph 3(1) of Schedule 4 enables any items required to be shown in a company's balance sheet or profit and loss account to be shown in greater detail than required by the format adopted.

35 Paragraph 3(2)(c) of Schedule 4 provides that a company's balance sheet or profit and loss account may include an item representing or covering the amount of any asset or liability, income or expenditure not otherwise covered by any of the items listed in the accounts format adopted. Cost of research shall not be treated as an asset in any company's balance sheet.

36 Paragraph 19(1) of Schedule 4 does not allow provision to be made for a temporary diminution in value other than for a fixed asset investment.

37 Paragraph 19(2) of Schedule 4 requires provision for diminution in value to be made in respect of any fixed asset which has diminished in value if the reduction is expected to be permanent (whether its useful economic life is limited or not) and the amount to be included in respect of it to be reduced accordingly. Any such provisions not shown in the profit and loss account shall be disclosed (either separately or in aggregate) in a note to the accounts.

38 Paragraph 19(3) requires that where the reasons for which any provision was made have ceased to apply to any extent, then the provision shall be written back to the extent that it is no longer necessary. Any amounts written back in accordance with this subparagraph which are not shown in the profit and loss account shall be disclosed (either separately or in aggregate) in a note to the accounts.

39 Paragraph 20(1) of Schedule 4 requires that notwithstanding that an item in respect of development costs is included under fixed assets in the balance sheet formats set out in Part 1 of Schedule 4, an amount may only be included in a company's balance sheet in respect of development costs in special circumstances.

40   Paragraph 20(2) of Schedule 4 requires that if any amount is included in a company's balance sheet in respect of development costs the following information shall be given in a note to the accounts:

(a)   the period over which the amount of those costs originally capitalised is being or is to be written off; and

(b)   the reasons for capitalising the development costs in question.

41   Paragraph 6(c) of Schedule 7 requires the Directors' Report to contain an indication of the activities (if any) of the company and its subsidiaries in the field of research and development.

42   Section 269(2)(b) of the Companies Act 1985 on the treatment of development costs requires that where the unamortised development expenditure carried forward is not treated as a realised loss when determining distributable reserves, the notes to the financial statements shall disclose:

(a)   the fact that the amount of the unamortised development expenditure is not to be treated as a realised loss for the purposes of calculating distributable profits; and

(b)   the circumstances that the directors relied upon to justify their decision not to treat the unamortised development expenditure as a realised loss.

PART 5 – NOTE ON LEGAL REQUIREMENTS IN THE REPUBLIC OF IRELAND

References are to the Companies (Amendment) Act 1986 and to the Schedule to that Act unless otherwise stated.

43   Section 4(5) of the Act enables any items required to be shown in a company's balance sheet or profit and loss account to be shown in greater detail than required by the format adopted.

44   Section 4(12) of the Act provides that the balance sheet, or profit and loss account, of a company may include an item representing or covering the amount of any asset or liability or income or expenditure not otherwise covered by any of the items listed in the format adopted but that costs of research shall not be treated as assets in the balance sheet of a company.

45   Paragraph 43(4) of the Schedule requires the amount expended on research and development in the financial year, and any amount committed in respect of research and development in subsequent years, to be stated.

46   Paragraph 43(5) of the Schedule provides that where, in the opinion of the directors, the disclosure of any information required by Paragraph 43(4) would be prejudicial to the interests of the company, that information need not be disclosed, but the fact that any such information has not been disclosed shall be stated.

47   Paragraph 7(1) of the Schedule does not allow provision to be made for a temporary diminution in value other than for a fixed asset investment.

48   Paragraph 7(2) of the Schedule requires provision for diminution in value to be made in respect of any fixed asset which has diminished in value if the reduction is expected to be permanent (whether its useful economic life is limited or not) and the amount to be included in respect of it shall be reduced accordingly. Any such provisions which are not shown in the profit and loss account shall be disclosed (either separately or in aggregate) in a note to the accounts.

49   Paragraph 7(3) of the Schedule requires that where the reasons for which any provision was made have ceased to apply to any extent, then the provision should be written back to the extent that it is no longer necessary. Any amounts written back in accordance with this sub-paragraph which are not shown in the profit and loss account shall be disclosed (either separately or in aggregate) in a note to the accounts.

50   Paragraph 8(1) of the Schedule requires that notwithstanding that an item in respect of development costs is included under fixed assets in the balance sheet formats set out in Part 1 of the Schedule, an amount may only be included in a company's balance sheet in respect of development costs in special circumstances.

51   Paragraph 8(2) of the Schedule requires that if any amount is included in a company's balance sheet in respect of development costs, the following information shall be given in a note to the accounts:

(a)   the period over which the amount of those costs originally capitalised is being or is to be written off, and

(b)   the reasons for capitalising the development costs in question.

52   Section 13(c) of the Act requires the Directors' Report to contain an indication of the activity, if any, of the company and its subsidiaries, if any, in the field of research and development.

53   Section 45A of the Companies (Amendment) Act 1983 on the treatment of development costs, provides that where development costs are shown in a company's accounts any amount shown as an asset in respect of those costs shall be treated as a realised loss for the purpose of determining profits available for distribution. This provision does not apply to any part of that amount representing an unrealised profit made on revaluation of these costs; nor does it apply if:

(a)   there are special circumstances justifying the directors of the company concerned in deciding that the amount mentioned in respect thereof in the company's accounts shall not be treated as a realised loss, and

(b)   the note to the accounts required by paragraph 8(2) of the Schedule states that the amount is not to be so treated and explains the circumstances relied upon to justify the decision of the directors to that effect.

PART 6 – COMPLIANCE WITH IAS 9 ACCOUNTING FOR RESEARCH AND DEVELOPMENT ACTIVITIES

54   The requirements of International Accounting Standard No. 9 *Accounting for research and development activities"* accord very closely with the content of the United Kingdom and Irish Accounting Standard No. 13 (Revised) *Accounting for research and development* and accordingly compliance with SSAP 13 (Revised) will ensure compliance with IAS 9 in all material aspects.

Department for
business, innovation
+ skills.

BIS Guidelines on the Meaning of Research and Development for Tax Purposes

Issued 5 March 2004, updated 6 December 2010

These Guidelines are issued by the Secretary of State for Trade and Industry for the purposes of Section 837A Income and Corporation Taxes Act 1988. They replace the previous Guidelines issued on 28 July 2000.	
	1. Research and development ('R&D') is defined for tax purposes in Section 837A Income and Corporation Taxes Act 1988[1]. This says the definition of R&D for tax purposes follows generally accepted accounting practice. SSAP 13 Accounting for research and development is the Statement of Standard Accounting Practice which defines R&D. The accountancy definition is then modified for tax purposes by these Guidelines, which are given legal force by Parliamentary Regulations. These Guidelines explain what is meant by R&D for a variety of tax purposes, but the rules of particular tax schemes may restrict the qualifying expenditure[2].
	2. In these Guidelines a number of terms are used which are intended to have a special meaning for the purpose of the Guidelines. Such terms are **highlighted** on first appearance and defined later.

1   For the purposes of research and development allowances (Part 6 Capital Allowances Act 2001) this definition is extended to include oil and gas exploration and appraisal as defined in Section 837B Income and Corporation Taxes Act 1988. These Guidelines apply to this extended definition as well.

2   The original footnotes 2 and 3 to the 2004 Guidelines (which were not themselves part of the Guidelines) have been removed. This is because those footnotes stated that the qualifying indirect activities (QIAs) listed in para 31 are R&D, but do not attract R&D tax credits. In fact, whether or not expenditure on the QIAs qualifies for R&D tax relief depends on a number of factors, but there is no blanket exclusion. For further explanation see, for example, HMRC guidance at http://www.hmrc.gov.uk/manuals/cirdmanual/CIRD83000.htm. These revised footnotes are not part of the Guidelines. Revised footnote prepared by Department for Business, Innovation and Skills in consultation with HMRC December 2010.

Appendix 2

	THE DEFINITION OF RESEARCH & DEVELOPMENT
	3. R&D for tax purposes takes place when a **project** seeks to achieve an **advance in science or technology.**
	4. The activities which **directly contribute** to achieving this advance in science or technology through the resolution of **scientific or technological uncertainty** are R&D.
	5. Certain **qualifying indirect activities** related to the project are also R&D. Activities other than qualifying indirect activities which do not directly contribute to the resolution of the project's scientific or technological uncertainty are not R&D.

	ADVANCE IN SCIENCE OR TECHNOLOGY
	6. An advance in science or technology means an advance in **overall knowledge or capability** in a field of **science** or **technology** (not a company's own state of knowledge or capability alone). This includes the adaptation of knowledge or capability from another field of science or technology in order to make such an advance where this adaptation was not readily deducible.
	7. An advance in science or technology may have tangible consequences (such as a new or more efficient cleaning product, or a process which generates less waste) or more intangible outcomes (new knowledge or cost improvements, for example).
	8. A process, material, device, product, service or source of knowledge does not become an advance in science or technology simply because science or technology is used in its creation. Work which uses science or technology but which does not advance scientific or technological capability as a whole is not an advance in science or technology.
	9. A project which seeks to, for example, (a) extend overall knowledge or capability in a field of science or technology; or (b) create a process, material, device, product or service which incorporates or represents an increase in overall knowledge or capability in a field of science or technology; or

	(c) make an **appreciable improvement** to an existing process, material, device, product or service through scientific or technological changes; or (d) use science or technology to duplicate the effect of an existing process, material, device, product or service in a new or appreciably improved way (e.g. a product which has exactly the same performance characteristics as existing models, but is built in a fundamentally different manner) will therefore be R&D.
	10. Even if the advance in science or technology sought by a project is not achieved or not fully realised, R&D still takes place.
	11. If a particular advance in science or technology has already been made or attempted but details are not readily available (for example, if it is a trade secret), work to achieve such an advance can still be an advance in science or technology.
	12. However, the routine analysis, copying or adaptation of an existing product, process, service or material, will not be an advance in science or technology.

[handwritten note in right margin: ie failed projects.]

SCIENTIFIC OR TECHNOLOGICAL UNCERTAINTY

	13. Scientific or technological uncertainty exists when knowledge of whether something is scientifically possible or technologically feasible, or how to achieve it in practice, is not readily available or deducible by a competent professional working in the field. This includes **system uncertainty**. Scientific or technological uncertainty will often arise from turning something that has already been established as scientifically feasible into a cost-effective, reliable and reproducible process, material, device, product or service.
	14. Uncertainties that can readily be resolved by a competent professional working in the field are not scientific or technological uncertainties. Similarly, improvements, optimisations and fine-tuning which do not materially affect the underlying science or technology do not constitute work to resolve scientific or technological uncertainty.

[handwritten note at bottom right: Competent Professional.]

OTHER DEFINITIONS	
Science	15. Science is the systematic study of the nature and behaviour of the physical and material universe. Work in the arts, humanities and social sciences, including economics, is not science for the purpose of these Guidelines. Mathematical techniques are frequently used in science, but mathematical advances in and of themselves are not science unless they are advances in representing the nature and behaviour of the physical and material universe.
	16. These Guidelines apply equally to work in any branch or field of science.
Technology	17. Technology is the practical application of scientific principles and knowledge, where 'scientific' is based on the definition of science above.
	18. These Guidelines apply equally to work in any branch or field of technology.
Project	19. A project consists of a number of activities conducted to a method or plan in order to achieve an advance in science or technology. It is important to get the boundaries of the project correct. It should encompass all the activities which collectively serve to resolve the scientific or technological uncertainty associated with achieving the advance, so it could include a number of different sub-projects. A project may itself be part of a larger commercial project, but that does not make the parts of the commercial project that do not address scientific or technological uncertainty into R&D.
Overall knowledge or capability	20. Overall knowledge or capability in a field of science or technology means the knowledge or capability in the field which is publicly available or is readily deducible from the publicly available knowledge or capability by a competent professional working in the field. Work which seeks an advance relative to this overall knowledge or capability is R&D.
	21. Overall knowledge or capability in a field of science or technology can still be advanced (and hence R&D can still be done) in situations where • several companies are working at the cutting edge in the same field, and are doing similar work independently; or • work has already been done but this is not known in general because it is a trade secret, and another company repeats the work; or

242

	• it is known that a particular advance in science or technology has been achieved, but the details of how are not readily available.
	22. However, the routine analysis, copying or adaptation of an existing process, material, device, product or service will not advance overall knowledge or capability, even though it may be completely new to the company or the company's trade.
Appreciable improvement	23. Appreciable improvement means to change or adapt the scientific or technological characteristics of something to the point where it is 'better' than the original. The improvement should be more than a minor or routine upgrading, and should represent something that would generally be acknowledged by a competent professional working in the field as a genuine and non-trivial improvement. Improvements arising from the adaptation of knowledge or capability from another field of science or technology are appreciable improvements if they would generally be acknowledged by a competent professional working in the field as a genuine and non-trivial improvement.
	24. Improvements which arise from taking existing science or technology and deploying it in a new context (e.g. a different trade) with only minor or routine changes are not appreciable improvements. A process, material, device, product or service will not be appreciably improved if it simply brings a company into line with overall knowledge or capability in science or technology, even though it may be completely new to the company or the company's trade.
	25. The question of what scale of advance would constitute an appreciable improvement will differ between fields of science and technology and will depend on what a competent professional working in the field would regard as a genuine and non-trivial improvement.
Directly contribute	26. To directly contribute to achieving an advance in science or technology, an activity (or several activities in combination) must attempt to resolve an element of the scientific or technological uncertainty associated with achieving the advance.
	27. Activities which directly contribute to R&D include: (a) activities to create or adapt software, materials or equipment needed to resolve the scientific or technological uncertainty, provided that the software, material or equipment is created or adapted solely for use in R&D;

	(b) scientific or technological planning activities; and (c) scientific or technological design, testing and analysis undertaken to resolve the scientific or technological uncertainty.
	28. Activities which do not directly contribute to the resolution of scientific or technological uncertainty include: (a) the range of commercial and financial steps necessary for innovation and for the successful development and marketing of a new or appreciably improved process, material, device, product or service; (b) work to develop non-scientific or non-technological aspects of a new or appreciably improved process, material, device, product or service; (c) the production and distribution of goods and services; (d) administration and other supporting services; (e) general support services (such as transportation, storage, cleaning, repair, maintenance and security); and (f) qualifying indirect activities.
System uncertainty	29. System uncertainty is scientific or technological uncertainty that results from the complexity of a system rather than uncertainty about how its individual components behave. For example, in electronic devices, the characteristics of individual components or chips are fixed, but there can still be uncertainty about the best way to combine those components to achieve an overall effect. However, assembling a number of components (or software sub-programs) to an established pattern, or following routine methods for doing so, involves little or no scientific or technological uncertainty.
	30. Similarly, work on combining standard technologies, devices, and/or processes can involve scientific or technological uncertainty even if the principles for their integration are well known. There will be scientific or technological uncertainty if a competent professional working in the field cannot readily deduce how the separate components or sub-systems should be combined to have the intended function.
Qualifying indirect activity	31. These are activities which form part of a project but do not directly contribute to the resolution of the scientific or technological uncertainty. They are: (a) scientific and technical information services, insofar as they are conducted for the purpose of R&D support (such as the preparation of the original report of R&D findings);

	(b) indirect supporting activities such as maintenance, security, administration and clerical activities, and finance and personnel activities, insofar as undertaken for R&D; (c) ancillary activities essential to the undertaking of R&D (e.g. taking on and paying staff, leasing laboratories and maintaining research and development equipment including computers used for R&D purposes); (d) training required to directly support an R&D project; (e) research by students and researchers carried out at universities; (f) research (including related data collection) to devise new scientific or technological testing, survey, or sampling methods, where this research is not R&D in its own right; and (g) feasibility studies to inform the strategic direction of a specific R&D activity.
	32. Activities not described in paragraph 31 are not qualifying indirect activities.

COMMENTARY ON PARTICULAR QUESTIONS WHICH ARISE	
Start and end of R&D	33. R&D begins when work to resolve the scientific or technological uncertainty starts, and ends when that uncertainty is resolved or work to resolve it ceases. This means that work to identify the requirements for the process, material, device, product or service, where no scientific or technological questions are at issue, is not R&D.
	34. R&D ends when knowledge is codified in a form usable by a competent professional working in the field, or when a prototype or pilot plant with all the functional characteristics of the final process, material, device, product or service is produced.
	35. Although the R&D for a process, material, device, product or service may have ended, new problems which involve scientific or technological uncertainty may emerge after it has been turned over to production or put into use. The resolution of these problems may require new R&D to be carried out. But there is a distinction to be drawn between such problems and routine fault fixing.

Planning as part of R&D	36. Scientific or technological planning activities associated with a project directly contribute to resolving the scientific or technological uncertainty associated with the project, and are therefore R&D. These include defining scientific or technological objectives, assessing scientific or technological feasibility, identifying particular scientific or technological uncertainties, estimating development time, schedule, and resources of the R&D, and high-level outlining of the scientific or technical work, as well as the detailed planning and management of the work.
	37. Elements of a company's planning activity relating to a project but not directly contributing to the resolution of scientific or technological uncertainty, such as identifying or researching market niches in which R&D might benefit a company, or examination of a project's financial, marketing, and legal aspects, fall outside the category of scientific or technological planning, and are therefore not R&D
Abortive projects	38. Not all projects succeed in their aims. What counts is whether there is an intention to achieve an advance in science or technology, not whether ultimately the associated scientific or technological uncertainty is completely resolved, or resolved to the degree intended. Scientific or technological planning activities associated with projects which are not taken forward (e.g. because of insurmountable technical or commercial challenges) are still R&D.
Prototypes, pilot plants	39. A prototype is an original model on which something new or appreciably improved is patterned, and of which all things of the same type are representations or copies. It is a basic experimental model possessing the essential characteristics of the intended process, material, device, product or service. The design, construction, and testing of prototypes generally fall within the scope of R&D for tax purposes. But once any modifications necessary to reflect the test findings have been made to the prototypes, and further testing has been satisfactorily completed, the scientific or technological uncertainty has been resolved and further work will not be R&D.
	40. Similarly the construction and operation of pilot plants while assessing their operations is R&D until the scientific or technological uncertainty associated with the intended advance in science or technology has been resolved.

Design	41. When achieving design objectives requires the resolution of scientific or technological uncertainty within a project, work to do this will be R&D. Design activities which do not directly contribute to the resolution of scientific or technological uncertainty within a project are not R&D.
Cosmetic and aesthetic effects	42. Cosmetic and aesthetic qualities are not of themselves science or technology, and so work to improve the cosmetic or aesthetic appeal of a process, material, device, product or service would not in itself be R&D. However, work to create a desired cosmetic or aesthetic effect through the application of science or technology can require a scientific or technological advance, and resolving the scientific or technological uncertainty associated with such a project would therefore be R&D.
Content delivered through science or technology	43. Information or other content which is delivered through a scientific or technological medium is not of itself science or technology. However, improvements in scientific or technological means to create, manipulate and transfer information or other content can be scientific or technological advances, and resolving the scientific or technological uncertainty associated with such projects would therefore be R&D.

EXAMPLES/ILLUSTRATIONS	
	Examples in these Guidelines are illustrative, designed to cast light on the principles explained in the Guidelines, and should be read in that context.
A. The R&D process	A1. A company conducts extensive market research to learn what technical and design characteristics a new DVD player should have in order to be an appealing product. This work is not R&D (paragraph 37). However, it does identify a potential project to create a DVD player incorporating a number of technological improvements which the company's R&D staff (who are competent professionals) regard as genuine and non- trivial. This project would be seeking to develop an appreciably improved DVD player (paragraphs 23–25) and would therefore be seeking to achieve an advance in science or technology (paragraph 9(c)).

247

	A2. The company then decides on a detailed specification for the desired new product, and devises a plan for developing it. Some elements of this plan involve planning of activities which directly contribute to resolving the project's scientific or technological uncertainties (such as the system uncertainty associated with an improved control mechanism for the laser that 'reads' the DVD). This element of planning is R&D (paragraph 36), as are the activities themselves (paragraph 4). Other elements of the plan focus on obtaining intellectual property protection or cosmetic design decisions, for example, which do not directly contribute to resolving the project's scientific or technological uncertainties and are not qualifying indirect activities (paragraph 31) and are therefore not R&D. Neither this planning (paragraph 37) nor these activities (paragraph 28) are R&D.
	A3. The scientific or technological work culminates in the creation of a series of prototype DVD players, and ultimately a 'final' prototype is produced and tested which possesses the essential characteristics of the intended product (circuit board design, performance characteristics, etc.). All the activities which directly contributed to resolving the scientific or technological uncertainty of creating the DVD player up to this point (such as the testing of successive prototypes) are R&D (paragraphs 34 and 39).
	A4. Several copies of this prototype are made (not R&D; paragraphs 4–5 and 26–28) and distributed to a group of consumers to test their reactions (not R&D; paragraph 28((a)). Some of these consumers report concerns about the noise level of the DVD player in operation. Additional work is done to resolve this problem. If this involves a routine adjustment of the existing prototype (i.e. no scientific or technological uncertainty) then it will not be R&D (paragraph 14); if it involves more substantial changes (i.e. there is scientific or technological uncertainty to resolve) then it will be R&D.
B. Equal applicability in any branch or field of science or technology	B1. The Guidelines apply equally to work in any branch or field of science or technology (paragraphs 15–18). This means that work in software engineering, for example, is subject to the same fundamental criteria for being R&D as work in textile science, or nanotechnology, or anything else.

	B2. This equality also applies to the methods used to resolve scientific or technological uncertainty. For example, it is sometimes possible to implement functionality in a product or process by means of software or of hardware. As long as the scientific or technological uncertainty cannot readily be resolved by a competent professional working in the field, hardware and software methods are both equally R&D in these circumstances.
C. Abortive projects	C1. Not all projects achieve the advance in science or technology they are seeking. For example, work to insert a particular gene into a gene sequence may simply fail, while an attempt to appreciably increase the life of a battery may only yield a marginal improvement. In both cases, the project seeks to achieve an advance in science or technology and work to resolve the scientific or technological uncertainty would be R&D (paragraph 10).
D. Advance in science or technology	D1. Searching for the molecular structures of possible new drugs would be an advance in science or technology, because it applies existing knowledge of science (which compounds are known to cause particular physiological effects) in search of new or improved active compounds (paragraph 9(b)). This is true even if the method used to search for those molecular structures (e.g. running a computer programme on a particular set of data) is itself entirely routine; the activity directly contributes to the resolution of scientific or technological uncertainty (paragraph 27(c)) and so would be R&D (paragraph 4) . Work to identify new uses of existing compounds would also be creative work in science or technology, because it seeks new scientific knowledge about those molecules (paragraph 9(a)).
	D2. However, the development of software intended for the analysis of market research data (which is not scientific or technological knowledge; paragraphs 15–18) which was not expected to result in the development of a scientific or technological advance in the field of software as a whole (such as an algorithm which extends overall knowledge or capability in the field of software) would not be R&D (paragraph 8). Work to adapt such software to analyse, say, customer spending patterns would also not be R&D.

	D3. An advance in science or technology need not imply an absolute improvement in the performance of a process, material, device, product or service. For example, the existence of high-fidelity audio equipment does not prevent a project to create lower-performance equipment from being an advance in science or technology (for instance, if it incorporated technological improvements leading to lower cost through more efficient circuit design or speaker construction) (paragraph 9(d)).
E. Scientific or technological uncertainty	E1. A firm's project involves finding a new active ingredient for weed-killer (an advance in overall knowledge or capability in the particular field of science or technology; paragraphs 6, 20), and developing a formula incorporating the new active ingredient for use in a commercial product (paragraph 9(b) or (c)). Both of these would constitute an advance in science or technology.
	E2. In order to achieve this advance, a programme of investigation by computer to pick likely ingredients and the systematic testing of possible ingredients and products based on those 'trial' ingredients is undertaken. The work involves the adaptation of existing software to tackle the specific problem, and product formulation and testing using established methods. This investigation and testing evaluates the weed-killing performance and other relevant characteristics of the formulations (for example, toxicity to humans and wildlife, water solubility, adhesion to weeds, damage done to other plants). All of these activities would therefore be R&D (paragraphs 4, 26, 27).
	E3. The company also does work to assess what characteristics a new weed-killing product should have in order to appeal to consumers. This activity does not directly contribute to the resolution of scientific or technological uncertainty (paragraph 28(a)) and is not a qualifying indirect activity (paragraph 31), and is therefore not R&D (paragraph 4).

F. Direct contribution to the resolution of scientific or technological uncertainty	F1. Work to compare the effectiveness of two possible designs for controlling part of a new manufacturing process would directly contribute to resolving the scientific or technological uncertainty inherent in the new process, and hence the activity would be R&D (paragraphs 4,26). But work to raise finance for the project, while indirectly contributing to the resolution of scientific or technological uncertainty (e.g. by paying for work) does not of itself help resolve the uncertainty, and hence is not R&D (paragraph 28(a)). Human Resources work to support the R&D is a qualifying indirect activity (paragraph 31) and hence is also R&D (paragraph 5), though it does not directly contribute to the resolution of scientific or technological uncertainty (paragraph 28(e) and (f))[3].
G. Testing as part of R&D	G1. Scientific or technological testing and analysis which directly contributes to the resolution of scientific or technological uncertainty is R&D (paragraph 26). So for example if testing work is carried out as part of the development of a pilot plant, this would be R&D, but once the design of the 'final' pilot plant had been finalised and tested, any further testing would not be R&D (paragraph 39). However, if flaws in the design became apparent later on, then work to remedy them would be R&D if they could not readily be resolved by a competent professional working in the field (in other words, if there was scientific or technological uncertainty around how to fix the problem; paragraph 14).
H. Cosmetic and aesthetic effects	H1. A company is seeking to make a water-breathable fabric for use in hiking gear. A test fabric with the required physical characteristics is produced through R&D. This new fabric is then produced in small quantities (not R&D) and market tested with a number of trial users. The user tests are not R&D, because they are concerned with testing the commercial potential of the new material and assessing its appeal to users (paragraph 42).
	H2. One of the results of these tests is that users do not like the feel of the new fabric against their skin, and dislike its shiny appearance. The company decides to investigate variants of its new fabric, which require significant changes to the material's weave and physical structure, to overcome these problems. Because there is scientific and technological uncertainty around whether a material with the desired physical characteristics can be made, the R&D continues.

3   See footnote 2.

J. Project, prototype and end of R&D	J1. A company develops new spark plugs for use in an existing petrol engine. The scientific or technological uncertainty associated with this work is resolved once prototype plugs have been fully tested in the engine. The activities directly contributing to this work, including the construction of prototypes and their testing in the engine, would be R&D.
	J2. The same company decides to design a new engine to incorporate the new spark plugs, involving a new combustion chamber design, lighter materials and other improvements such that the overall engine is appreciably improved (it uses less petrol to achieve slightly greater power output performance, and generates less pollution than current models). The activities directly contributing to this work, including the design of the separate components (not all of which need be different from those used in previous models) and their integration into a new engine, are R&D. The uncertainty associated with this work is resolved, and R&D is complete once a functionally final prototype has been tested.

Appendix 3

Commission Recommendation of 6 May 2003 concerning the definition of micro, small and medium-sized enterprises

(notified under document number C(2003) 1422)

(Text with EEA relevance)

(2003/361/EC)

THE COMMISSION OF THE EUROPEAN COMMUNITIES,

Having regard to the Treaty establishing the European Community, and in particular Article 211, second indent, thereof,

Whereas:

(1) In a report submitted to the Council in 1992 at the request of the 'Industry' Council held on 28 May 1990, the Commission had proposed limiting the proliferation of definitions of small and medium-sized enterprises in use at Community level. Commission Recommendation 96/280/EC of 3 April 1996 concerning the definition of small and medium-sized enterprises[1] was based on the idea that the existence of different definitions at Community level and at national level could create inconsistencies. Following the logic of a single market without internal frontiers, the treatment of enterprises should be based on a set of common rules. The pursuit of such an approach is all the more necessary in view of the extensive interaction between national and Community measures assisting micro, small and medium-sized enterprises (SME), for example in connection with Structural Funds or research. It means that situations in which the Community focuses its action on a given category of SMEs and the Member States on another must be avoided. In addition, it was considered that the application of the same definition by the Commission, the Member States, the European Investment Bank (EIB) and the European Investment Fund (EIF) would improve the consistency and effectiveness of

policies targeting SMEs and would, therefore, limit the risk of distortion of competition.

(2) Recommendation 96/280/EC has been applied widely by the Member States, and the definition contained in the Annex thereto has been taken over in Commission Regulation (EC) No 70/2001 of 12 January 2001 on the application of Articles 87 and 88 of the EC Treaty to State aid to small and medium-sized enterprises[2]. Apart from the need to adapt Recommendation 96/280/EC to economic developments, pursuant to Article 2 of the Annex thereto, consideration must be given to a number of difficulties of interpretation which have emerged in its application, as well as the observations received from enterprises. In view of the number of amendments now requiring to be made to Recommendation 96/280/EC, and for the sake of clarity, it is appropriate to replace the Recommendation.

1 OJ L 107, 30.4.1996, p. 4.
2 OJ L 10, 13.1.2001, p. 33.

(3) It should also be made clear that, in accordance with Articles 48, 81 and 82 of the Treaty, as interpreted by the Court of Justice of the European Communities, an enterprise should be considered to be any entity, regardless of its legal form, engaged in economic activities, including in particular entities engaged in a craft activity and other activities on an individual or family basis, partnerships or associations regularly engaged in economic activities.

(4) The criterion of staff numbers (the 'staff headcount criterion') remains undoubtedly one of the most important, and must be observed as the main criterion; introducing a financial criterion is nonetheless a necessary adjunct in order to grasp the real scale and performance of an enterprise and its position compared to its competitors. However, it would not be desirable to use turn- over as the sole financial criterion, in particular because enterprises in the trade and distribution sector have by their nature higher turnover figures than those in the manufacturing sector. Thus the turnover criterion should be combined with that of the balance sheet total, a criterion which reflects the overall wealth of a business, with the possibility of either of these two criteria being exceeded.

(5) The turnover ceiling refers to enterprises engaged in very different types of economic activity. In order not to restrict unduly the usefulness of applying the definition, it should be updated to take account of changes in both prices and productivity.

(6) As regards the ceiling for the balance sheet total, in the absence of any new element, it is justified to maintain the approach whereby the turnover ceilings are subjected to a coefficient based on the statistical ratio between the two variables. The statistical trend requires a greater increase to be made to the turnover ceiling. Since the trend differs according to the size-category of the enterprise, it is also appropriate to adjust the coefficient in order to reflect the economic trend as closely as possible and not to penalise microenterprises

and small enterprises as opposed to medium-sized enterprises. This coefficient is very close to 1 in the case of microenterprises and small enterprises. To simplify matters, there- fore, a single value must be chosen for those categories for the turnover ceiling and balance sheet total ceiling.

(7) As in Recommendation 96/280/EC, the financial ceilings and the staff ceilings represent maximum limits and the Member States, the EIB and the EIF may fix ceilings lower than the Community ceilings if they wish to direct their measures towards a specific category of SME. In the interests of administrative simplification, the Member States, the EIB and the EIF may use only one criterion – the staff headcount – for the implementation of some of their policies. However, this does not apply to the various rules in competition law where the financial criteria must also be used and adhered to.

(8) Following the endorsement of the European Charter for Small Enterprises by the European Council of Santa Maria da Feira in June 2000, microenterprises – a category of small enterprises particularly important for the development of entrepreneurship and job creation – should also be better defined.

(9) To gain a better understanding of the real economic position of SMEs and to remove from that category groups of enterprises whose economic power may exceed that of genuine SMEs, a distinction should be made between various types of enterprises, depending on whether they are autonomous, whether they have holdings which do not entail a controlling position (partner enterprises), or whether they are linked to other enterprises. The current limit shown in Recommendation 96/280/EC, of a 25% holding below which an enterprise is considered autonomous, is maintained.

(10) In order to encourage the creation of enterprises, equity financing of SMEs and rural and local development, enterprises can be considered autonomous despite a holding of 25% or more by certain categories of investors who have a positive role in business financing and creation. However, conditions for these investors have not previously been specified. The case of 'business angels' (individuals or groups of individuals pursuing a regular business of investing venture capital) deserves special mention because – compared to other venture capital investors – their ability to give relevant advice to new entrepreneurs is extremely valuable. Their investment in equity capital also complements the activity of venture capital companies, as they provide smaller amounts at an earlier stage of the enterprise's life.

(11) To simplify matters, in particular for Member States and enterprises, use should be made when defining linked enterprises of the conditions laid down in Article 1 of Council Directive 83/349/EEC of 13 June 1983 based on Article 54(3)(g) of the Treaty on consolidated accounts[1], as last amended by Directive 2001/65/EC of the European Parliament and of the Council[2], in so far as these conditions are suitable for the purposes of this Recommendation. To strengthen the incentives for investing in the equity funding of an SME, the presumption of absence of dominant influence on the enterprise in question was introduced, in pursuance of the criteria of Article 5(3), of Council

Appendix 3

Directive 78/660/EEC of 25 July 1978 based on Article 54(3)(g) of the Treaty on the annual accounts of certain types of companies[3], as last amended by Directive 2001/65/EC.

(12)   Account should also be taken, in suitable cases, of relations between enterprises which pass through natural persons, with a view to ensuring that only those enterprises which really need the advantages accruing to SMEs from the different rules or measures in their favour actually benefit from them. In order to limit the examination of these situations to the strict minimum, the account taken of such relationships has been restricted to the relevant market or to adjacent markets – reference being had, where necessary, to the Commission's definition of 'relevant markets' in the Commission notice on the definition of relevant market for the purposes of Community competition law[4].

1   OJ L 193, 18.7.1983, p. 1.
2   OJ L 283, 27.10.2001, p. 28.
3   OJ L 222, 14.8.1978, p. 11.
4   OJ C 372, 9.12.1997, p. 5.

(13)   In order to avoid arbitrary distinctions between different public bodies of a Member State, and given the need for legal certainty, it is considered necessary to confirm that an enterprise with 25% or more of its capital or voting rights controlled by a public body is not an SME.

(14)   In order to ease the administrative burden for enter- prises, and to simplify and speed up the administrative handling of cases for which SME status is required, it is appropriate to allow enterprises to use solemn declarations to certify certain of their characteristics.

(15)   It is necessary to establish in detail the composition of the staff headcount for SME definition purposes. In order to promote the development of vocational training and sandwich courses, it is desirable, when calculating staff numbers, to disregard apprentices and students with a vocational training contract. Similarly, maternity or parental leave periods should not be counted.

(16)   The various types of enterprise defined according to their relationship with other enterprises correspond to objectively differing degrees of integration. It is therefore appropriate to apply distinct procedures to each of those types of enterprise when calculating the quantities representing their activities and economic power,

HEREBY RECOMMENDS:

Article 1

1.   This Recommendation concerns the definition of micro, small and medium-sized enterprises used in Community policies applied within the Community and the European Economic Area.

2. Member States, the European Investment Bank (EIB) and the European Investment Fund (EIF), are invited:

(a)   to comply with Title I of the Annex for their programmes directed towards medium-sized enterprises, small enter- prises or microenterprises;

(b)   to take the necessary steps with a view to using the size classes set out in Article 7 of the Annex, especially where the monitoring of their use of Community financial instruments is concerned.

Article 2

The ceilings shown in Article 2 of the Annex are to be regarded as maximum values. Member States, the EIB and the EIF may fix lower ceilings. In implementing certain of their policies, they may also choose to apply only the criterion of number of employees, except in fields governed by the various rules on State aid.

Article 3

This Recommendation will replace Recommendation 96/280/ EC as from 1 January 2005.

Article 4

This Recommendation is addressed to the Member States, the EIB and the EIF.

They are requested to inform the Commission by 31 December 2004 of any measures they have taken further to it and, no later than 30 September 2005, to inform it of the first results of its implementation.

Done at Brussels, 6 May 2003.

For the Commission

Erkki LIIKANEN

Member of the Commission

ANNEX TITLE I

DEFINITION OF MICRO, SMALL AND MEDIUM-SIZED ENTERPRISES ADOPTED BY THE COMMISSION

Article 1

Enterprise

An enterprise is considered to be any entity engaged in an economic activity, irrespective of its legal form. This includes, in particular, self-employed persons and family businesses engaged in craft or other activities, and partnerships or associations regularly engaged in an economic activity.

Article 2

Staff headcount and financial ceilings determining enterprise categories

1.   The category of micro, small and medium-sized enterprises (SMEs) is made up of enterprises which employ fewer than 250 persons and which have an annual turnover not exceeding EUR 50 million, and/or an annual balance sheet total not exceeding EUR 43 million.

2.   Within the SME category, a small enterprise is defined as an enterprise which employs fewer than 50 persons and whose annual turnover and/or annual balance sheet total does not exceed EUR 10 million.

3.   Within the SME category, a microenterprise is defined as an enterprise which employs fewer than 10 persons and whose annual turnover and/or annual balance sheet total does not exceed EUR 2 million.

Article 3

Types of enterprise taken into consideration in calculating staff numbers and financial amounts

1.   An 'autonomous enterprise' is any enterprise which is not classified as a partner enterprise within the meaning of paragraph 2 or as a linked enterprise within the meaning of paragraph 3.

2.   'Partner enterprises' are all enterprises which are not classified as linked enterprises within the meaning of paragraph 3 and between which there is

the following relationship: an enterprise (upstream enterprise) holds, either solely or jointly with one or more linked enterprises within the meaning of paragraph 3, 25% or more of the capital or voting rights of another enterprise (downstream enterprise).

However, an enterprise may be ranked as autonomous, and thus as not having any partner enterprises, even if this 25% threshold is reached or exceeded by the following investors, provided that those investors are not linked, within the meaning of paragraph 3, either individually or jointly to the enterprise in question:

(a) public investment corporations, venture capital companies, individuals or groups of individuals with a regular venture capital investment activity who invest equity capital in unquoted businesses ('business angels'), provided the total investment of those business angels in the same enterprise is less than EUR 1 250 000;

(b) universities or non-profit research centres;

(c) institutional investors, including regional development funds;

(d) autonomous local authorities with an annual budget of less than EUR 10 million and fewer than 5 000 inhabitants.

3. 'Linked enterprises' are enterprises which have any of the following relationships with each other:

(a) an enterprise has a majority of the shareholders' or members' voting rights in another enterprise;

(b) an enterprise has the right to appoint or remove a majority of the members of the administrative, management or supervisory body of another enterprise;

(c) an enterprise has the right to exercise a dominant influence over another enterprise pursuant to a contract entered into with that enterprise or to a provision in its memorandum or articles of association;

(d) an enterprise, which is a shareholder in or member of another enterprise, controls alone, pursuant to an agreement with other shareholders in or members of that enterprise, a majority of shareholders' or members' voting rights in that enterprise.

There is a presumption that no dominant influence exists if the investors listed in the second subparagraph of paragraph 2 are not involving themselves directly or indirectly in the management of the enterprise in question, without prejudice to their rights as stakeholders.

Enterprises having any of the relationships described in the first subparagraph through one or more other enterprises, or any one of the investors mentioned in paragraph 2, are also considered to be linked.

Enterprises which have one or other of such relationships through a natural person or group of natural persons acting jointly are also considered linked enterprises if they engage in their activity or in part of their activity in the same relevant market or in adjacent markets.

An 'adjacent market' is considered to be the market for a product or service situated directly upstream or downstream of the relevant market.

4. Except in the cases set out in paragraph 2, second subparagraph, an enterprise cannot be considered an SME if 25% or more of the capital or voting rights are directly or indirectly controlled, jointly or individually, by one or more public bodies.

5. Enterprises may make a declaration of status as an autonomous enterprise, partner enterprise or linked enterprise, including the data regarding the ceilings set out in Article 2. The declaration may be made even if the capital is spread in such a way that it is not possible to determine exactly by whom it is held, in which case the enterprise may declare in good faith that it can legitimately presume that it is not owned as to 25% or more by one enterprise or jointly by enterprises linked to one another. Such declarations are made without prejudice to the checks and investigations provided for by national or Community rules.

Article 4

Data used for the staff headcount and the financial amounts and reference period

1. The data to apply to the headcount of staff and the financial amounts are those relating to the latest approved accounting period and calculated on an annual basis. They are taken into account from the date of closure of the accounts. The amount selected for the turnover is calculated excluding value added tax (VAT) and other indirect taxes.

2. Where, at the date of closure of the accounts, an enterprise finds that, on an annual basis, it has exceeded or fallen below the headcount or financial ceilings stated in Article 2, this will not result in the loss or acquisition of the status of medium-sized, small or microenterprise unless those ceilings are exceeded over two consecutive accounting periods.

3. In the case of newly established enterprises whose accounts have not yet been approved, the data to apply is to be derived from a bona fide estimate made in the course of the financial year.

Article 5

Staff headcount

The headcount corresponds to the number of annual work units (AWU), i.e. the number of persons who worked full-time within the enterprise in question or on its behalf during the entire reference year under consideration. The work of persons who have not worked the full year, the work of those who have worked part-time, regardless of duration, and the work of seasonal workers are counted as fractions of AWU. The staff consists of:

(a)   employees;

(b)   persons working for the enterprise being subordinated to it and deemed to be employees under national law;

(c)   owner-managers;

(d)   partners engaging in a regular activity in the enterprise and benefiting from financial advantages from the enterprise.

Apprentices or students engaged in vocational training with an apprenticeship or vocational training contract are not included as staff. The duration of maternity or parental leaves is not counted.

Article 6

Establishing the data of an enterprise

1.   In the case of an autonomous enterprise, the data, including the number of staff, are determined exclusively on the basis of the accounts of that enterprise.

2.   The data, including the headcount, of an enterprise having partner enterprises or linked enterprises are determined on the basis of the accounts and other data of the enterprise or, where they exist, the consolidated accounts of the enter- prise, or the consolidated accounts in which the enterprise is included through consolidation.

To the data referred to in the first subparagraph are added the data of any partner enterprise of the enterprise in question situated immediately upstream or downstream from it. Aggregation is proportional to the percentage interest in the capital or voting rights (whichever is greater). In the case of cross-holdings, the greater percentage applies.

To the data referred to in the first and second subparagraph is added 100% of the data of any enterprise, which is linked directly or indirectly to the enterprise in question, where the data were not already included through consolidation in the accounts.

3.   For the application of paragraph 2, the data of the partner enterprises of the enterprise in question are derived from their accounts and their other data, consolidated if they exist. To these is added 100% of the data of enterprises which are linked to these partner enterprises, unless their accounts data are already included through consolidation.

For the application of the same paragraph 2, the data of the enterprises which are linked to the enterprise in question are to be derived from their accounts and their other data, consolidated if they exist. To these is added, pro rata, the data of any possible partner enterprise of that linked enterprise, situated immediately upstream or downstream from it, unless it has already been included in the consolidated accounts with a percentage at least proportional to the percentage identified under the second subparagraph of paragraph 2.

4.   Where in the consolidated accounts no staff data appear for a given enterprise, staff figures are calculated by aggregating proportionally the data from its partner enterprises and by adding the data from the enterprises to which the enterprise in question is linked.

TITLE II

SUNDRY PROVISIONS

Article 7

Statistics

The Commission will take the necessary measures to present the statistics that it produces in accordance with the following size-classes of enterprises:

(a)   0 to 1 person;

(b)   2 to 9 persons;

(c)   10 to 49 persons;

(d)   50 to 249 persons.

Article 8

References

1.   Any Community legislation or any Community programme to be amended or adopted and in which the term 'SME', 'microenterprise', 'small enterprise' or 'medium-sized enterprise', or any other similar term occurs, should refer to the definition contained in this Recommendation.

2.   As a transitional measure, current Community programmes using the SME definition in Recommendation 96/280/EC will continue to be implemented for the benefit of the enterprises which were considered SMEs when those programmes were adopted. Legally binding commitments entered into by the Commission on the basis of such programmes will remain unaffected.

Without prejudice to the first subparagraph, any amendment of the SME definition within the programmes can be made only by adopting the definition contained in this Recommendation in accordance with paragraph 1.

Article 9

Revision

On the basis of a review of the application of the definition contained in this Recommendation, to be drawn up by 31 March 2006, and taking account of any amendments to Article 1 of Directive 83/349/EEC on the definition of linked enterprises within the meaning of that Directive, the Commission will, if necessary, adapt the definition contained in this Recommendation, and in particular the ceilings for turnover and the balance-sheet total in order to take account of experience and economic developments in the Community.

Eligible R&D costs At a Glance – SME & Large Company Schemes

INTRODUCTION

This Chapter is deliberately short of detail. It provides a simple checklist of R&D costs from the detailed explanations of eligible R&D costs covered at Chapters 2, 4 and 5.

Costs Eligible for both SME and Large Companies

2013/14:

Present in Alphabetical order

Contributions to independent research

CTA 2009 / S1079

Limited to large company scheme relief.

Contributions towards funded research programmes by large companies are eligible for relief where incurred on payments to qualifying bodies, individuals or partnerships. The parties must not be connected.

Staffing Costs

S1123 1124

Eligible for Both SME and Large Company schemes

Emoluments paid to project personnel directly contributing to the resolution of technical project uncertainties.

This includes salary, Employers National Insurance contributions, pension and bonus payments and reimbursed expenses which are directly relevant to project expenditure.

Where staff indirectly contribute towards the R&D project, costs are eligible as 'Qualifying indirect activity' even where these are of an administrative or supporting nature.

Group companies can sometimes arrange payrolls to be run through one company – this will not prevent relief being available in another group company, provided the staffing costs reflect bona fide R&D activity.

Externally provided workers

S1127 – 1132

Eligible for Both SME and Large Company schemes

Introduced for expenditure incurred on / after 08 April 2003 [SME schemes], / 01 September 2003 [large companies].

65% of the expenditure paid by the claimant in respect of the worker will be eligible for relief. Where the parties are connected, the relief is limited to the 'relevant' expenditure.

EPW's are costs incurred in engaging workers supplied by third parties. Very detailed rules apply to the engagement contract. These are based upon the Regulations at S 44 ITEPA / 2003 which require companies to operate PAYE directly upon workers provided to third party clients.

FA 2012 relaxed the tripartite arrangement conditions where more than three entities were involved, but there must still be at least three parties to any engagement.

The operation of PAYE will be evident and EPW payments will exclude payments to freelance consultants and subcontractor payments or management charges between group companies.

Subcontractor costs

SME Schemes – any third party bona fide subcontractor
ss 1133–1136

Large company schemes – payments to qualifying bodies, individuals or partnerships only S 1078 / 1079

The company may claim 65% of the cost of payments made to unconnected parties. Where the subcontractor and claimant are connected, the relevant cost must be identified from the subcontractors accounting data.

Software and consumable items 1125/1126/cta 2009

Costs incurred upon computer software or consumable items:

Materials used or 'consumed' within project work will be allowable for R&D purposes. Heat, light, power and water are included within the definition.

Expenditure is apportioned where the costs are incurred for dual purposes.

This updated the historical category of 'consumable stores'.

Production costs are not eligible for relief as 'consumable' items.

No territorial limit applies to any of the above expenditure categories

SME & Large Company Schemes:

Cost ineligible for RDTR [put in alphabetical order]
Employee Expenses:

- Reimbursed expenses paid as general allowances and not linked to specific project expenditure

- Redundancy payments: HMRC cite the case of Nichols. From this it can be assumed that other legally based payments such as ex gratia payments or compensation would not attract relief.

- Share incentivisation awards: Paper for paper incentivisation does not represent a 'payment' to project staff despite the fact that PAYE and national insurance contributions may be exigible upon the award of various share based awards.

- Dividends Dividend payments are a distribution of profits or reserves and are not deductible in the company's accounts for tax purposes.

- National Insurance Contributions: Class 4 NIC Contributions, Employees National Insurance contributions

- Benefits in Kind (A loophole existed during FY 2003 and was closed.

- *Freelance/Self Employed Consultants*

- Payments to freelance consultants do not represent payments to either 'subcontractors' or 'externally provided workers'

- *Management charges* Inter company account 'payments' do not fall within the heading of staffing costs or payment to externally provided workers or subcontractors (although they may represent payments for any or all of these costs by a related company)

- *Directors Remuneration* Where this is unpaid 9 months after the company's accounting period

- *Admin Expenses* Administration staff can indirectly contribute toward R&D work, but mainstream administrative costs are not eligible

Rent / Lease payments		These costs are not regarded as 'consumables'
Finance costs		These costs are not regarded as 'consumables' and may constitute a 'subsidy' towards R&D work.
Marketing costs		No 'technical objective' will be apparent
Legal costs		No 'technical objective' will be apparent
Depreciation		Not recognised as a corporation tax deduction
Intellectual property:		The Cost of registering intellectual property and similar rights created as a result of R&D project work etcare not eligible for relief. The costs will represent 'capital' expenditure of the company and in any case be ineliglbe as a cost heading for RDTR.
Negative Goodwill	[Intangible Asset 'expenditure']:	Negative Goodwill represents a book entry and although fundamental to the value of intangible assets in the balance sheet will not be within the scope of S 53.
Acquired know-how:		Intangible asset expenditure. The acquisition of know how is likely to have an enduring benefit and will represent capital expenditure.
		It is unlikely that it will be possible to 'acquire' another company's previous project costs upon a takeover forR& D tax relief purposes.

Professional fees:		As above, payments to bona fide subcontractors are eligible for relief. Depending upon their nature, professional costs attached to the purchase of capital assets / equipment for which a Research Development Allowance claim is made may be eligible for inclusion in the value of the asset concerned.
Recruitment commission		For externally provided workers, or staff
Production costs		Once technical uncertainty has been resolved, the collection of staffing costs and other project costs will stop even where minor adjustments or testing / certification continues.

RD6 Industry sector analysis of number and cost of R&D tax credit claims, 2011–12[1,2,3,4]

| | SME R&D scheme | | Large companies R&D scheme | | | | All schemes | |
| | | | Large companies | | SME sub-contractors | | Numbers: actual / Amounts: £ million | |
Industry sector	Number of claims	Amount claimed	Number of claims	Amount claimed	Number of claims	Amount claimed	Number of claims	Amount claimed
Agriculture & Fishing	30	–	5	5	–	–	40	–
Mining & quarrying	25	–	25	25	5	–	55	25
Manufacturing	2,490	95	870	300	90	–	3,450	395
Distribution of gas, electricity & water	15	–	30	15	–	–	45	15
Construction	140	5	65	10	5	–	210	15
Wholesale & retail trade, Hotels & restaurants	485	10	95	15	20	–	600	25

	SME R&D scheme		Large companies R&D scheme				All schemes	
			Large companies		SME sub-contractors		Numbers: actual Amounts: £ million	
Industry sector	Number of claims	Amount claimed	Number of claims	Amount claimed	Number of claims	Amount claimed	Number of claims	Amount claimed
Transport, storage & communication	135	5	35	5	5	–	170	10
Financial Intermediation	30	5	25	15	–	–	55	20
Business Services	2,930	175	535	270	180	5	3,655	450
Public administration & Defence	5	–	5	20	–	–	10	20
Education, Health & Social Work	75	5	20	5	15	–	105	10
Other activities	275	10	50	30	10	–	335	35
All	**6,630**	**310**	**1,755**	**705**	**325**	**10**	**8,720**	**1,025**

1 Industry sector is based on primary SIC2003 coding of registered company. This coding might not correspond to the industry sector of the R&D activity, so caution must be exercised when interpreting these figures.

2 Figures exclude claims where industry sector is not known.

3 Numbers are rounded to the nearest 5; those below 3 are suppressed.

4 Amounts are rounded to the nearest £5m; those below £2.5m are suppressed.

The R&D Timeline

FA 2000 to FA 2013

UK R&D legislation has developed through sequential Finance Acts. The publication of CTA in 2009 consolidated many of these changes, but the Finance Acts of 2011 and 2012 introduced seminal changes to the reliefs. Other legislation has brought in key incentives for corporate intangible assets, such as the Patent Box, which runs alongside but impacts upon the main R&D reliefs.

2000

FA 2000

02.04.2000	SME R&D Scheme introduced tax relief as a 150% enhancement for expenditure incurred after 01 04 2000. £25,000 de minimis limit.
28.07.2000	DTI Guidelines 'The Definition of R&D for tax purposes' is published

The Mainstream corporation tax rate is 30% and remains unchanged until FY 2008.

The small company rate is 20%, and then remains at 19% from FY 2002 through to FY 2007.

2002

FA 2002

01.04.2002	The 'Large company' R&D Scheme is introduced, for expenditure incurred on or after 01/04/2002.

2003

FA 2003

- The project de minimis limits are lowered for both SME and Large Schemes [£10,000 and £25,000], FA 2003, Sch 31, paras 2 and 9.

- Inclusion of a new category of qualifying expenditure – expenditure on externally provided workers.

- Introduction of ITEPA: Change to the definition of staffing costs to *include* certain benefits in kind. Quickly abolished by FA 2004, Sch 17, para 7(1).

- Large companies able to claim relief for Externally Provided workers

- FA 2003, Sch 31, para 3.

- Removal of the 80:20 arrangements for expenditure on staffing costs incurred on or after 9 April 2003 under the large company scheme 27 September 2003 for SMEs.

- An extension of the large company scheme to subsidised SMEs that were barred from claiming under the rules of the SME scheme (FA 2003, Sch 31, para 15).

2004

- FA2004 – Introduction of new category of R&D expenditure, 'consumable items and software' to replace 'consumable stores'; for expenditure incurred on or after 1 4 04: S141/FA 2004.

BIS Guidelines restated, providing 'clearer' definitions of R&D published in the 'BIS Guidelines', 5 March 2004 given effect by Statutory Instrument, SI 2004/712.

Rules on when capitalised R&D expenditure can qualify for relief included in Finance Act. Providing clarity for the treatment of intangible assets qualifying for RDTR, where the adoption of International Accounting Standards or UK GAAP might otherwise obscure or delay relief: Key clauses: S 53/FA 2004.

2005

01 January 2005: New EC definition of an SME becomes effective, 2003/361 EC.

Reith Lecture: 'Technology will determine the future of the human race'.

2006

FA 2006

- R&D relief for payments to participants in clinical trials legislated: 01 April 2006 for Large Companies; 01 August 2008 for SME's; FA 2006, s 28 ; Sch 2.

- Claim time limits for R&D tax relief aligned to deadlines for claiming R&D tax credits for accounting periods ending on or after 01 April 2006 FA 2006, s 29; Sch 3.

- 01/04/06 Large company scheme: expenditure on clinical trials allowable.

November 06 HMRC R&D Units set up.

2007

Small company rate of corporation tax increases to 20 % FY 2007.

FA 2007:	SME rate of Vaccine research relief set at 50%
	SME Thresholds uplifted to 500 persons / balance sheet total E86m/ turnover total E100m
	Significant extensions to HMRC penalty powers for errors in records, documents and company tax returns

2008

The mainstream corporation tax rate is reduced to 28% FY 2008 through to FY 2011.

The small company rate increases to 21% for FY 2008 to FY 2010.

01.04.08	New category of expenditure in SME scheme – clinical trials
01.04.08	Large company scheme rate increased from 125% to 130%
01.08.08	SME rate of relief increased from 150% to 175%,

SME Repayable tax credit rate reduced to 14 from 16%.

01.08.08	'Going concern' condition applied to SME and vaccine rates of relief
01.08.08	Project cap of E7.5m total aid applied to SME and vaccine expenditure by project
01.08.08	Rate of vaccine research relief reduced from 50 to 40%
01.08.08	Extension of staffing costs to include overseas NI
01.12.08	Transitional rules for SME's entering large scheme clarified

2009

26.03.09	Enactment CTA 2009
	SME intellectual property requirement abolished, CTA 2009, ss 1052.53.1139

2010

Dyson Report published: 'Ingenious Britain – Making the UK the leading exporter of technology, James Dyson March 2010.

2011

01.04.2011	Mainstream rate of corporation tax reduced to 26% FY 2011
	Small company rate of corporation tax reduced to 20%

SME R&D tax relief enhanced to 200%, repayable tax credit reduced to 12.5%.

2012

01.04.2012	Mainstream rate of corporation tax reduced to 24% FY 2012

FA 2012, Sch 3:

- 01.04.2012 SME R&D tax relief enhanced to 125%, repayable tax credit reduced to 11%
  - De minimis project limit of £10,000 abolished
  - Going concern condition clarified to include companies in liquidation or administration

- PAYE Cap abolished (SME scheme)
- Abolition of SME Vaccine reliefs
- Tripartite rules upon externally provided workers relaxed and modified

2013

01.04.2013	Mainstream rate of corporation tax reduced to 23% FY 2013

FA 2013

S 36 Announcement of TV Production and Video Games Development reliefs Schedule 15 – Large company scheme:

- Introduction of RD Expenditure Credit, for expenditure incurred on or after 01 April 2013.
- Abolition of large company 'legacy', enhanced deduction scheme by 31 3 2016 announced

August 2013	National Statistics Office publish 2011/12 HMRC Claims data
October 2013	HMRC publish detailed RDEC guidance
November 2013	European Commission publish EU R&D Scoreboard, UK placed second behind Germany in large company activity
November 2013	European Commission publishes details of long term R&D support
	Horizon 2020 Grant/subsidy scheme for R&D formulated

Summary of corporation tax rates/RDTR/Tax Credit Rates

FY (01.04)	2000	2001	2002	2003	2004	2005	2006	2007	2008	2009	2010
Main rate	30%	30%	30%	30%	30%	30%	30%	30%	28	28	28
Small company rate	20%	19%	19%	19%	19%	19%	19%	19%	21%	21%	21%
R&D											
SME rate of enhancement	150%	150	150	150%	150%	150%	150%	150%	01 Aug 08 175%	175%	175%
Tax Credit											
Large Company	–	–	125%	125%	125%	125%	125%	125%	01.Apr 08: 130%	130%	130%

Appendix 7

	2011	2012	2013	2014
Main rate	26	24	23	22
Small company rate	20	20	20	20
R&D:				
SME Enhancement:	01 Apr 11: 200%	01 Apr 12: 225% De minimis limit abolished	225%	225%
Large company enhancement	130%	130%De minimis limit abolished	130%	130%
RDEC	–	–	01 Apr 13: 10	

Appendix 8

HMRC R&D units

Postcode list

From 1 November 2006, companies whose main R&D activities are located in one of the following postcodes should send their corporation tax returns containing R&D tax credit or relief claims to the appropriate office listed below.

AB Cardiff	DG Cardiff	IP Cambridge	OL Manchester	SY Cardiff
AL Cambridge	DH Manchester	IV Cardiff	OX Solent	TA Cardiff
B Leicester	DL Manchester	KA Cardiff	PA Cardiff	TD Cardiff
BA Cardiff	DN Leicester	KT Croydon	PE Cambridge	TF Leicester
BB Manchester	DT Solent	KW Cardiff	PH Cardiff	TN Croydon
BD Manchester	DY Leicester	KY Cardiff	PL Cardiff	TQ Cardiff
BH Solent	E Cambridge	L Manchester	PO Solent	TR Cardiff
BL Manchester	EC Cambridge	LA Manchester	PR Manchester	TS Manchester
BN Solent	EH Cardiff	LD Cardiff	RG Solent	TW Croydon
BR Croydon	EN Cambridge	LE Leicester	RH Croydon	UB Croydon
BS Cardiff	EX Cardiff	LL Cardiff	RM Cambridge	W Croydon
BT Croydon	FK Cardiff	LN Leicester	S Leicester	WA Manchester
CA Manchester	FY Manchester	LS Manchester	SA Cardiff	WC Croydon
CB Cambridge	G Cardiff	LU Cambridge	SE Croydon	WD Cambridge
CF Cardiff	GL Cardiff	M Manchester	SG Cambridge	WF Manchester
CH Manchester	GU Solent	ME Croydon	SK Manchester	WN Manchester
CM Cambridge	HA Cambridge	MK Cambridge	SL Croydon	WR Cardiff
CO Cambridge	HD Manchester	ML Cardiff	SM Croydon	WS Leicester
CR Croydon	HG Manchester	N Cambridge	SN Solent	WV Leicester
CT Croydon	HP Croydon	NE Manchester	SO Solent	YO Manchester
CV Leicester	HR Cardiff	NG Leicester	SP Solent	ZE Cardiff
CW Manchester	HS Cardiff	NN Leicester	SR Manchester	
DA Croydon	HU Manchester	NP Cardiff	SS Cambridge	
DD Cardiff	HX Manchester	NR Cambridge	ST Manchester	
DE Leicester	IG Cambridge	NW Croydon	SW Croydon	

(HMRC Manual CIRD80360)

Specialist Unit contact details

Cambridge R&D Unit	Eastbrook Shaftsbury Road Cambridge CB2 2DJ Telephone 03000 542 315
Croydon R&D Unit	Local Compliance S1137 PO Box 3900 Glasgow G70 6AA Telephone 03000 511 811
Leicester R&D Unit	Local Compliance S0563PO Box 3900 Glasgow G70 6AA Telephone 0116 253 5402
Manchester R&D Unit	Local Compliance S0717PO Box 3900 Glasgow G70 6AA Telephone 03000 510 190
Solent R&D Unit	Local Compliance S0793PO Box 3900 Glasgow G70 6AA Telephone 03000 530476
Cardiff R&D Unit (Wales, Scotland and Northern Ireland)	Local Compliance S0970PO Box 3900 Glasgow G70 6AA Telephone 03000 582420

(HMRC Manual CIRD80350)

Appendix 9

Sources used in this book

NAO	R&D Funding for Science & Innovation in the UK	June 2013
BIS	Innovation and Research Strategy for Growth	December 2011
J Dyson	Ingenious Britain	March 2010
European Commission	The 2013 EU Industrial R&D Investment Scoreboard	September 2013
OECD	Frascati Manual – Standardisation practice for R&D surveys 2002	

HM Revenue & Customs, Research and Development (R&D) Relief for Corporation Tax 2012.

Office for National Statistics, Business Enterprise Research and Development, 2011.

European Commission, Europe 2020 targets.

Organisation for Economic Cooperation and Development, OECD Science, Technology and Industry Scoreboard 2011, September 2011.

Thomson Reuters, Top 100 Global Innovators, 2012, 2012.

Appendix 10

Linked and Partner Enterprises

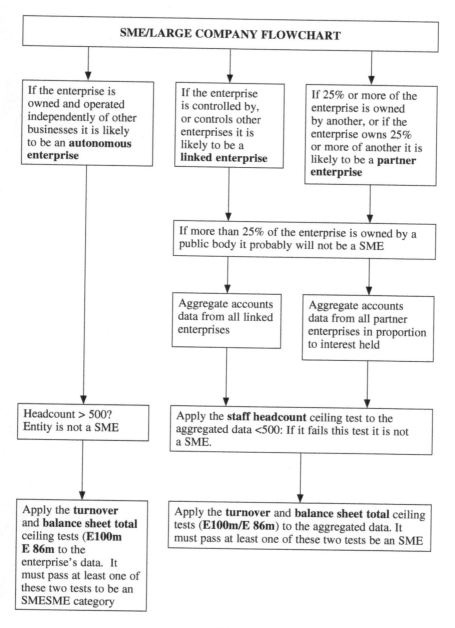

| SME/LARGE COMPANY FLOWCHART |

If the enterprise is owned and operated independently of other businesses it is likely to be an **autonomous enterprise**

If the enterprise is controlled by, or controls other enterprises it is likely to be a **linked enterprise**

If 25% or more of the enterprise is owned by another, or if the enterprise owns 25% or more of another it is likely to be a **partner enterprise**

If more than 25% of the enterprise is owned by a public body it probably will not be a SME

Aggregate accounts data from all linked enterprises

Aggregate accounts data from all partner enterprises in proportion to interest held

Headcount > 500? Entity is not a SME

Apply the **staff headcount** ceiling test to the aggregated data <500: If it fails this test it is not a SME.

Apply the **turnover** and **balance sheet total** ceiling tests (**E100m E 86m** to the enterprise's data. It must pass at least one of these two tests to be an SMESME category

Apply the **turnover** and **balance sheet total** ceiling tests (**E100m/E 86m**) to the aggregated data. It must pass at least one of these two tests be an SME

Linked and Partner Enterprises

SQUARE A COMPANY FLOWCHART

Appendix 11

SME definition: text of 1996/280/EC

COMMISSION RECOMMENDATION (1996/280/EC)

of 3 April 1996 concerning the definition of small and medium-sized enterprises

THE COMMISSION OF THE EUROPEAN COMMUNITIES

Having regard to the Treaty establishing the European Commission, and in particular Article 155, second indent, thereof,

Whereas the implementation of the Integrated Programme in Favour of Small and Medium-Sized Enterprises (SMEs) and the Craft Sector (hereinafter referred to as 'the Integrated Programme') (1), in accordance with the White Paper on Growth, Competitiveness and Employment, requires the establishment of a coherent, visible and effective framework within which the enterprise policy in favour of SMEs can take its place;

Whereas, well before the implementation of the Integrated Programme, various Community policies were targeted at SMEs, each policy using different criteria to define them; whereas a number of Community policies have developed gradually with no joint approach or overall consideration of what, objectively, constitutes an SME; the result being a diversity of criteria used to define an SME and thus, a multiplicity of definitions currently in use at Community level in addition to the definitions used by the European Investment Bank (EIB) and the European Investment Fund (EIF) together with a rather wide range of definitions in the Member States;

Whereas many Member States have no general definition and operate ad hoc with rules based on local practice or which apply to particular sectors; whereas others adhere rigidly to the definition contained in the Community guidelines on State aid to SMEs (2);

Whereas the existence of different definitions at Community level and at national level can create inconsistencies and can also distort competition between enterprises; whereas the Integrated Programme aims at a more forceful coordination between, on the one hand, the different Community initiatives in favour of SMEs and, on the other hand, between these and the initiatives which exist at national level; whereas these objectives cannot be realized successfully unless the question of the definition of SMEs is clarified;

Whereas the Commission's Report to the European Council meeting in Madrid on 15 and 16 December 1995 has underlined that a refocused effort in favour of SMEs is required in order to create more jobs across all sectors of the economy;

Whereas the 'Research' Council of 29 September 1994 agreed that preferential treatment for SMEs should be accompanied by a clearer definition of what was meant by a small or medium-sized enterprise; therefore it has requested the Commission to re-examine the criteria to be selected for defining SMEs;

Whereas, in a first Report presented in 1992 at the request of the 'Industry' Council held on 28 May 1990, the Commission had already proposed limiting the proliferation of definitions in use at Community level; specifically, it favoured the adoption of the following four criteria: number of persons employed, turnover, balance-sheet total and independence, while proposing thresholds of 50 and 250 employees for small and for medium-sized enterprises respectively;

Whereas this definition has been adopted in the Community guidelines on State aid for SMEs and in all the other guidelines or communications concerning State aid which have been adopted or revised since 1992 (it applies in particular to the Commission Communication to the Member States on the accelerated clearance of aid schemes for SMEs and of amendments of existing schemes (3), the guidelines on State aid for environmental protection (4) and the guidelines on State aids for rescuing and restructuring firms in difficulty (5);

Whereas other measures adopt this definition wholly or in part, notably the Fourth Council Directive (78/660/EEC) of 25 July 1978 based on Article 54 (3) (g) of the Treaty on the annual accounts of certain types of companies (6), as last amended by Directive 94/8/EC (7), Council Decision 94/217/EEC of 19 April 1994 on the provision of Community interest subsidies on loans for small and medium-sized enterprises extended by the European Investment Bank under its temporary lending facility (8), and the Commission's Communication (9) on the Community SME Initiative under the Structural Funds;

Whereas, however, full convergence has not yet been achieved; some programmes still fix very varied thresholds or disregard certain criteria, such as independence;

Whereas it is appropriate that this convergence continues and is completed on the basis of the rules set out in the Community guidelines on State aids for SMEs, and that the Commission should apply, in all the policies it administers, the same criteria and the same thresholds which it requires Member States to observe;

Whereas in a single market without internal frontiers, the treatment of enterprises must be based on a set of common rules, particularly as regards State support – national or Community;

Whereas this approach is all the more necessary in view of the extensive interaction between national and Community measures assisting SMEs, for example as regards Structural Funds and research; it means that situations in which the Community targets its action on a certain category of SMEs and the Member States on another must be avoided;

Whereas application of the same definition by the Commission, the Member States, the EIB and the EIF would reinforce the consistency and effectiveness of policies targeting SMEs and would, therefore, limit the risk of distortion of competition; whereas, moreover, many programmes intended for SMEs are co-financed by the Member States and the EC and, in some cases, by the EIB and the EIF;

Whereas before proposing thresholds for defining SMEs, it should be pointed out that this attempt to rationalize and lay down a reference standard does not mean that enterprises which exceed these thresholds do not deserve State or Community attention; however it would be more appropriate to solve this problem through specific measures in the framework of the relevant programmes, in particular international cooperation programmes, rather than by adopting or maintaining a different SME definition;

Whereas the criterion of number of persons employed is undoubtedly one of the most important and must be regarded as imperative but that introducing a financial criterion is a necessary complement in order to grasp the real importance and performance of an enterprise and its position compared to its competitors;

Whereas, however, it would not be desirable to adopt turnover as the sole financial criterion because enterprise in the trade and distribution sector have by their nature higher turnover figures than those in the manufacturing sector, thus the turnover criterion should be combined with that of the balance sheet total, a criterion which represents the overall wealth of a business, with the possibility of one of these two financial criteria being exceeded;

Whereas independence is also a basic criterion in that an SME belonging to a large group has access to funds and assistance not available to competitors of equal size; whereas there is also a need to rule out legal entities composed of SMEs which form a grouping whose actual economic power is greater than that of an SME;

Whereas, in respect of the independence criterion, the Member States, the EIB and the EIF should ensure that the definition is not circumvented by those enterprises, which, whilst formally meeting this criterion, are in fact controlled by one large enterprise or jointly by several large enterprises;

Whereas stakes held by public investment corporations or venture capital companies do not normally change the character of a firm from that of an SME, and may therefore be disregarded; the same applies to stakes held by institutional investors, who usually maintain an 'arm's-length' relationship with the company in which they have invested;

Whereas a solution must be found to the problem of joint stock enterprises which, although they are SMEs, cannot state with any accuracy the composition of their share ownership due to the way in which their capital is dispersed and the anonymity of their shareholders and cannot therefore know whether they meet the condition of independence;

Whereas, therefore, fairly strict criteria must be laid down for defining SMEs if the measures aimed at them are genuinely to benefit the enterprises for which size represents a handicap;

Whereas the threshold of 500 employees is not truly selective, since it encompasses almost all enterprises (99,9 % of the 14 million enterprises) and almost three-quarters of the European economy in terms of employment and turnover; furthermore, an enterprise with 500 employees has access to human, financial and technical resources which fall well outside the framework of the medium-sized enterprise, namely ownership and management in the same hands, often family-owned, and lack of a dominant position on the market;

Whereas, not only do enterprises between 250 and 500 employees often have very strong market positions but they also possess very solid management structures in the fields of production, sales, marketing, research and personnel management, which clearly distinguish them from medium-sized enterprises with up to 250 employees; whereas in the latter group, such structures are far more fragile; whereas the threshold of 250 persons employed is therefore a more meaningful reflection of the reality of an SME;

Whereas this threshold of 250 employees is already the most prevalent among the definitions used at Community level and whereas it has been taken up in the legislation of many Member States as a result of the Community guidelines on State aid for SMEs; whereas the EIB had also decided to use this definition for a substantial part of the loans granted in the framework of the 'SME facility' provided for in Decision 94/217/EEC;

Whereas, according to Eurostat figures, the turnover of an enterprise with 250 employees does not exceed ECU 40 million (1994 figures); whereas it would therefore appear reasonable to apply a threshold for turnover of ECU 40 million; whereas recent calculations show that the average ratio between turnover and balance sheet total is 1:5 or SMEs and small enterprises (10), whereas, as a result, the threshold for the balance-sheet total should be fixed at ECU 27 million;

Whereas, however, a distinction must be drawn, within SMEs, between medium-sized enterprises, small enterprises and micro-enterprises; whereas the latter should not be confused with craft enterprises, which will continue to be defined at national level due to their specific characteristics;

Whereas thresholds for small enterprises must be fixed in the same way, meaning thresholds of ECU 7 million for turnover, and ECU 5 million for balance sheet total;

Whereas the thresholds chosen do not necessarily reflect the average SME or small enterprise but represent ceilings designed to allow all enterprises having the characteristics of an SME or a small enterprise to be included within one or other of the categories;

Whereas the turnover and balance-sheet total thresholds laid down for defining SMEs should be revised as the need arises to take account of changing economic circumstances such as price levels and increases in the productivity of enterprises;

Whereas the Community guidelines on State aids for SMEs will be aligned by replacing the currently used definitions with a reference to those set out in this Recommendation;

Whereas it is necessary to provide that when the Fourth Council Directive 78/660/EEC, which affords Member States the right to exempt SMEs from certain obligations relating to the publication of their accounts, is next amended, the Commission will propose that the existing definition be replaced by a reference to this Recommendation;

Whereas it would also be desirable for evaluations made of measures in favour of SMEs that the Commission, the Member States, the EIB and the EIF state exactly which enterprises benefit from them, distinguishing various categories of SME according to size, as greater knowledge of the recipients makes it possible to adjust and better target the measures proposed for SMEs, and consequently renders them more effective;

Whereas, given that a certain degree of flexibility must be permitted to the Member States, the EIB and the EIF to fix thresholds lower than the Community thresholds if they wish to direct their measures towards a specific category of SME, these thresholds represent only maximum limits;

Whereas it is also possible for the Member States, the EIB and the EIF, for reasons of administrative simplification, to retain only one criterion, notably that of the number of employees, for the implementation of some of their policies. However, this flexibility does not apply to the various State aid frameworks where the financial criteria must also be respected;

Whereas this Recommendation concerns only the definition of SMEs used in Community policies applied within the Community and the European Economic Area,

MAKES THIS RECOMMENDATION:

Article 1

Member States, the European Investment Bank and the European Investment Fund are invited:

- to comply with the provisions set out in Article 1 of the Annex for their programmes directed towards 'SMEs', 'medium-sized enterprises', 'small enterprises' or 'micro-enterprises',

- to comply with the ceilings chosen for the turnover and balance-sheet total where they are amended by the Commission in accordance with Article 2 of the Annex,

- to take the necessary steps with a view to using the size classes set out in Article 3 (2) of the Annex, especially where the monitoring of Community financial instruments is concerned.

Article 2

The thresholds specified in Article 1 of the Annex are to be regarded as ceilings. Member States, the European Investment Bank and the European Investment Fund may, in certain cases, choose to fix lower thresholds. In implementing certain of their policies, they may also choose to apply only the criterion of number of employees, except in fields to which the various rules on State aid apply.

Article 3

To enable the Commission to evaluate what progress has been made, Member States, the European Investment Bank and the European Investment Fund are invited to inform the Commission, before 31 December 1977, of the measures they have taken to comply with this Recommendation.

Article 4

This Recommendation concerns the definition of SMEs in Community policies applied within the Community and the European Economic Area and is addressed to the Member States, the European Investment Bank and the European Investment Fund.

Done at Brussels, 3 April 1996.

For the Commission

Christos PAPOUTSIS

Member of the Commission

(1) COM(94) 207 final.

(2) OJ No C 213, 19. 8. 1992, p. 2.

(3) OJ No C 213, 19. 8. 1992, p. 10.

(4) OJ No C 72, 10. 3. 1994, p. 3, footnote 16.

(5) OJ No C 368, 23.12. 1994, p. 12.

(6) OJ No L 222, 14. 8. 1978, p. 11.

(7) OJ No L 82, 25. 3. 1994, p. 33.

(8) OJ No L 107, 28. 4. 1994 p. 57; see Commission Report on this matter (COM(94) 434 final of 19 October 1994).

(9) OJ No C 180, 1. 7. 1994, p. 10.

(10) Source: 'BACH' (harmonized accounts) database.

ANNEX

DEFINITION OF SMALL AND MEDIUM-SIZED ENTERPRISES ADOPTED BY THE COMMISSION

Article 1

1. Small and medium-sized enterprises, hereinafter referred to as 'SMEs', are defined as enterprises which:
   - have fewer than 250 employees, and
   - have either,
     - an annual turnover not exceeding ECU 40 million, or
     - an annual balance-sheet total not exceeding ECU 27 million,
   - conform to the criterion of independence as defined in paragraph 3.

2. Where it is necessary to distinguish between small and medium-sized enterprises, the 'small enterprise' is defined as an enterprise which:
   - has fewer than 50 employees, and
   - has either,
     - an annual turnover not exceeding ECU 7 million, or
     - an annual balance-sheet total not exceeding ECU 5 million,
   - conforms to the criterion of independence as defined in paragraph 3.

3.   Independent enterprises are those which are not owned as to 25% or more of the capital or the voting rights by one enterprise, or jointly by several enterprises, falling outside the definition of an SME or a small enterprise, whichever may apply. This threshold may be exceeded in the following two cases:

   •   if the enterprise is held by public investment corporations, venture capital companies or institutional investors, provided no control is exercised either individually or jointly,

   •   if the capital is spread in such a way that it is not possible to determine by whom it is held and if the enterprise declares that it can legitimately presume that it is not owned as to 25% or more by one enterprise, or jointly by several enterprises, falling outside the definitions of an SME or a small enterprise, whichever may apply.

4.   In calculating the thresholds referred to in paragraphs 1 and 2, it is therefore necessary to cumulate the relevant figures for the beneficiary enterprise and for all the enterprises, which it directly or indirectly controls through possession of 25% or more of the capital or of the voting rights.

5.   Where it is necessary to distinguish micro-enterprises from other SMEs, these are defined as enterprises having fewer than 10 employees.

6.   Where, at the final balance sheet date, an enterprise exceeds or falls below the employee thresholds or financial ceilings, this is to result in its acquiring or losing the status of 'SME', 'medium-sized enterprise', 'small enterprise' or 'micro-enterprise' only if the phenomenon is repeated over two consecutive financial years.

7.   The number of persons employed corresponds to the number of annual working units (AWU), that is to say, the number of full-time workers employed during one year with part-time and seasonal workers being fractions of AWU. The reference year to be considered is that of the last approved accounting period.

8.   The turnover and balance sheet total thresholds are those of the last approved 12-month accounting period. In the case of newly established enterprises whose accounts have not yet been approved, the thresholds to apply shall be derived from a reliable estimate made in the course of the financial year.

Article 2

The Commission will amend the ceilings chosen for the turnover and balance-sheet total as the need arises and normally every four years from the adoption of this Recommendation, to take account of changing economic circumstances in the Community.

Article 3

1. The Commission undertakes to adopt the appropriate measures to ensure that the definition of SMEs, as set out in Article 1, applies to all programmes managed by it in which the terms 'SME', 'medium-sized enterprise', 'small enterprise' or 'micro-enterprise' are mentioned.

2. The Commission undertakes to adopt the appropriate measures to adapt the statistics that it produces in line with the following size-classes:

    0 employees,

    1 to 9 employees,

    10 to 49 employees,

    50 to 249 employees,

    250 to 499 employees,

    500 employees plus.

3. Current Community programmes defining SMEs with criteria other than those mentioned in Article 1 will continue, during a transitional period, to be implemented to the benefit of the enterprises, which were considered SMEs when these programmes were adopted. Any modification of the SME definition within these programmes can be made only by adopting the definition contained herein and by replacing the divergent definition with a reference to this Recommendation. This transitional period should in principle end at the latest on 31 December 1997. However, legally binding commitments entered into by the Commission on the basis of these programmes will remain unaffected.

4. When the Fourth Council Directive 78/660/EEC is amended, the Commission will propose that the existing criteria for defining SMEs be replaced by a reference to the definition contained in this Recommendation.

5. Any provisions adopted by the Commission which mention the terms 'SME', 'medium-sized enterprise', 'small enterprise' or 'micro-enterprise, or any other such term, will refer to the definition contained in this Recommendation.

GRIPPLE LIMITED v THE COMMISSIONERS FOR HM REVENUE AND CUSTOMS

[2010] EWHC 1609 (Ch)

Mr Justice Henderson:

Introduction

1.   This appeal raises a short question about the entitlement of a company which is a small or medium-sized enterprise ('SME') to enhanced tax relief for expenditure on research and development ('R&D tax relief') pursuant to provisions which were first enacted in section 69 of, and schedule 20 to, the Finance Act 2000, and are now contained (together with provisions relating to certain other reliefs of a similar nature) in Part 13 of the Corporation Tax Act 2009 (sections 1039 to 1142).

2.   The issue, shortly stated, is whether the appellant, Gripple Limited ('Gripple'), was entitled to claim R&D tax relief in its three accounting periods being the calendar years 2004, 2005 and 2006 respectively, in respect of payments which it made to an associated company, Loadhog Limited ('Loadhog'), for R&D services provided to it by Loadhog. Those services took the form of work carried out by Mr Hugh Facey, who was at all material times a director of both Gripple and Loadhog. As I understand it, he was also the founder of Gripple's business, and in conjunction with a family trust he was Gripple's controlling shareholder.

3.   It is common ground that Gripple satisfied all but one of the conditions for grant of the relief, and that it was entitled to claim it if, but only if, the sums so paid by Gripple to Loadhog constituted expenditure on 'staffing costs' within the meaning of paragraph 5(1) of schedule 20 to the 2000 Act. So far as material, paragraph 5 provides as follows:

'5(1) For the purposes of this Schedule the staffing costs of a company are –

(a)   the emoluments paid by the company to directors or employees of the company, including all salaries, wages, perquisites and profits whatsoever other than benefits in kind;

(b)   the secondary Class 1 national insurance contributions paid by the company; and

      (c)   the contributions paid by the company to any pension fund ... operated for the benefit of directors or employees of the company.

         ...

    (2)   The staffing costs of a company attributable to relevant research and development are those paid to, or in respect of, directors or employees directly and actively engaged in such research and development.'

The wording of paragraph 5(1)(a) which I have quoted was substituted by the Finance Act 2004 with effect for expenditure incurred after 31 March 2004, with the object of excluding benefits in kind from the definition of staffing costs. Before the substitution, paragraph 5(1)(a) simply referred to 'the earnings paid by the company to directors and employees of the company'. It is agreed that for present purposes nothing turns on this change in wording.

4.   Gripple prepared its tax computations, and paid corporation tax under the corporate self-assessment regime, on the footing that it was entitled to claim the relief for the full amounts invoiced to it by Loadhog in respect of Mr Facey's work on R&D. HMRC disagreed, and in due course the issue came before the General Commissioners for the Division of Sheaf and Don on the hearing of appeals by Gripple against (a) HMRC's amendment of Gripple's self-assessment return for its 2004 accounting period, and (b) discovery assessments by HMRC in respect of the two following accounting periods. The hearing took place on 27 January 2009. Gripple was represented by an accountant, Mr T Holmes of Holmes Widlake Accountants. Mr Facey gave oral evidence, but there were no other witnesses. HMRC were represented by two officers, Mrs Ann Green and Mr Alan Bamford. The documents before the Commissioners consisted of a schedule of R&D statistics provided by Mr Facey, and a number of extracts from Gripple's accounts and tax returns for the relevant years, and from Mr Facey's personal tax returns, produced by HMRC.

5.   The General Commissioners dismissed the appeals, having accepted HMRC's submission that the relevant sums paid by Gripple to Loadhog were not staffing costs within the meaning of schedule 20 paragraph 5. Gripple expressed dissatisfaction with the decision, and requested the Commissioners to state a case for the opinion of the High Court. The case stated was duly signed by the Commissioners on 4 November 2009, and the appeal came on for hearing before me on 11 May 2010. Both sides were now represented by counsel, Mr Keith Gordon and Ms Ximena Montes Manzano for Gripple and Mr David Yates for HMRC.

6.   It is appropriate to record that this must be one of the last tax appeals to come before the High Court by way of case stated. It does so because the hearing below took place some two months before the First-tier Tribunal (Tax Chamber) came into existence on 1 April 2009 and took over the first-instance jurisdiction in respect of direct tax appeals previously

exercised by the Special and General Commissioners. Unlike the Special Commissioners and the VAT and Duties Tribunal, the General Commissioners were not automatically abolished on 1 April 2009, and by virtue of paragraph 4 of the Tribunals Courts and Enforcement Act 2007 (Commencement No. 6 and Transitional Provisions) Order 2008 (SI 2008/2696) they remain in existence where there is a statement of case for the opinion of the High Court under section 56 of the Taxes Management Act 1970, so that (for example) the matter may still be remitted to them by the High Court.

7.   By virtue of section 56(6), the appeal to the High Court lies only on questions of law arising on the case stated. The question of law formulated in paragraph 12 of the case stated in the present case is:

> 'Whether we have misdirected ourselves as to the application of Schedule 20 Finance Act 2000 in respect of the expenditure of [Gripple] relating to the cost of the services provided by Mr Hugh Facey.'

Legislation

8.   R&D tax relief was introduced in 2000, with the evident purpose of providing a fiscal incentive to SMEs to incur expenditure on R&D. So long as such expenditure is incurred wholly and exclusively for the purposes of a trade carried on by the company, its full amount will be deductible in accordance with normal principles in computing the taxable profits of the trade: see section 74(1)(a) of the Income and Corporation Taxes Act 1988. Where, however, a company was entitled to claim R&D tax relief, the deductible amount of qualifying R&D expenditure was treated 'as if it were an amount equal to 150% of the actual amount': schedule 20 paragraph 13. So a deduction was allowed for one and a half times the amount of the actual expenditure.

9.   The basic conditions of entitlement to the relief were set out in paragraph 1 of schedule 20. (Here, as elsewhere in this judgment, I refer to the legislation as amended and in force in 2005, unless the contrary is stated). For present purposes, the details are unimportant. The company has to be a SME (defined in paragraph 2 by reference to Commission Recommendation 2003/361/EC of 6 May 2003, subject to certain qualifications). There is a minimum amount of qualifying R&D expenditure (£10,000 for a 12 month accounting period), and it has to be deductible in computing the profits of a trade carried on by the company. If the company is not yet carrying on a trade, it suffices if the expenditure would be deductible if the company were carrying on a trade consisting of the activities to which the expenditure relates.

10.   Paragraph 3 then defines 'qualifying R&D expenditure':

> '3(1) For the purposes of this Schedule "qualifying R&D expenditure" of a company means expenditure that meets the following conditions.

(2)   The first condition is that the expenditure is not of a capital nature.

(3)   The second condition is that the expenditure is attributable to relevant research and development (see paragraph 4) directly undertaken by the company or on its behalf.

(4)   The third condition is that the expenditure –

    (a)   is incurred on staffing costs (see paragraph 5),

    (b)   is incurred on software or consumable items (see paragraph 6),

    (c)   is qualifying expenditure on externally provided workers (see paragraphs 8A to 8E), or

    (d)   is qualifying expenditure on sub-contracted research and development (see paragraphs 9 to 12).

(5)   The fourth condition is that any intellectual property (see paragraph 7) created as a result of the research and development to which the expenditure is attributable is, or will be, vested in the company (whether alone or with other persons).

(6)   The fifth condition is that the expenditure is not incurred by the company in carrying on activities the carrying on of which is contracted out to the company by any person.

(7)   The sixth condition is that the expenditure is not subsidised (see paragraph 8).'

11.   The remaining paragraphs in Part I of the schedule then explain and amplify the conditions set out in paragraph 3. I have already quoted the relevant parts of paragraph 5, which deals with staffing costs. I should also refer to the provisions relating to qualifying expenditure on externally provided workers, the material parts of which are as follows:

'8A(1)   The provisions of paragraphs 8C to 8E have effect for determining the amount of the qualifying expenditure of a company ("the company") on externally provided workers.

(2)   ...

(3)   For the purposes of this Schedule the company incurs expenditure on externally provided workers if it makes a payment (a "staff provision payment") to another person (the "staff provider") in respect of the supply to the company, by or through the staff provider, of the services of any externally provided workers.

(4)   Qualifying expenditure on externally provided workers is attributable to relevant research and development if the externally provided workers are directly and actively engaged in such research and development.

...

8B   For the purposes of this Schedule a person is an "externally provided worker" in relation to the company if the following conditions are satisfied –

(a) he is an individual,

(b) he is not a director or employee of the company,

(c) he personally provides, or is under an obligation personally to provide, services to the company,

(d) he is subject to (or to the right of) supervision, direction or control by the company as to the manner in which those services are provided,

(e) his services are supplied to the company by or through the staff provider (whether or not he is a director or employee of the staff provider or of any other person),

(f) he provides, or is under an obligation to provide, those services personally to the company under the terms of a contract between him and the staff provider,

(g) the provision of those services does not constitute the carrying on of activities contracted out by the company.'

12. It is unnecessary for me to cite any further provisions of schedule 20. I would, however, make the general point that the provisions form a detailed and meticulously drafted code, with a series of defined terms and composite expressions, and a large number of carefully delineated conditions, all of which have to be satisfied if the relief is to be available. The schedule runs to 26 paragraphs, and occupies ten pages in Tolley's Yellow Tax Handbook for 2005/06. I emphasise this point because one of Mr Gordon's submissions for Gripple is that the schedule evinces a general intention to provide enhanced relief for expenditure on R&D, and that a generous construction should where possible be adopted in order to further that general aim. I am unable to accept this submission. It seems to me, on the contrary, that a detailed and prescriptive code of this nature leaves little room for a purposive construction, and there is no substitute for going through the detailed conditions, one by one, to see if, on a fair reading, they are satisfied. It also needs to be remembered, in this context, that the relief is a generous one, which grants a deduction for notional expenditure which has not actually been incurred. Even if the relief is not available, there will be nothing to prevent the company from deducting its actual R&D expenditure in full in the computation of its trading profits, provided only that the normal 'wholly and exclusively' test is satisfied.

The Facts

13. The facts found by the General Commissioners are set out in paragraph 5 of the case stated, as follows:

'5. As a result of the oral and documentary evidence adduced before us, the following facts were proved.

5.1 [Gripple] is an engineering company based in Sheffield which incurs expenditure in research and development. Mr Hugh Facey at all times was and is a director of that company.

5.2 Until 31 December 2003 [Loadhog] was a wholly owned subsidiary of [Gripple], thereafter it was a wholly owned subsidiary of Loadhog Holdings Ltd. Mr Hugh Facey at all times during the relevant period was and continues to be a director of those companies.

5.3 Prior to the 1 January 2004 Mr Facey's salary had been paid entirely by [Gripple] and charged to [Gripple] and both parties agreed this was a cost in respect of which the company could claim R&D tax relief pursuant to the Schedule.

5.4 From 1 January 2004, Mr Facey divided his time between [Gripple] and [Loadhog] and the companies reached an agreement that one half of Mr Facey's salary should be met by [Gripple] and one half of Mr Facey's salary should be met by [Loadhog].

5.5 From 1 January 2004 until 31 December 2006 Mr Facey's salary was wholly paid by [Loadhog]. [Loadhog] invoiced [Gripple], by way of recharge, in respect of the salary costs of Mr Facey that were to be met by [Gripple].'

14. These findings of fact are consistent with the documents produced by HMRC. The relevant extracts from Mr Facey's personal tax returns show that he returned employment income of £135,675 from Gripple for the tax year ended 5 April 2004, and employment income of £50,000 from Loadhog during the same year. In the two following tax years he returned no employment income at all from Gripple, and employment income of £200,000 from Loadhog. In the year to 5 April 2007, he still returned no employment income from Gripple, but his employment income from Loadhog was reduced to £183,333. The extracts from Gripple's 2004, 2005 and 2006 returns included details of expenses recharged by Loadhog to Gripple in the following total amounts, but without any breakdown or explanation of the arrangement pursuant to which the expenses were recharged: £83,220 (2004), £171,002 (2005) and £160,419 (2006).

15. Although nothing turns on the point, I should mention that the relationship between Gripple, Loadhog and Loadhog Holdings Ltd was not quite as simple as the Commissioners say in paragraph 5.2 of the case stated. Without objection from counsel for Gripple, I was shown a letter from Gripple's accountants to the Inland Revenue's Business Tax Clearance Team dated 29 September 2005 seeking clearance in respect of a proposed reacquisition of Loadhog by Gripple. It appears from this letter that clearance had been given for an earlier de-merger of Loadhog from Gripple which took effect in January 2004. Since that date, Loadhog had struggled and had made substantial losses, but two new products were under development which it was hoped would turn the business round. In those circumstances, the directors of both companies

were of the view that Loadhog should be brought back into Gripple's ownership, and steps were proposed in order to achieve that goal. I was told that Loadhog again became a wholly-owned subsidiary of Gripple in or about November 2005.

The Commissioners' Decision

16.   After setting out the rival contentions of the parties, the Commissioners gave their reasons for dismissing the appeal in paragraph 10 of the case stated:

'10.   We the Commissioners heard the appeal and decided:

10.1   The appeal of [Gripple] should be refused. We heard that Mr H D Facey is a director of [Gripple] and also a director of a subsidiary company [Loadhog].

10.2   For several years [Gripple] had claimed research and development tax relief under the Schedule in connection with remuneration paid to Mr Facey. During this time Mr Facey was a director of only [Gripple].

10.3   Mr Facey became a director of [Loadhog] at the time [Loadhog] was created. He provided approximately half of his time to [Gripple] and half of his time to [Loadhog]. For convenience, his salary was paid solely by [Loadhog] and [Loadhog] invoiced [Gripple] for the services of Mr Facey to recover one half of Mr Facey's salary and national insurance contributions.

10.4   HMRC sought to disallow the claim for R&D relief by [Gripple] by finding that Mr Facey was an externally provided worker provided by Loadhog to Gripple. As a result of Mr Facey being a director, Gripple could not claim the R&D allowance due to the provisions of the Schedule. HMRC also reviewed whether the payments were a staffing cost or expenditure on subcontracted R&D but the payments did not qualify under either of those requirements.

10.5   Having regard to the above facts we had sympathy for [Gripple]. Having looked at the legislation, we asked the parties to consider an alternative: that Loadhog acted only as a payment or salary agent in respect of one half of the salary paid to Mr Facey. We heard representations from both parties on this point.

10.6   It was with reluctance that we found in favour of HMRC in the current circumstances.'

17.   Although the Commissioners do not say so expressly, it is implicit in their decision that they rejected the alternative analysis referred to in paragraph 10.5, and counsel for Gripple did not seek to argue the contrary. For his part, counsel for HMRC accepted that, if the true position had been that Loadhog acted only as a payment or salary agent

on behalf of Gripple, the relief would indeed have been available. He submitted, however, that such an analysis was impossible to reconcile with the primary facts found by the Commissioners, and with the evidence of Mr Facey's personal tax returns. In my judgment that is right, and although I can understand why the Commissioners wished to hear submissions on the point, I have no doubt that their conclusion on it was correct.

Discussion

18. In their written submissions in support of the appeal, counsel for Gripple argued that the General Commissioners interpreted paragraph 5(1)(a) of schedule 20 too narrowly and restrictively, and in particular that they failed to interpret it in the light of the wording of paragraph 5(2) which refers to staffing costs 'paid to, or in respect of, directors or employees …'. They submitted that the purpose and intention of the legislation, which had remained essentially unchanged since its introduction in 2000, was to provide relief for expenditure on R&D undertaken by a SME. In those circumstances, paragraph 5 should be construed so as to include emoluments paid indirectly by a company to a relevant director or employee, and the recharge arrangement in the present case, between two closely related companies, should be characterised as an indirect payment of emoluments by Gripple to Mr Facey.

19. In the alternative, counsel argued that this was an appropriate case for the court to lift the veil of incorporation and to treat Gripple and Loadhog as a single commercial entity that was undertaking R&D. The two companies were working in conjunction with each other, and in order to achieve a common goal. In support of this submission they referred to the decision of the Court of Appeal in *D. H. N. Ltd v Tower Hamlets* [1976] 1 WLR 852, a compulsory purchase case concerning the payment of compensation for disturbance in respect of a wholesale grocery business carried on by a group of three closely associated companies, one of which owned the land which had been compulsorily acquired, the second of which owned the business and the third of which owned the vehicles. The companies which owned the land and the vehicles were both wholly-owned subsidiaries of the third company which ran the business, and the directors of all three companies were the same. Against this background it was held by all three members of the Court of Appeal (Lord Denning MR, Goff LJ and Shaw LJ) that it would be appropriate to lift the corporate veil. At 860 C Lord Denning said this:

> 'This group is virtually the same as a partnership in which all the three companies are partners. They should not be treated separately so as to be defeated on a technical point. They should not be deprived of the compensation which should justly be payable for disturbance. The three companies should, for present purposes, be treated as one, and the parent company D. H. N. should be treated as that one. So D. H. N. are entitled to claim

compensation accordingly. It was not necessary for them to go through a conveyancing device to get it.'

Lord Denning's reference to a conveyancing device was a reference to the fact that the companies could easily have arranged matters (by conveying the land to the parent company) in such a way as to put themselves in an unassailable position to claim not only the value of the land but also compensation for disturbance: see 858 E – G. Goff LJ agreed with Lord Denning MR, but emphasised that he did so in reliance on the particular facts of the case: see 861 D – E. Shaw LJ also stressed 'the complete identity of commercial interest and personality' between the three companies at 867 D – E.

20.   In his oral submissions, Mr Gordon clarified his case on this point. He did not argue that the court should ignore the separate corporate existence of Loadhog, nor did he contend that the court should treat R&D carried out by one company in the group as if it were carried out by another. His argument was, rather, that a similar spirit of commercial realism should inform the construction of paragraph 5(1), and although as a matter of form Mr Facey received his remuneration in the three years from Loadhog, and half of it was recharged to Gripple, the commercial reality was that Gripple paid half his remuneration and channelled it to him through Loadhog.

21.   Mr Gordon also referred me to the decision of Templeman J, as he then was, in *Harmel v Wright* [1974] 1 WLR 325, where the question was whether certain sums received by the taxpayer in the United Kingdom in the form of interest-free loans from a South African company were to be treated as emoluments received by him in the United Kingdom under Case III of Schedule E, then contained in section 156 of the Income Tax Act 1952. In an attempt to avoid the application of this charge, the taxpayer entered into arrangements whereby his South African employers paid his salary to him in South Africa, he then used the money to buy shares in a South African company which he controlled, the proceeds of sale were lent to a second South African company in which he held no shares, and the money was then lent to him in the United Kingdom. Templeman J had little difficulty in holding that the attempt failed, and said at 328F that the case depended 'on keeping one's eye on the emoluments, on the original sum of £25,000, and seeing what happened to it'. He then continued:

> 'It is true that it was paid over at one stage as purchase price for shares, and it is true that one cannot normally identify money, but in the present case you can; you do not need to get behind the corporate veil to perceive and know that the £25,000 which went in as purchase price for shares came out on the instant in the form of the loan to Lodestar. In my judgment, on the wording of section 156, one does not need to strip aside the corporate veil if you find that emoluments, which means money, come in at one end of a conduit pipe and pass through certain traceable pipes until they come out at the other end to the taxpayer.'

22.   Mr Gordon relied on this passage as providing support for his submission that the court should make a commercially realistic assessment of the manner in which Mr Facey was remunerated by Gripple. However, the case is in my judgment too far removed from the present context to be of any assistance. The statutory provisions in issue were entirely different, and notably included a direction (contained in paragraph 8 of schedule 2 to the Finance Act 1956) that for the purposes of Case III 'emoluments shall be treated as received in the United Kingdom if they are paid, used or enjoyed in or in any manner or form transmitted or brought to the United Kingdom ...'. In the light of that express provision, it is hardly surprising that Templeman J held that the taxpayer's South African emoluments had been transmitted or brought to the United Kingdom.

23.   I am equally unable to accept Mr Gordon's submissions about lifting the corporate veil, even in the more moderate form in which he advanced them orally. It is a commonplace of United Kingdom tax law that companies in a group, however closely related, are normally to be treated as separate entities. Indeed, it is precisely for this reason that special provision has to be made, for example by the provision of group or consortium relief, to enable the tax treatment of a group to correspond more closely with the underlying commercial structure. I am aware of no authority, and none was cited to me, which provides any support for the notion that the court should somehow coalesce separate corporate entities in construing fiscal legislation, unless, of course, the legislation properly construed permits such an approach. It is enough for present purposes to say that I can find no encouragement at all for such an approach in the detailed and meticulously drafted code of schedule 20. On the contrary, there are detailed provisions relating to connected persons (for example in paragraphs 8C to 8E and paragraphs 10 to 12) which show that the draftsman was well aware of the existence of corporate groups and the need to fit them within the structure of the relief. In the absence of express provision, I have no doubt that the general principle must be to respect the separate corporate identity of group members, and that the question whether the preconditions for grant of relief have been satisfied must be answered accordingly.

24.   Once Mr Gordon's more adventurous submissions have been disposed of, the answer to the present case is in my judgment clear. The sums recharged by Loadhog to Gripple in respect of Mr Facey's services cannot be treated as staffing costs within the meaning of paragraph 5(1)(a), for the simple reason that they were not emoluments paid by Gripple to Mr Facey. All Mr Facey's emoluments, during the relevant three year period, were paid to him by Loadhog. The position would be different if Loadhog had merely acted as a payroll agent on behalf of Gripple, but as I have already said this possibility was considered and rightly rejected by the Commissioners. It just does not accord with the evidence which was before them.

25.   Nor, in my judgment, can Gripple gain any assistance from the wording of paragraph 5(2). The purpose of this subparagraph is not to expand

the meaning of 'staffing costs', which has already been exhaustively defined in paragraph 5(1), but rather to explain which staffing costs (as already defined) are to be treated as 'attributable to relevant research and development', that being the second of the six qualifying conditions laid down in paragraph 3 of the schedule. The subparagraph provides an illustration of the rather laborious way in which the draftsman states a condition, here that the expenditure must be attributable to relevant research and development, and then provides further definitions in order to flesh out the content of the condition. 'Relevant research and development' is defined in paragraph 4, and paragraph 5(2) tells us when such expenditure is to be treated as attributable to staffing costs, namely when it is 'paid to, or in respect of, directors or employees directly and actively engaged in such research and development'. The words 'or in respect of' are there because not all staffing costs, as defined in paragraph 5(1), are paid to directors or employees. Staffing costs within paragraph 5(1)(b) and (c), that is to say secondary class 1 national insurance contributions paid by the company, and contributions paid by the company to any pension fund operated for the benefit of directors or employees of the company, are payments 'in respect of' directors or employees, but are not payments to them.

26.   It is common ground that the payments in issue could not be 'qualifying expenditure on externally provided workers' within the meaning of paragraphs 8A to 8E, because Mr Facey's position as a director of Gripple meant that he could not qualify as an 'externally provided worker' within the meaning of paragraph 8B. The words 'he is not a director or employee of the company' in paragraph 8B(b) are clear and unambiguous, and they clearly apply to Mr Facey.

27.   The Commissioners reached their conclusion with avowed reluctance. I can understand their feelings, because the group could easily have arranged matters in such a way as to attract relief for the full amounts paid to Mr Facey. Gripple was not attempting any form of tax avoidance, but inadvertently failed to obtain the maximum relief to which it might otherwise have been entitled. However, as the Commissioners rightly appreciated, their duty was to apply the law to the transactions which the parties had actually entered into, and not to some alternative transactions which they might have entered into with the benefit of better advice. The mere fact that the same economic result could have been achieved in a different, and more fiscally attractive, manner cannot avail the taxpayer where the clear words of the relevant legislation preclude the grant of relief for the transaction which the taxpayer has actually undertaken.

Conclusion

28.   For these reasons Gripple's appeal will be dismissed.

Index

[All references are to paragraph numbers.]

A

Accounting for R&D (SSAP 13), *see*
Relief framework
Advance in science or technology 3.6,
3.18
adapting existing technology 3.10
appreciable improvement 3.11
capability based R&D 3.8, 3.9
case study 3.39
knowledge based R&D 3.7, 3.9
R&D scenarios
'appreciable improvement' 3.20–
3.22
projects duplicating scientific
or technological effects
3.23
Animation production companies,
see Creative industry reliefs; TV
production relief (TPTR)
Anti-avoidance
claims under R&D tax credit schemes
6.10
Appreciable improvement
BIS definition 3.34
**Automotive industry and automotive
parts**
case study 9.9

B

BIS 'Gateway' tests
definition of R&D 3.3
identifying claim 3.4
R&D review 3.5
R&D scenarios, *see* R&D scenarios
resolution of scientific or
technological uncertainty (test
two) 3.12, 3.18
how technical uncertainty occurs
3.14
inferior technology 3.16
origin of uncertainty in commercial
context 3.17
system uncertainty 3.15
uncertainty defined 3.13

BIS 'Gateway' tests – *contd*
resolution of scientific or
technological uncertainty (test
two) – *contd*
seeking an advance in science or
technology (test one) 3.6, 3.18
adapting existing technology 3.10
appreciable improvement 3.11
capability based R&D 3.8, 3.9
knowledge based R&D 3.7, 3.9
BIS Guidelines
case studies, *see* Case studies
competent professional 3.37
definition 3.34
definition of R&D for tax purposes
2.14, 3.1, App 3
BIS 'Gateway' tests, *see* BIS
'Gateway' tests
context 3.2
extension of overall knowledge and
capability 3.36
glossary of definitions 3.33
purposive construction of terms
3.34
advance in science or technology
3.34
appreciable improvement 3.34
competent professional 3.34
directly contributing activity 3.34
overall knowledge and capability
3.34
project 3.34
science 3.34
scientific or technological
uncertainty 3.34
system uncertainty 3.34
technology 3.34
practical points 3.42
production costs 3.35

C

Capital allowances
research development allowances
(RDAs) 2.13

315